A Will Is Not Enough
In California
2nd Edition

SIMPLE, PRACTICAL THINGS
A CALIFORNIA RESIDENT CAN DO TO

- ✦ PRESERVE ASSETS
- ✦ AVOID PROBATE
- ✦ AVOID GUARDIANSHIP
- ✦ PROVIDE FOR HEALTH CARE
- ✦ PROVIDE FOR THE FAMILY'S CARE

By AMELIA E. POHL, ESQ.
and
California Attorney
MARY S. FALK

EAGLE PUBLISHING COMPANY OF BOCA

The purpose of this book is to provide the reader with an informative overview of the subject; but laws change frequently and are subject to different interpretations as courts rule on the meaning or effect of a law. This book is sold with the under standing that neither the authors, nor the editors, nor the publisher, nor the distributors of this book are engaging in, or rendering, legal, accounting, financial planning, or any other professional service. Pursuant to Internal Revenue Service guidance, be advised that any federal tax advice in this publication was not intended or written to be used, and it cannot be used, by any person or entity for the purpose of avoiding penalties imposed under the Internal Revenue Code (IRS Circular 230 Disclaimer). If you need legal, accounting, financial planning or any other expert advice, you should seek the services of a licensed professional.

This book is intended for use by the consumer for his or her own benefit. If you use this book to counsel someone about the law or tax matters, that may be considered to be an unlicensed and illegal practice.

Web sites, telephone numbers and addresses appear throughout the book for the convenience of the reader; however, this information is subject to change as agencies move. Publication of a Web site is not an endorsement of that site by the authors, editors or publishers of this book.

EAGLE PUBLISHING COMPANY OF BOCA
4199 N. Dixie Highway, #2
Boca Raton, FL 33431 E-mail: info@eaglepublishing.com
Printed in the United States of America ISBN 1-892407-96-5
Library of Congress Catalog Card Number: 2002106004

A Will Is Not Enough In California

2nd Edition

CONTENTS

Introduction

Over the years, as we practiced law, we noticed that the questions people have about Wills, Trusts, powers of attorney, avoiding probate and guardianship, preserving assets, providing health care for themselves and their families, are much the same client to client. Many people are concerned about who will control their finances should they become too aged or too ill to do so themselves. Of even more concern is their health care:

Who will make my medical decisions if I can't do so myself?

How can I pay for my health care?

How much and what type of insurance should I have?

How can I avoid guardianship?

Others worry about the care of family members. Those with minor children worry:

Who will care for my minor child if I become incapacitated or die?

Is there a way to make sure my child has enough money to see him through college?

Those with elderly parents worry:

How can I manage my parent's finances should my parent become too aged or ill to do so?

Can my parent qualify for MEDI-CAL?

If my parent dies, will I need to go through Probate?

Is there a way to avoid Probate?

We agreed that a book answering such questions would be of service to the general public. We wish to thank all of the clients, whom we have had the honor and pleasure to serve, for providing us with the impetus to write this book.

Mary S. Falk, Esq,

MARY S. FALK received her Juris Doctor degree in 1988 from Santa Clara University Law School. She practiced law with a firm in San Jose for eight years, then decided to form her own firm in 1996. She joined forces with Daniel Cornell, an attorney she worked with over the years. They formed the law firm of Falk, Cornell & Associates, LLP, concentrating exclusively on Estate Planning.

The firm regularly provides free educational seminars to the community on the subject of Estate Planning.

As a principal of the firm, Mary S. Falk devotes herself to practicing law with integrity, providing her clients with the type of quality legal service that she herself would seek from an attorney.

Ms. Falk is married to Harry Falk, a Certified Public Accountant. They have three children. Their daughter Serra E. Falk has joined the law firm of Falk, Cornell & Assoc. LLP as an Estate Planning attorney. Their sons Taylor and Harry live in the San Francisco area. Their first grandchild, Harry Falk, V, was born in 2004. Mary and her family are devoted fans of the San Francisco 49ers football team.

Mary S. Falk is a member of the Palo Alto Bar Association., the San Mateo County Bar Association, and a member of the Estate Planning, Probate and Trust Section of the Santa Clara County Bar Assoc.

MARY S. FALK is a member of the AMERICAN ACADEMY OF ESTATE PLANNING ATTORNEYS, and serves as past member of their Board of Governors.

About the Academy

The American Academy of Estate Planning Attorneys is a member organization serving the needs of legal professionals concentrating on Estate Planning. Through the Academy's comprehensive training and educational programs on state-of-the-art Estate Planning law and techniques, it fosters excellence in Estate Planning among its members and helps them deliver the highest possible service to their clients. The Academy provides its members with excellent legal education, and top notch practice management support. In addition, each member is required to attain thirty-six units of continuing legal education in tax and Estate Planning annually.

The American Academy of Estate Planning Attorneys serves law firms in over 150 geographic areas in forty-four states. Clients who chose an attorney who is a member of the Academy can feel confident that they have an attorney who is dedicated to bringing them the highest quality of service.

The Academy is also committed to educating consumers on vital Estate Planning issues that touch their lives. Through its series of publications, educational programs and its consumer Web site, the Academy seeks to create a public armed with the information they need to become wise consumers of Estate Planning services.

 THE AMERICAN ACADEMY OF
ESTATE PLANNING ATTORNEYS
http://www.aaepa.com

Amelia E. Pohl, Esq.

Before becoming an attorney in 1985, AMELIA E. POHL taught mathematics on both the high school and college level. During her tenure as Associate Professor of Mathematics at Prince George's Community College in Maryland, she wrote several books including

Probability: A Set Theory Approach
Principals of Counting

Ms. Pohl, graduated from Nova Law School in Florida and established an Elder Law practice. Over the years she observed that many people want to reduce the high cost of legal fees by performing or assisting with their own legal transactions. Attorney Pohl found that, with a bit of guidance, people are able to perform many legal transactions for themselves. Attorney Pohl utilizes her background as teacher, author and attorney to provide that "bit of guidance" to the general public in the form of self-help legal books that she has written. Amelia E. Pohl is currently completing this series for the remaining states:

Guiding Those Left Behind in Maine
Guiding Those Left Behind In Utah
Guiding Those Left Behind In Nevada, etc.

Acknowledgment

Many thanks to California attorney TIMOTHY P. MURPHY for his editorial review of the Medi-Cal chapters (10 and 11) of this book. He is an estate planning and Elder Law Attorney whose practice emphasizes helping people to build, preserve and pass on their wealth.

Mr. Murphy has practiced in the Sacramento area for almost 25 years—first with a large law firm and then with his own firm since 1987. He has written a regular column on legal issues for *Senior Magazine*. He also was a regular featured guest on the *Money Experts* radio program. He has been quoted by the *Sacramento Bee* and the *Sacramento Business Journal* on estate planning and related topics.

Timothy P. Murphy graduated magna cum laude from the University of Colorado and earned his law degree from the University of California, Hastings College Of The Law, where he served as Managing Editor of the Law Review. He was also elected into Phi Beta Kappa, the National Honor Society.

Mr. Murphy has been awarded the top AV rating by the Martindale-Hubbell Law Directory, the legal profession's preeminent rating service for attorneys. The AV rating is the highest rating and is earned by only a small number of attorneys considered to have "Very High to Preeminent Legal Ability" with the highest standard of ethical and professional conduct.

Mr. Murphy is active in numerous professional activities. He serves as an arbitrator and pro tem judge for the local courts and he is a member of the State Bar of California Estate Planning Section.

Reading the Law

Where applicable, we identified the state statute or federal statute that is the basis of the discussion. We did this as a reference, and also to encourage the reader to look at the law as it is written. Prior to the Internet the only way you could look up the law was to physically take yourself to the local courthouse law library or the law section of a public library. Today all of the state and federal statutes are literally at your finger tips. They are just a mouse click away on the Internet. To look up a statute all you need is the address of the Web site and the identifying number of the statute.

FEDERAL STATUTES
http://www4.law.cornell.edu/uscode

CALIFORNIA STATUTES
http://www.leginfo.ca.gov

California has organized their statutes into 29 different codes, including:
BUSINESS & PROFESSIONAL CODE ("Bus. & Prof."),
CIVIL CODE ("Civ."),   CODE OF CIVIL PROCEDURE ("Civ. Proc.")
CORPORATIONS ("Corp.")   FAMILY CODE ("Fam.")
HEALTH AND SAFETY CODE ("Health & Safety")
PROBATE CODE ("Prob.")
REVENUE & TAXATION ("Rev & Tax")   VEHICLE CODE ("Veh.")
WELFARE & INSTITUTIONS ("Welf. & Inst.")

Each Code is divided into numbered sections. When referring to a statute we give the name of the Code and the section of the code. For example, To look up (Fam. 297.5) go to Family Code section of the California statute Web site and look up section 297.5. If you come across a topic that you think is important, you may find it both interesting and profitable to read the law as it is actually written.

When You Need A Lawyer

The purpose of the book is to give the reader a basic understanding of California law as it relates to Wills and other methods of Estate Planning. It is not intended as a substitute for legal counsel or any other kind of professional advice. If you have a legal question, you should seek the counsel of an attorney. When looking for an attorney, consider three things:

EXPERTISE, COST and PERSONALITY.

EXPERTISE

THE STATE BAR OF CALIFORNIA has *Legal Specialization* programs in AppellateLaw, Bankruptcy Law, Criminal Law, Estate Planning, Trust and Probate Law, Immigrant and Nationality Law, Taxation Law, and Workers' Compensation Law.

To be a *certified specialist* in any of the above areas of law, the attorney must pass a written examination, demonstrate a high level of experience in the field, be favorably evaluated by other attorneys and judges familiar with his work. Once certified, the attorney must fulfill ongoing educational requirements to remain current with the law. To find an attorney who is specialized in the area of law that you seek, call the State Bar of California toll free at (866) 442-2529. Out of state call (415) 538-2250.

Legal Specialization is just one of the criteria to consider. Many fine attorneys are experienced in an area of law, but have not taken the time, effort and expense to become certified as a specialist in that area of law by the California Bar. If the attorney is not certified in that branch of law, ask how long he has practiced that type of law and what percentage of his practice is devoted to that branch of law.

One of the most reliable ways to find an attorney is through personal referral. Ask your friends, family or business acquaintances if they used an attorney for the field of law that you seek and whether they were pleased with the results. It is important to employ an attorney who is experienced in the area of law you seek. Your friend may have a wonderful Estate Planning attorney, but if you suffered an injury to your body, then you need an attorney experienced in Personal Injury.

Before employing an attorney, ask how long he has practiced in that field of law and what percentage of his practice is devoted to that type of law.

COST

In addition to the attorney's experience, it is important to check what it will cost in attorney fees. When you call for an appointment ask what the attorney will charge for the initial consultation and the approximate cost for the service you seek. Ask whether there will be additional costs such as filing fees, accounting fees, expert witness fees, etc. If the least expensive attorney is out of your price range, you can call your local Legal Aid Society, or the State Bar of California Bar at (415) 538-2247 for a referral to the Legal Services office nearest you.

You can also find a directory of California Legal Services Programs at the General Public Resources section of The American Bar Association Web site.

 AMERICAN BAR ASSOCIATION
http://www.abanet.org

PERSONALITY

Of equal importance to the attorney's experience and legal fees, is your relationship with the attorney. How easy was it to reach the attorney? Did he promptly return your call or did you have to go through layers of receptionists and legal assistants before being allowed to speak to the attorney? If you had difficulty reaching the attorney on your first call, you can expect similar problems should you employ that attorney.

Did the attorney treat you with respect? Did the attorney treat you paternally with a "father knows best" attitude or did he treat you as an intelligent person with the ability to understand the options available to you and the ability to make your own decision based on the information provided to you?

Were you able to understand and easily communicate with the attorney? Was he speaking to you in plain English or was his explanation of the matter so full of legalese to be almost meaningless to you?

Do you find the attorney's personality to be pleasant or grating? If you come away from your first visit feeling annoyed or uncomfortable, then he is not right for you. Find another attorney.

It is worth the effort to take the time to interview as many attorneys as it takes to find one with the right expertise, fee schedule and personality for you.

The Organization of the Book

Many people who have a Will think they have their affairs in order, reasoning that should they die everything will go to the people named in the Will and somehow things will all be taken care of. But this is a simplistic view. There are many more things to consider.

1. What exactly will your beneficiaries inherit?
2. How will your property be transferred?
3. Can you (should you) avoid Probate?
4. Can you avoid a challenge to your Will?

The first four chapters of this book deal with these basic issues. Once you read these chapters you will have an understanding of what will happen to your property should you die, regardless of whether you do, or do not, have a Will.

The rest of the book deals with things a Will <u>cannot</u> do:

Chapter 5. Manage your personal debt
Chapter 6. Limit your business debt
Chapter 7. Provide care for a minor or disabled child
Chapter 8. Appoint someone to make your health care decisions should you be unable to do so
Chapter 9. Appoint someone to handle your finances should you be unable to do so
Chapter 10. Help you qualify for MEDI-CAL should the need arise
Chapter 11. Protect your home should you need to apply for MEDI-CAL
Chapter 12. Help your family settle your Estate.

A Will can't do these things but you will be able to do so once you read these chapters and understand what options are available to you under California law.

GLOSSARY

This book is designed for the average reader. Legal terminology has been kept to a minimum. There is a glossary at the end of the book in case you come across a legal term that is not familiar to you.

FICTITIOUS NAMES AND EVENTS

The examples in this book are based loosely on actual events; however, all names are fictitious; and the events, as portrayed, are fictitious.

MALE GENDER USED

Rather than use he/she or himself/herself, for simplicity, we used the male gender.

THE BOOK COVER

LUBOSH CECH designed the cover of this book. Lubosh Cech is the founder of OKO DESIGN STUDIO located in Portland, Oregon. He designs promotional materials for print and digital media. He has received numerous awards for both graphic design and painting. For more information about Mr. Cech and the OKO Design Studio visit his Web site. http://www.okodesignstudio.com

The photograph on the cover is that of the Golden Gate Bridge. The photographer is Larry Brownstein.

Your Financial Check-up 1

To understand why *A Will is Not Enough in California* you need to know what a Will can and cannot do. One thing a Will can do is make a gift of all you own (your *Estate*). One of the things a Will cannot do is preserve and protect your property during your lifetime. For that, you need to think about risks to your property (poor investments, theft, loss through acts of nature, etc.) and what you can do to minimize or eliminate such risks. In other words, you need an *Estate Plan* for the care and management of your property during your lifetime.

The average person may be thinking "I don't have an Estate — never mind an Estate Plan." But you do. Every-one who owns property, has an Estate Plan. You may not have verbalized your Estate Plan, or even thought about it, but it's there none-the-less. Take the case of the college student purchasing his first car. If his parents bankroll the purchase, the son may offer to hold the car jointly with them. In such case, the son's Estate consists of his car. His Estate Plan is to hold the car jointly with his parents so that they will own the car should anything happen to him.

This may not be the best Estate Plan. Holding the car jointly with his parents may make them liable for injuries or damages should the car be involved in an accident. If the young man's parents are familiar with California law, they would be wise to refuse the offer and reassure their son "You can make a Will and make us the beneficiary of your car. But even if you die without a Will, we are your heirs under California law. Either way, we will inherit the car. Just make sure to drive carefully and carry enough car insurance."

This is a better Estate Plan. It gives the young man maximum control over his Estate (i.e., his car) during his lifetime. He can sell the car, mortgage it, or trash it, all as he sees fit. If he follows his parent's advice, of driving carefully and purchasing sufficient insurance, his Estate will have maximum protection. If he dies *intestate* (without a Will), and is single and without children, under California's LAWS OF INTESTATE SUCCESSION, his parents will inherit his Estate. And that is just the way the son wants things at this stage of his life.

Simple situation, simple Estate Plan. But, for most of us, life isn't all that simple. We may own many items of value and have loved ones who rely on us. At some point in our lives, we need to ask:

How can I make sure that my property will be inherited by my choice of beneficiary?

How can I arrange to have my property inherited quickly and at minimum cost?

How can I achieve these goals and yet have maximum control and protection of my property during my lifetime?

We will explore the different ways to answer these questions so that you can decide on an Estate Plan that is best for you. But before doing so you need to know what property you own; i.e., how much your Estate is worth. If you are married and your spouse handles all of the finances, it may be that you have no idea of the value of your Estate.

That was the case with Kristin. She met Matt when they were both at the pinnacle of their careers, but they had no more insight into their precarious position than fireworks in a summer sky just before self-destruct.

A Will Is Not Enough In California

Kristin was a model. Not the best, nor the most beautiful, but she made a comfortable living. She moved in a circle of famous models. She reflected off of their radiance, making her appear more attractive than she actually was.

Matt worked in middle management for one of those high tech companies. Like Kristin, he was not particularly gifted but he happened to be in Silicon Valley just at the time the high stakes investors were showing extraordinary, if not misguided, confidence in the industry. The good times were rolling. It never crossed Matt's mind that this would one day end. He spent the money as fast as it came in.

Kristin was impressed with the lavish gifts Matt gave to her. She, and her family, thought she made quite a catch when she announced her engagement. After the wedding she continued to model, but it took a lot of traveling and Matt resented her time away. Eventually, she agreed to stop working altogether. After all, why should she, the wife of a wealthy man, need to continue with the rigors of a model's life of diet and exercise?

Matt never told Kristin about his financial difficulties. All she knew was that he was drinking quite a bit. Her suspicion that he also was into drugs was verified when he died, suddenly, because of an overdose. Her shock and sadness turned to anger when she discovered that all he owned was mortgaged and he was heavily in debt. He even borrowed money from her family without her knowledge!

Matt's creditors took it all. The house, the boat, the Porsche, everything. If only Kristin had investigated the true state of their finances, she could have arranged to set aside the money she earned prior to her marriage and not end up as she did, a destitute widow, past her prime.

DETERMINING YOUR NET WORTH

Even if you are single you may not know the value of your Estate because you have not taken the time to actually sit down and figure it out. To get maximum benefit from this book, you need to take a few minutes to determine your *Net Worth*, i.e. the current value of your Estate.

ASSETS

$_____	Cash (certificates of deposit, bank accounts, etc.)
$_____	Tangible personal property (jewelry, motor vehicles, private art, stamp or coin collections, etc.)
$_____	Cash value of insurance policies
$_____	Securities (stocks, bonds, etc.)
$_____	Cash value of pension plans, IRAs, etc.
$_____	Cash value of a partnership or other business interest
$_____	Real property (residence, time share, lot, condo, cooperatives, etc.)
$_____	TOTAL VALUE OF ASSETS

It may be that you have a loan on your car or home, or any of the above items. You need to subtract away monies you owe to get the bottom line value of what you own.

LIABILITIES

$_____	Private loans
$_____	Mortgage Balance
$_____	Credit card debt
$_____	Car loan or car lease balance
$_____	TOTAL LIABILITIES

A simple subtraction gives you the value of your Estate.
ASSETS — LIABILITIES = NET WORTH

If you are married and hold all property jointly with your spouse, divide by 2 to get the value of your own Net Worth.

Your Net Worth is the value of all that you own, and that is how much your beneficiaries can inherit. Who will inherit your property depends on how your property is *titled* (held or owned).

There are three basic ways to title property:
⇨   **IN YOUR NAME ONLY**
Property held *in your name only*, and no provision for a transfer to a beneficiary after death, becomes part of your Probate Estate. It will be inherited by the beneficiary named in your Will. If you do not have a Will, the property will go to your heirs according to California's Laws of Intestate Succession.

⇨   **JOINTLY WITH ANOTHER**
Property you own *jointly* will belong to the surviving joint owner(s) of that property.

⇨   **IN TRUST FOR ANOTHER**
Property you hold *in Trust* will go to those you name as the beneficiary of the Trust.

NOTE ⇨ If you are in a legal relationship, your spouse, or registered Domestic Partner, may have rights in your property regardless of the way your property is titled.

We will examine each of these types of ownership in detail so that you can give yourself an Estate Planning check-up, i.e., you can check whether the way you are currently holding your property accomplishes your Estate Planning goals.

MINE, ALL MINE

There's much to be said about holding property in your name only and not jointly or in trust for another. There's maximum control. You can sell it, trade it, mortgage it, with no one to account to, or ask "may I?" How you protect your assets depends on how much security you require. Again, it's all up to you.

As discussed, there are three things to consider when setting up an Estate Plan:

CONTROL   How to control and protect your
             Estate during your lifetime.
BENEFICIARY How to be sure your Estate goes
             to the beneficiary of your choice.
COST   How to transfer your Estate to your
             beneficiaries at lowest cost.

Holding all of your property in your name only should give you maximum control and protection; but such an Estate Plan may present problems with the cost of transferring your property upon your death. More than likely it will take some sort of court procedure to transfer that property once you die. The name of the court procedure is *Probate*.

In California, Probate is conducted in the Probate Department of the Superior Court (Prob. 7050). The Superior Court handles civil and criminal matters as well as Probate. For simplicity, we will refer to the court that handles Probate as the *Probate Court*. We will refer to property that is transferred to your beneficiary by means of a Probate procedure as your *Probate Estate* and the person appointed by the Court to settle your Estate, as your *Personal Representative*.

Probate can be expensive, so if you keep all of your property in your name only there could be a significant cost to transfer your property to the beneficiary of your Estate.

Holding property in your name should not create a problem with having your beneficiary of your choice inherit your Estate, provided you have a Will. But if you die without a valid Will the Probate Court will use the California Laws of Intestate Succession to determine who is entitled to inherit your property. Of course it could be that the beneficiaries of your Estate under the Laws of Intestate Succession are exactly who you would have wanted had you taken the time to prepare a Will.

To help you determine if this is the case, we will take a few pages to explain the Law. Those who have a Will might want to skip over the section, however, this information is good to know in the event someone in your family dies without a Will. Once you read the section you will know whether you have a right to inherit their property.

THE FAMILY'S RIGHT TO INHERIT

The state of California recognizes the right of the family to inherit property left by the *decedent* (the person who died), so the Laws of Intestate Succession cover all possible relationships beginning with the surviving spouse. In order for the decedent's spouse to inherit property under the Laws of Intestate Succession, the state of California needs to recognize the union as a valid marriage.

BEING MARRIED IN CALIFORNIA

To be married in California means that a woman and a man have obtained a license to marry from the state and then solemnized the marriage by a state or religious ceremony. A Certificate of Registry of Marriage must be returned to the Clerk of the Court (Fam. 300).

The parties must be at least 18 when they marry; but someone under the age of 18 can marry provided their parent gives written consent AND the Court, after learning all of the facts of the case, issues an order granting them permission to marry (Fam. 302).

☒ BIGAMY

It is illegal for a married person to marry without first obtaining a divorce. No license can be granted if one of the parties is currently married — with the exception of someone whose spouse has been missing for five successive years or who is generally believed to be dead (Fam. 2201).

California law does not bar marriages between cousins, but the law prohibits the marriage of those who are:

☒ *ancestors* (parent, grandparents, etc.) or *descendants* (child, grandchild, etc.) of each other

☒ aunt and nephew or uncle and niece

☒ brother and sister. This includes siblings of the *half blood*; i.e. they have only one parent in common. (Fam. 2200).

☒ THE COMMON LAW MARRIAGE

A Common Law marriage is one that has not been solemnized by ceremony. It is more than just living together. The couple must agree to live together as man and wife, and then publicly hold themselves out as being married. California abolished Common Law marriages in 1895, however California does respect the laws of other states and countries. If a couple enter into a Common Law marriage in a state that recognizes such union as a valid marriage, and the couple later move to California, then their marriage is recognized as being valid in the state of California (Fam. 308).

☒ SAME SEX MARRIAGES

In 1998, the federal government passed the Defense of Marriage Act, saying that for purposes of federal law, marriage is a legal union between one man and one woman (28 U.S.C. 1738C). However, for purposes of state law, whether you can marry, who you can marry; and how you can marry, are determined by the laws of the state in which you live.

There is much variation state to state. Connecticut and Vermont have approved same-sex *Civil Unions*. Massachusetts allows gay marriages. Several other states, including California, have passed statutes, specifically denying marital status to couples of the same gender regardless of whether that marriage is valid in any other state or country. California statute (Family Law 308.5) states:

> Only marriage between a man and a woman is valid or recognized in California.

THE DOMESTIC PARTNER REGISTRATION

Although the state of California does not recognize the same sex marriages, as of January 1, 2000, people of the same sex who are 18 or older may become **Registered Domestic Partners** by filing a Declaration of Domestic Partner. The County Clerk provides the Declaration form. Once the form is completed and the filing fee paid, the Declaration is filed with the Secretary of State who then enters the Declaration in a registry for Domestic Partnerships.

Recognizing that there are elderly people who do not want to jeopardize their Social Security or widow(er) pension by marriage, the statute extended the Domestic Partner registration to heterosexual couples over the age of 62.

There is a Notice of Termination of Domestic Partnership that can be filed with the Secretary of State in the event that things don't work out (Fam. 297, 298, 298.5).

Initially, the statute provided few rights or responsibilities for the couple, however as of January 1, 2005, section 297.5 of the Family Code is amended to read:

> Registered domestic partners shall have the same rights, protections, and benefits, and shall be subject to the same responsibilities, obligations, and duties under law, whether they derive from statutes, administrative regulations, county rules, government policies, common law, or any other provision or sources of law, as are granted to and imposed upon spouses.

Registered Domestic Partners now have the same rights and responsibilities as does a spouse within the state of California, so in this book we will use the designation "Spouse/RDP" to indicate that the discussion applies to those couples whose marriage is recognized as being valid in the state of California, as well as to those couples who are registered as Domestic Partners with the California Secretary of State. We will use the word "union" to indicate that the partners are either married or are Registered Domestic Partners.

Now that you know whether the State of California considers you to be married or a Domestic Partner, the next question is whether the state recognizes anyone as your descendant.

Who Is Your Child?

Medical technology has made important contributions to solving the problem of infertility. There are all sorts of solutions, from hormone therapy, to sperm banks that provide donations anonymously, to frozen sperm or ova to be thawed and used at a later date, to women who become a surrogate or gestational mother. Solving a set of medical problems opened the door to a new set of legal problems.

Used to be, the only question was "Who's the father?" Now it could well be "Who's the mother?

To answer these questions, the State of California has passed laws to legally establish the parentage of children whose conception was assisted by medical technology. We will examine the law as it relates to the right of the child to inherit property.

CHILD OF ARTIFICIAL INSEMINATION

Under California law, a husband who consents to his wife being artificially inseminated with semen donated by another man is treated in law as if he were the child's natural father of the child. The consent must be in writing and signed by the husband and his wife. The physician who performs the procedure is required to keep the consent form confidential and in a sealed file. The file can be opened only on court order (Fam. 7613).

A child born to a married couple using any other form of assisted conception has the same rights as a child conceived the old fashioned way. It is presumed that the husband consented to the assisted conception procedure. If that is not the case, and he is not the father of the child, he can *petition* (ask) the court to terminate his parental rights and responsibilities. If the husband is successful, the child will not be able to inherit from the husband, nor from his family.

FROZEN SPERM AND THE AFTERBORN CHILD

Under California law a child conceived prior to death and born to the surviving spouse after the death, has the same right to inherit as any other natural child of the decedent (Prob. 6407). But suppose the child was conceived after death. Does that child have the same rights? That question is becoming more of an issue as couples are freezing sperm, ovum or pre-embryo (fertilized cell) for use at a later date. Often the procedure is done to protect the cell from damage during cancer treatments. If the treatment is unsuccessful, the surviving parent may decide to go ahead with the pregnancy using the frozen reproductive cell. This raises issues of whether the surviving parent has the right to do that without the written consent of the deceased donor; and whether a child born of such procedure is entitled to inherit from the deceased donor.

This inheritance issue has important consequences, not only on the state level but on the federal level as well. A minor child who has lost a parent is entitled to Social Security benefits, but those benefits are based on the state's Laws of Intestate Succession. Section 216 of the Social Security Act provides "a child's insurance benefits can be paid to a child who could inherit under the State's intestate laws." Specifically, a child cannot receive Social Security benefits, unless the child is entitled to inherit under the state's Laws of Intestate Succession. This issue was brought before the Superior Court in New Jersey. The Court ruled that a child conceived and born after the death of a parent can inherit under New Jersey's Laws of Intestate Succession (*In Re Estate of Kolacy*, 322 N.J. Super. 593 (2000)). Other states have passed laws on the issue. For example, under Virginia law, the child may not inherit from the deceased donor, unless prior to death the decedent agreed, in writing, to the implantation.

As of mid 2006, the issue of whether a child conceived after the death of the donor parent can inherit from that parent, has not been raised in California. If you decided to freeze your reproductive cells, it is important that you express, in writing, whether you want your cells used after your death and whether you intend that a child born of the reproductive cell be entitled to inherit your Estate. For those who are married, it is important that your Spouse/RDP join in the writing and agree to honor your wishes. That written agreement should include a provision about what will be done with the cells in the event of a divorce or the death of either party.

Still another legal issue raised because of modern technology is the question of the rights of the Surrogate mother as opposed to the rights of the biological parent who contracted with the Surrogate to bear his child.

THE SURROGATE PARENT CONTRACT

A *Surrogate Parent Contract* is an agreement, usually between a married couple (the intended parents) and a woman (the gestational or Surrogate mother), in which the woman agrees to be the birth mother of a child conceived with the sperm of the husband, or the egg cell of the wife, or the embryo of the married couple, or none of these. This means that the husband or wife might be, but is not necessarily, the biological parent of the child born of the Surrogate mother.

Some states consider a Surrogate Parent Contract to be against public policy and have passed laws restricting their use. Other states, such as Florida and Virginia, allow a couple to contract with a woman to have their baby, provided it is done according to the law of the state. As of mid 2006, there is no California statute dealing with Surrogate Parent Contract. A child born to a Surrogate mother has the same rights as any other child born to the mother. If she is married, and her husband agreed to the procedure, then he is the legal father of the child (Fam. 7613). After birth the surrogate parent(s) can agree to the adoption of the child by the intended parents. Adoption is necessary, regardless of whether either (or both) of the intended parents happen to be the genetic parent of the child. If the child is later adopted, the child will have the same status as any other adopted child.

If there is a disagreement regarding a surrogacy contract it will need to be settled by a Court. That was the case with a couple who contracted with a woman to bear a child produced from an egg cell from the intended mother, and fertilized by the sperm of the intended father. When the child was born, the surrogate mother refused to surrender the child, stating that she was the child's natural mother.

The California's Supreme Court ruled that the intended couple were the child's natural parents, and that the surrogate mother had no parental rights (*Johnson v. Calvert*, 5 Cal. 4th 84 (1993), 851 P.2d 776). Using this case as a precedent, a child born to a surrogate mother using the fertilized egg of the intended parents is the natural child of those parents, and not the child of the surrogate mother. But the Court's decision in this case was not unanimous. Justice Kennard wrote a 16 page dissent. Other situations, such as using the surrogate mother's egg and the intended father's sperm might lead to a different result.

THE ADOPTED CHILD
An adopted child has the same right to inherit from an adoptive parent as does a natural child. The adopted child cannot inherit from a natural parent or a relative of a natural parent, unless the adoption took place after the death of one of his parents and the child was adopted by the spouse of his natural parent (Prob. 6451).

THE FOSTER CHILD, THE STEPCHILD, THE EQUITABLE CHILD
Sometimes a foster child or a stepchild is raised by someone who treats the child with all the love and care of a natural parent. In such cases, it is only equitable (fair) that the child be allowed to inherit from the foster parent or step-parent under the Laws of Intestate Succession. Under California law if the parent-child relationship began before the child was 18 and continued up until the death AND evidence shows that there would have been an adoption except for some legal barrier, the child can inherit under California's Laws of Intestate Succession (Prob. 6454). The law is not restricted to a foster child or stepchild. A California court can find that a child was "equitably" adopted whenever some special circumstance justifies that conclusion (Prob. 6455). See *Estate Of Ford*, 82 P.3d 747 (Cal. 2004) for a detailed discussion of what constitutes an equitable adoption in the state of California.

NON-MARITAL CHILD

A child born out of wedlock has the same rights to inherit from his/her natural father as does one born in wedlock, provided the relationship is established according to California law. The law includes the following methods:

☑ the child is born while his parents are married or within 300 days from the date the marriage was terminated because of divorce, death, legal separation, etc. - or -

☑ the parents marry after the child's birth and with the father's consent, he is identified on the birth certificate as the father - or -

☑ the parents marry after the child's birth and the father is obliged to support the child by signing a voluntary promise to do so, or by court order - or -

☑ the father takes the child into his home and openly acknowledges the child as his own (Fam. 7611) - or -

☑ a Court order is entered during the father's lifetime declaring the paternity (Prob. 6453).

Under California law neither the father of a child born out of wedlock or any relative of the father can inherit the child's property unless:

⇨ the parent or relative of the parent acknowledges the child AND

⇨ the parent or relative of the parent contribute to the support or care of the child (Prob. 6450, 6452).

The Laws of Intestate Succession are based on the right of family members to inherit property from the decedent. Now that we know who the state of California considers to be your Spouse/RDP and child, we can examine what part of your Probate Estate each is entitled to inherit.

If you are married or a Domestic Partner, your Spouse/ RDP may have marital rights in your Probate Estate, so we first need to determine what property is covered by the California Laws of Intestate Succession. California is a Community Property state. This means that if you are married or a Domestic Partner, property acquired by either you or your Spouse/RDP while you are in the union and living in California is *Community Property.* It includes monies either of you earn during the union. It does not include property either of you acquire as a gift or through an inheritance. Once a Spouse/RDP dies, the surviving Spouse/RDP owns half of their Community Property. The other half becomes part of the decedent's Estate (Prob. 100).

If you lived in another state during the course of your marriage, property you acquired as a married couple in another state is called *Quasi-community property* (Fam. 125, 760). The laws relating to Quasi-community property are much the same as those for Community property. For simplicity, we will use the term "Community Property" understanding that the law quoted applies to Quasi-community property as well.

Separate Property is anything you owned before you married and anything you acquired during the marriage as a gift or an inheritance. Any profit or increase in value of Separate Property is also Separate Property. For example, if you owned rental property prior to your marriage, any money you receive as rent during your marriage is your Separate Property. If your rental property appreciates in value, that increase in value is also Separate Property. If you separate from your Spouse/RDP, money you earn while you are living separately, is also Separate Property (Fam. 770, 771, 772).

Couples contemplating marriage, or a Domestic Partnership can decide whether they want property that they acquire during their union to be Community Property or whether they want to hold all or certain of their property separately. They can enter into a *Premarital* or *Prepartnership Agreement* stating what they consider to be their Separate Property and what property will be their Community Property. If they wish, they can agree that all of their property is Separate Property; i.e., they will own no Community Property. In the absence of an Agreement, property earned by the Spouse/RDP during the marriage is Community Property. However, at any time during the union, the couple can sign an Agreement identifying certain of their property as being separately owned by either partner. Any transfer of Community Property to Separate Property or vice-versa Separate Property to Community Property must be in writing (Fam. 852).

A Spouse/RDP can own property together with a partner as Joint Tenants (with right of survivorship), or as Tenants In Common (without right of survivorship), or as Community Property (Fam. 750). Property owned by the couple as Joint Tenants cannot also be owned as Community Property, so if a deed identifies the couple as Joint Tenants, it is presumed that they have agreed that the property is not their Community Property *(Gudelj v. Gudelj,* 41 P 2d 202 (Cal. 1953)).

As we will see later in this book, how a couple owns property has important consequences. For a married couple, it has federal tax consequences. Inheritance rights and creditor protection for a Spouse/RDP depends on whether property is owned as Community Property or Separate Property.

THE LAWS OF INTESTATE SUCCESSION

If you leave property in your name only and you do not have a Will, the state of California provides one for you in the form of its Laws of Intestate Succession. If you are single the Laws apply to all of your Probate Estate. If you are married or a Registered Domestic Partner, the Laws of Intestate Succession apply to:

⇨   all of your Separate Property, and

⇨   your half of the Community Property.

For purposes of this discussion, we will assume that in addition to having no Will, you have no written Agreement with your Spouse/RDP to distribute your intestate property any differently than as stated in California's Law of Intestate Succession.

THE DECEASED SPOUSE/RDP

California is unique in that the family of a deceased Spouse/RDP has rights in your Probate Estate, provided you did not remarry or become a RDP after the death. To inherit your *real property* (residence, condominium, lot, etc.) your Spouse/RDP must have died within 15 years of your death. To inherit your *personal property* (bank account, securities, car, etc., your Spouse/RDP must have died within 5 years of your death. A death beyond those time limits has no effect on your intestate Probate Estate. When we refer to a *Deceased Spouse/RDP* in this section, we mean a deceased Spouse/RDP who died within the time limits.

SINGLE, WITH DESCENDANTS

If, you have a surviving descendant (child, grandchild, etc.) and no Spouse/RDP or Deceased Spouse/RDP, your children inherit your Probate Estate, in equal shares, *per stirpes*, meaning that if all of your children are alive, they each take an equal share of your Estate, but if a child dies before you, the share intended for the deceased child is inherited by his children, in equal shares.

If the deceased child dies without descendants, your surviving children will share equally in your Probate Estate.

SINGLE WITHOUT DESCENDANTS

If you have no surviving descendants, or a Spouse/RDP or Deceased Spouse/RDP, your Probate Estate will go to your parents, equally, or to the survivor of them. If neither parent survives you, your Probate Estate is inherited by your brothers and sisters, in equal shares, per stirpes; i.e., the share intended for a deceased sibling goes to his surviving descendant (your nieces or nephews).

Relatives of half-blood inherit the same as if they were whole blood. For example, if you have a brother from the same set of parents and a brother with the same father and a different mother, both brothers inherit an equal share (Prob. 6402, 6406).

If you have no surviving parents or their descendants, your Probate Estate is shared equally by your surviving grandparents. If you have no surviving grandparent, then to their descendants (your aunts and uncles), in equal shares, per stirpes.

SURVIVING SPOUSE/RDP

You surviving Spouse/RDP inherits your entire Probate Estate, provided you are not survived by a descendant, parent, sibling or descendant of a sibling (Prob. 6401).

If you have a surviving Spouse/RDP and one child, your Spouse/RDP inherits your half of the Community Property, and half of your Separate Property and your only child, the other half. If your only child dies before you, the child's half goes to his descendants in equal shares, per stirpes.

If you have a surviving Spouse/RDP and more than one child, your Spouse/RDP is entitled to all of your Community Property and one-third of your Separate Property. Your children inherit the other two-thirds in equal shares, per stirpes. If none of your children, or their descendants survive you, your family inherits the two-thirds share of your Separate Property in the same manner as if you were single without descendants (Prob. 6401).

These same rules apply if you have a deceased Spouse/RDP. For example, if you have a deceased Spouse, and one child, your child inherits half of your Probate Estate. The descendants of your deceased Spouse inherit the other half, in equal shares, per stirpes. If the deceased Spouse has no surviving descendants, the half goes to his parents, and if no surviving parents, to the descendants of his parents. The line of inheritance proceeds in the same manner as described on the previous page under the heading of SINGLE WITH DESCENDANTS (Prob. 6402.5).

CALIFORNIA: HEIR OF LAST RESORT
Property that is either unclaimed or abandoned, goes to the state; so if you die without a Will and absolutely no one has the right to inherit your Probate Estate under the Laws of Intestate Succession, your property is "inherited" by the state of California (Prob. 6404).

THERE'S MORE TO THE LAW
If you think the California Laws of Intestate Succession is difficult to understand — it is. Worse yet, this discussion is abridged. There is much more to the Law.

But why let the state of California decide who and how much goes to your family members? Why chance having your property go to someone you may not even know or like? Best to prepare a Will and have your property inherited the way you want.

THE COST OF PROBATE

Holding property in your name only gives you maximum control and protection during your lifetime. If you do not like the way your property will be distributed should you die without a Will, then you can control who inherits your property by preparing a Will. But there is still the question of what it will cost to transfer your Estate to your beneficiaries. In all probability, a Probate procedure will be necessary. How much of your Estate will need to be spent to Probate your Estate?

TRANSFERRING REAL PROPERTY WORTH $20,000 OR LESS

There is no need to be concerned about Probate if all you own in your name only is real property with a gross value that does not exceed $20,000. The beneficiary of your property can file an *Affidavit* (a written statement, signed and sworn to before a Notary Public) in the county of your residence. If you are not a resident of California at the time of your death, the Affidavit can be filed in the county where the property is located.

The Clerk of the Superior Court will give the beneficiary the Affidavit to complete. Once the Clerk verifies that the information contained in the Affidavit is true, he will issue a certified copy of the Affidavit. The certified copy of the Affidavit is then given to the County Recorder who will record the change of ownership of the real property (Prob. 13200, 13202).

Although the law allows for the transfer of real property without the need for Probate, this statute is of no practical use. Where can you find land in California for less than $20,000???

An Affidavit can be used to transfer *personal property* (stocks, bonds, bank accounts, etc.) provided that the total value of your real and personal property in the state of California is no more than $100,000. This value does not include property that can be transferred directly to your beneficiary without the need for Probate; for example, property held jointly, or property held in trust. California statute (Prob. 13050) gives a list of all of the items that you do not need to include as part of the $100,000.

The person signing the Affidavit must verify that the following statements are true:

1. At least 40 days have elapsed since the date of death.

2. No proceeding is now being or has been conducted in California for administration -or - if commenced the Personal Representative has consented in writing to the use of this procedure.

3. The current gross fair market value of the decedent's real and personal property in California, excluding property described in Section 13050 of the California Probate Code is not greater than $100,000.

4. Affiant is the successor of the decedent and to the decedent's interest in the described property, and no other person has a superior right to the interest of the decedent in the property (Probate 13100, 13101).

This seems almost too easy. The reader may be thinking "You mean that all my beneficiary needs to do is go to a brokerage office, or bank, give them an Affidavit and they will hand over my personal property?"

The answer is "yes, but..."

▶ THE TRANSFER CAN BE REFUSED ◀

The person in possession of the property might refuse to accept the Affidavit from anyone other than a court appointed Personal Representative. In such case, your beneficiary can either go through the Probate procedure, or sue the person in possession to compel the transfer. If the Court finds that the person in possession acted unreasonably, the beneficiary can get the property, and be reimbursed for his attorney's fees (Prob. 13105).

▶ BENEFICIARY IS RESPONSIBLE FOR DEBTS ◀

Whoever uses the Affidavit becomes responsible to pay monies owed on that item. For example, suppose you borrowed $25,000 and used your $50,000 Certificate of Deposit as collateral. Your beneficiary will need to pay the $25,000 before he can get the CD. If your CD was not used to secure any debt, but you owe money, whoever takes the CD becomes personally liable for your debts up to the value of the CD.

And if someone uses an Affidavit to transfer your property and it turns out that another person had a superior right to that property then the property must be turned over to the proper beneficiary. If the person took the property fraudulently, i.e., he knew he had no right to that property but he took it anyway, the beneficiary has the right to demand the property and three times its market value (Prob. 13110).

For most people these are not major concerns. If all you own is personal property worth $100,000 and you have only one or two beneficiaries, the cost of Probate should be $0. The two heirs can get your property by signing a joint Affidavit.

The Affidavit may not be a practical choice if you leave your property to several different beneficiaries. And a full Probate may be necessary if you owe money to several different creditors. In such case it is better to have a Personal Representative appointed to settle the Estate. He will give notice to your creditors to come forward and present their *claims* (i.e. demands for payment) for money you owe (Prob. 9050). Once all valid claims are paid, the Personal Representative will distribute whatever remains to your beneficiaries.

Of course an Affidavit is not an option if you own real property in your name worth more than $20,000; or if the total value of your Probate Estate is more than $100,000.

NO ADMINISTRATION IF ALL TO SPOUSE/RDP

A full Probate procedure is not necessary if all of your property is inherited by your Spouse/RDP either according to the Laws of Intestate Succession and through your Will. Your Spouse/RDP can file a petition asking the Court to issue an order stating that NO ADMINISTRATION is necessary and that all of the property described in the petition be turned over to the Spouse/RDP.

Before issuing an order the Court will want to know all of the facts of the case to be sure that your Spouse/RDP is entitled to inherit all of your property. Obtaining the order is much simpler than Probate, but it does require preparing the petition according to California law and working through the Court system to obtain the order. Your Spouse/RDP will probably want to employ an attorney to get the order. Still, the cost of the procedure should be minimal (Prob. 13500, 13651).

THE FULL PROBATE PROCEDURE

The full Probate procedure can be involved and time consuming; not to mention, expensive. Administration of the Estate can take anywhere from several months to more than a year, depending on the size and complexity of the Estate. Someone must be appointed by the Court to serve as Personal Representative. Whoever is named as Executor of the Will gets the job. California statute gives an order of priority for appointing a Personal Representative for those who die without a Will, with the Spouse/ RDP having top priority (Prob. 8461).

Your Personal Representative will take possession of your Probate Estate. Within four months of his appointment he must prepare an inventory of the Estate and file it with the Court Clerk together with an appraisal of property listed in the inventory (Prob. 8800).

The Personal Representative will publish notice of your death and will notify known creditors, in writing, that they have a right to come forward and file a claim for money you owe (Prob. 8121, 9050, 9052).

Debts are paid from the Probate Estate and not from the Personal Representative's pocket; but if he makes a mistake, he may be responsible to pay for it. The Personal Representative needs to employ an attorney to guide him through the process. It then becomes the job of the attorney for the Personal Representative to see to it that the Estate is administered properly and without any personal liability to the Personal Representative.

THE PERSONAL REPRESENTATIVE'S FEES

The Personal Representative is entitled to compensation for his efforts. California statute has a schedule of fees for the Personal Representative:

> 4% on the first $100,000
> 3% on the next $100,000
> 2% on the next $800,000
> 1% on the next nine million dollars
> .5% on the next fifteen million dollars

The Court determines the fee for values over $25,000,000 (Prob. 10800).

This fee schedule is based on the ***gross value*** of the Probate Estate. For example, suppose all you own in your name only is a home worth $400,000. If you have a mortgage of $300,000, the fee is based on the $400,000. The Personal Representative would be entitled to a fee of $11,000:

> $4,000 (1st $100,000) + $3,000 (next $100,000)
> + $4,000 (2% of the remaining $200,000) = $11,000

THE ATTORNEY'S FEES

Under California law, the attorney for the Personal Representative is entitled to the same rate of compensation as is the Personal Representative. The Court can award the Personal Representative and/or his attorney, additional fees for extraordinary services, such defending a challenge to the Will, or a claim made by a creditor that is contested by the Personal Representative (Prob. 10810, 10811).

Using the statutory fee as set by California law, a relatively modest Estate with a gross value of $200,000, and no special problem, will pay $7,000 in Personal Representative and $7,0000 in attorney fees.

The Personal Representative and attorney's fees are significant charges to the Probate Estate; but they are not the only charges against the Estate. A Probate proceeding can incur some or all of the following expenses:

$$ Court filing fees

$$ The cost of a bond that the Court may order for the protection of your Probate Estate

$$ The cost of notifying your creditors which may include publishing notice, or mailing notice to them by registered or certified mail

$$ The cost of an appraisal

$$ Accounting fees to prepare an inventory, and account for monies spent during Probate

$$ The cost of transferring property to the proper beneficiary; i.e., recording fees, broker fees to sell securities or real estate.

Once the above costs, Personal Representative fees, attorney fees, taxes and all valid claims are paid, the Personal Representative will distribute whatever is left to the proper beneficiary and then close the Estate.

You may be thinking that Probate is a good thing to avoid. Why should your Personal Representative go through all that effort to settle your Estate? Why should your beneficiaries wait months or maybe years, and pay all these fees to inherit your Estate? There are ways to arrange your Estate so that your beneficiaries can immediately inherit your Estate without incurring unnecessary costs. In the next two chapters we will examine different methods that can be used to achieve this goal.

Is Probate Necessary? 2

Many people think that only wealthy people need to make plans to avoid Probate, yet each year, beneficiaries of relatively modest estates, spend thousands of dollars to settle an Estate. A bit of Estate Planning could have eliminated most, if not all, of the cost (and hassle) suffered by those families.

It is not difficult to arrange your finances to eliminate the need for Probate if you have a small Estate and only one or two beneficiaries. All you need do is title your property so that it automatically goes to your beneficiaries. There are many ways to arrange your finances to achieve this result. The most common method is to hold property jointly with another. Such an arrangement is the Estate Plan of choice for married couples and/or Domestic Partners. The couple hold all of their property jointly with right of survivorship, so that the surviving Spouse/RDP has complete and immediate ownership of the property without any need for Probate.

As we will see in this Chapter, holding property jointly may not be the most desirable method for the single person. There are other ways to ensure that your property is inherited quickly and without cost to your heirs. We will explore the pros and cons of different methods of holding property so that it can be transferred quickly and without the need for Probate.

PROPERTY OWNED JOINTLY

Bank accounts, securities, motor vehicles, real property can all be owned by two or more people. If one of the owners dies, the survivor(s) continue to own their share of the property. Who owns the share belonging to the decedent depends on California law and how ownership of the property was set up.

THE JOINT BANK ACCOUNT

When a bank account is opened in two or more names, the parties sign an agreement with the bank stating who is to have access to the account during the lifetime of the account owners; i.e. whether each owner has full authority to make a withdrawal, or whether two signatures are required. A **Joint Account** is an account that is payable to either party on request (Prob. 5130)

Unless there is clear evidence of a different intent, during their lifetime, each joint owner is entitled to as much as their **net contribution** (amount deposited, less amount withdrawn, plus a pro rata share of interest or dividends on the account) (Prob. 5301, 5302). Upon the death of a joint owner it is presumed that each joint owner had an equal share in the account (Prob. 5134).

An account can be set up with or without the right of the surviving owners to inherit the monies in the account:

JOINT ACCOUNT WITH RIGHT OF SURVIVORSHIP
To set up a joint account with **right of survivorship**, the contract with the bank should say:

> This account or certificate is owned by the named parties. Upon the death of any of them, ownership passes to the survivor(s) (Prob. 5203).

ACCOUNT HELD AS TENANTS IN COMMON

An account that is set up as *Tenants In Common* has no right of survivorship. Each owner of the account owns his share of the account without any claim to the share owned by the other tenants. The contract with the bank should say:

> This account or certificate is owned by the named parties as tenants in common. Upon the death of any party, the ownership interest of that party passes to the named pay-on-death payee(s) of that party or, if none, to the Estate of that party (Prob. 5203).

Once the bank is notified of the death of a Tenant In Common, the bank will freeze the account until the beneficiaries of the decedent's share of the account can be established. If a surviving owner withdraws all of the money from the account either before or after death, he may be liable to the beneficiary of the account for monies improperly withdrawn.

THE COMMUNITY PROPERTY ACCOUNT

An account opened by a husband and wife, or Registered Domestic Partners is presumed to be *Community Property Account* with each owning half of the account. Should one of them die, half of the account remains the property of the surviving spouse. The other half belongs to the Estate of the decedent, to be distributed according to his Will or if no Will, according to the Laws of Intestate Succession (Prob. 100, 5305).

The Community Property Account operates as a Tenancy-In-Common unless the couple sets up the account so that the surviving Spouse/RDP owns the entire account. In such case the contract should say:

> This account or certificate is owned by the named parties as husband and wife (or Domestic Partners), and is presumed to be their Community Property. Upon the death of either of them, ownership passes to the survivor (Prob. 5203).

The benefit of a joint account is that whatever remains in the account goes directly to the surviving joint owners of the account without the need to go through a Probate procedure to get that money. Married couples often own a bank account jointly for just that reason.

A single parent whose only asset is a bank account might decide that a simple way to avoid Probate is to make his child joint owner of the account. But there are potential problems associated with holding an account jointly with a child.

⊠ OVERREACHING

Making your child a joint owner of the account gives the child free access to the account. Monies may be withdrawn without your knowledge or authorization. You may be thinking that couldn't happen because you would immediately know of the withdrawal, and you could force the child to return the money. That may be true when you are healthy and alert. But in this ever aging society, it is likely that you will live to an advanced age and not be as aware as you are today. And if you have two children and decided to hold your account jointly with them, then there may be a problem with how the funds are distributed should you die.

That was the case with Amanda. All she had when her husband died, was a bank account worth $50,000. She wanted to be sure that the money would go to her two sons, Robert and Leon, without the need for Probate. She went to the bank with her two sons and opened a new survivorship account with all three names on the account as joint owners.

Several years passed without incident. As Amanda aged, her health began to fail, and she became more and more dependent on Robert. She needed his assistance to take her to the doctor, to do her shopping, and of course take care of her finances. Robert had a wife and two children, so it was hard for him to care for his family and his mother as well. Leon was single, yet he never seemed to have the time to help care for his mother. And Robert resented that.

Finally, Amanda died.

After the funeral, Leon asked Robert about the bank account "Didn't Mom have a joint account in our names?"

"Yeah, but I closed it out. There was only a few thousand left, and I used it for her funeral."

Leon thought it strange that all of the money was gone, so he went to the bank and asked to see the record of withdrawals. He found that over the last two years Robert had written several large checks to himself. There was only $7,000 left in the account when Robert closed it out, within a week of her death.

Leon fumed for several weeks before he brought up the subject. Robert's face flushed when Leon asked about the money. Leon did not know if it was from anger or embarrassment. He soon learned that it was both when Robert asked "Where were you for the past two years? You never once helped. Did you know she became incontinent at the end? Who cleaned up? Not you. She blessed me every day. She often said she would have been dead long ago if it wasn't for me. She wanted me to have that money!"

"Mom never said anything to me about wanting you to have the money. She never asked for my help and neither did you. It isn't right for you to throw this up to me now."

The boys never spoke of the money again. But then there were few times that they ever spoke to each other after that.

Overreaching isn't the only problem with a joint account, there is also the problem of liability.

⊠   POTENTIAL LIABILITY
If you hold a bank account jointly with your adult child and that child is sued or gets a divorce, then the child may need to disclose his ownership of the joint account. In such a case, you may find yourself spending money to prove that the account was established for convenience only and that all of the money in that account really belongs to you.

Because of these inherent problems, you might want to hold the funds so that your beneficiary does not have access to the monies unless you die while the account is open. You can do so by opening a *Beneficiary Account*.

As explained, the terms of a bank account are established when a bank account is opened. Your agreement gives directions about who can access your account during your lifetime, but it can also give directions about what to do with the account should you die. If you hold the account in your name only and do not give any such directions, then should you die while the account is open, the monies in your account will become part of your Probate Estate and will be distributed in the same way as any other item that you hold in your name only.

One way to avoid Probate of the account, yet retain full control of the account during your lifetime, is to name one or more persons to be the beneficiary of your account. There are two forms of beneficiary account. You can have a contract with the bank that directs the bank to **Pay-On-Death** ("POD") all of the money in the account to one or more beneficiaries that you name — or you can direct the bank to hold your account **In Trust For** ("ITF") one or more beneficiaries that you name (Prob. 5139, 5140). The ITF account is also known as a *Totten Trust* (Prob. 80). With both the POD and ITF account, unless your contract with the bank says differently:

⇨ The beneficiary does not have access to the account during your lifetime.

⇨ You, as the owner of the account, have complete control over the account. You can add to it or close it or change beneficiaries without asking anyone's permission to do so (Prob. 5301).

You may want to hold the account jointly with your Spouse /DP with directions to the bank to give the funds to one or more beneficiaries that you name.

For example, the contract with the bank may state:

> This Joint Account is owned by ELDON CONNORS and LORRAINE CONNORS. Upon the death of any of them, ownership passes to survivor. Upon the death of all of them, ownership passes to SAM CONNORS AND FRED CONNORS (Prob. 5203).

Unless the contract with the bank says differently, if either parent dies, the surviving party owns the account, and is free to close the account or change the beneficiary of the account without notifying either of their children. If the account is not changed, once both parents are deceased, their sons share the money in the account equally. Should one son die before his parent, the remaining son will inherit the entire account (Prob. 5301, 5302).

TRANSFER ON DEATH

The California law for securities is similar to the statute for bank accounts. You can instruct the holder of the security to **Transfer On Death** ("TOD") to a named beneficiary. As with the Pay-On-Death account, the Transfer On Death designation has no effect on the ownership of the security until the owner of the security dies. The security can be held jointly with another with instructions that once both owners of the security die, the security is to be transferred to a named beneficiary. This is a convenient way of owning a security for a couple who want their child to inherit the security without going through a Probate procedure. For example, a security can be titled as:

TIM REILLY and OLIVIA REILLY,
AS JOINT TENANTS WITH RIGHT OF SURVIVORSHIP
TOD STUART REILLY

Stuart has no right to the security until both his parents die. His parents are free to change the beneficiary of the security at any time during their lifetime. If no change is made Stuart will inherit the security once both parents are deceased. All he needs to do to transfer the securities to his name is produce a certified copy of the death certificate. If Stuart dies before his parents and no other provision made, the security will go to the Estate of the last parent to die (Prob. 5504, 5506, 5507).

CAR, BOAT, MOBILE HOME

The TOD registration is available under California law for cars, trucks, boats and mobile homes. You can have title to the vehicle in your name followed by the words "transfer on death to" or just the abbreviation TOD followed by the name of the beneficiary. The only difference between the TOD registration for securities and the TOD registration for vehicles, is that California law limits the TOD registration for vehicles to just one owner and just one beneficiary. In other words, to have a TOD title to your car, boat, truck or mobile home, you must own the vehicle in your name only, and the TOD registration must be to one beneficiary only (Veh. 4150.7, 9852.7, Health & Safety 18080.2)

You can use any of these Beneficiary Registrations (*In Trust For, Pay-On-Death, Transfer On Death*) to transfer your property to your beneficiaries without the need for Probate. More importantly, a Beneficiary Registration affords you maximum control and protection of those funds during your lifetime.

REAL PROPERTY OWNED JOINTLY

If you own real property together with another, then who will own the property upon your death depends on how the current owner is identified on the face of the deed. The top paragraph of the deed should identify the **Grantor** i.e. the person who transferred the property to you. The person to whom the property was transferred is called the **Grantee**. The deed might read something like:

ROBERT TRAYNOR, a single man,
for value received, hereby grants to
SUSAN CODY, a married woman
and HENRY TRAYNOR, a single man,
AS JOINT TENANTS
all that real property situated in the county of
Los Angeles, state of California
described as follows . . .

In California, property held as JOINT TENANTS means that each Grantee owns an equal share of the property, and that each has a right of survivorship (Civ. 683). Should either Susan or Henry die, the survivor will own the property 100% Nothing need be done to establish that ownership, but the name of the deceased joint owner remains on the deed.

See page 43 for an explanation of what documents can be recorded so that anyone who examines the title to the property will know that the survivor is now the sole owner of the property.

🗐 DEED HELD AS TENANTS IN COMMON

You might have a deed that names you and another person as Grantee, followed by **TENANTS IN COMMON**. In such case, there is no right of survivorship. Should you die, your share will go to whomever you name as beneficiary in your Will. If you die without a Will, California's Laws of Intestate Succession determine who will inherit your share of the property.

If a deed names two or more people as Grantees, but does not state that they own the property:
> "IN JOINT TENANCY"   or   "AS JOINT TENANTS"   or
> "AS JOINT TENANTS WITH RIGHT OF SURVIVORSHIP"

the property is a Tenancy In Common (Civ. 683).

🗐 DEED HELD AS HUSBAND AND WIFE

In many states, a deed held as husband and wife means that the surviving partner owns the property. This is not the case in California. It is presumed that real property held as husband and wife is Community Property with each partner owning half. If you and your spouse own real property as:

> HUSBAND AND WIFE AS COMMUNITY PROPERTY

should one of you die, the decedent's "half" may need to go through a Probate procedure in order to transfer the property to the proper beneficiary. No Probate is necessary if the surviving spouse inherits that half, either as a beneficiary of the Will or according to the Laws of Intestate Succession (Prob. 13500). The spouse will inherit the property at a *step-up in basis* ** i.e., the property is inherited at the fair market value as of the date of death.

** The step-up in basis is federal law, and does not apply to a Registered Domestic Partner.

This could result in a substantial tax savings, especially if the property has appreciated significantly over the years. The surviving spouse can immediately sell the property and not pay any Capital Gains Tax on that increase in value. But if a married couple hold property as:

JOINT TENANTS WITH RIGHT OF SURVIVORSHIP

there is a step-up in basis in decedent's half only. Should the surviving spouse decide to sell the property, there might be a Capital Gains Tax on the increase in value of the share owned by the surviving spouse.

The California legislature created a new method of holding Community Property that results in a step-up in basis for the entire property and not just half. Effective July 1, 2001, Community Property can be transferred to the surviving spouse without any need for Probate and with 100% step-up in basis if the deed identifies the property as:

COMMUNITY PROPERTY WITH RIGHT OF SURVIVORSHIP

This designation can be used with other property owned by the couple (Civ. 682.1). For example, securities can be owned as Community Property With Right of Survivorship.

Those of you who are married and own property as Joint Tenants With Right of Survivorship may be tempted to change to the new designation to take advantage of the step-up in basis; but if you or your spouse have a creditor problem (i.e., you owe more than you own), consider that Community Property With Right of Survivorship is still Community Property for purposes of paying monies owed by you or your spouse. Joint tenancy might provide better asset protection with respect to the debts of a deceased spouse. See Chapter 5 for a discussion of Community Property Liability.

CAUTION FEDERAL LAWS RELATING TO MARRIED COUPLES
DO NOT APPLY TO DOMESTIC PARTNERS

Registered Domestic Partners may own property in the same manner as a married couple:

REGISTERED DOMESTIC PARTNERS AS COMMUNITY PROPERTY

or

JOINT TENANTS WITH RIGHT OF SURVIVORSHIP

or

COMMUNITY PROPERTY WITH RIGHT OF SURVIVORSHIP.

However, the Registered Domestic Partner relationship is a product of the California legislature. The federal government does not recognize the relationship as qualifying for any tax break that may be granted to a married couple. In particular, if Registered Domestic Partners own property as Community Property With Right of Survivorship, the federal government will consider this to be the same as Joint Tenants With Right of Survivorship and just allow a step-up in basis on the share owned by the decedent.

▤ DEED WITH A LIFE ESTATE

A *Life Estate* interest in real property means that the person who owns the Life Estate has the right to live in that property until he/she dies. You can identify a Life Estate interest by examining the face of the deed. If somewhere on the face of the deed you see the phrase RESERVING A LIFE ESTATE, then the Grantee cannot take possession of the property until the owner of the Life Estate dies. For example, suppose the granting paragraph of the deed reads:

> ROSE CAVALLO, a single woman for value received,
> hereby grants to
> SALVATORE CAVALLO, a married man
>
> . . .
> RESERVING A LIFE ESTATE
> TO ROSE CAVALLO
>
> . . .

Rose is the owner of the Life Estate. Salvatore is the owner of the *Remainder Interest*. Rose has the right to occupy the premises during her lifetime or to rent it out and receive the income from the property. During Rose's lifetime, Salvatore has no right to the possession of, or the income from, the property. Once Rose dies, Salvatore will own the property and is free to take possession of the property and to lease, sell or transfer it, as he sees fit.

If you are an owner of the Life Estate interest, upon your death, no Probate procedure will be necessary to transfer the property to the owner of the Remainder Interest.

No Probate procedure will be necessary if you hold property in California:

⇨   as the owner of a Life Estate - or -

⇨   as a Joint Tenant with right of survivorship - or -

⇨   as Community Property with right of survivorship.

No Probate procedure is necessary for Community property inherited by your surviving spouse according to the Laws of Intestate Succession or even as a beneficiary of your Will (Prob. 13500). In each of these cases, upon your death, the surviving owner will own the property 100%. All the surviving owner needs to do is to keep a certified copy of the death certificate available in the event the owner wishes to sell or transfer the property.

Even though nothing need be done to establish the ownership of the surviving owner, it is a good idea to have an attorney prepare and record documents to notify anyone examining title to the property, of the death. The attorney can prepare an **AFFIDAVIT OF DEATH OF JOINT TENANT** for the survivor to sign. The attorney will also have the survivor complete a **PRELIMINARY CHANGE OF OWNER-SHIP** form which is then forwarded to the County Assessor for tax purposes. Once the Affidavit and decedent's death certificate are recorded, and the Preliminary Change of Ownership Report filed, the decedent's name is, in effect, removed from the deed.

If you own California property in your name only, or as a Tenant In Common, it will take a Probate procedure to transfer property to your intended beneficiary. As explained in Chapter 1, the type of Probate procedure will depend on the size of your Estate.

OUT OF STATE PROPERTY

This chapter relates only to real property you own in the state of California. If you own property in another state or country, the laws of that state or country determine who has the right to inherit your property.

RIGHT OF SURVIVORSHIP

Whether or not there is a right of survivorship depends on the laws of that state. Some states require that the deed specifically state that there is a right of survivorship. In such states, a deed held as Joint Tenants (and no stated right of survivorship) is the same as a Tenancy In Common. In other states, including California, a deed that identifies the owners as Joint Tenants has a right of survivorship even though the deed may not specify such right. If you own out of state property jointly with another, it is important that you check with an attorney in that state to be verify that your interest in the property will go to the person of your choice.

SPOUSAL RIGHTS

If you are married, and own real property in another state, you need to be aware that your spouse may have rights in that property, even though the deed is in your name only. That is the case in Community Property states. In other states, a surviving spouse may have Dower rights or other statutory rights. And of course, a Registered Domestic Partner is a relationship recognized in California only. Your Domestic Partner does not have any marital rights in property you own in that state.

In the next chapter, we will discuss the rights of a surviving spouse in real property located in California. If you are married, and own property in another state, you need to determine the rights of your spouse in that state as well.

Still another concern is whether a Probate procedure will be necessary to transfer out of state property that you own to your beneficiary. Each state is in charge of the way real property located in that state is transferred. Most state laws are similar to California, namely, property you own as a Joint Tenant With Right of Survivorship or property in which you hold a Life Estate interest are transferred without the need for Probate. Property you own as a Tenant In Common or in your name only may require a Probate procedure in order to transfer the property to your beneficiary.

If you own property in your name only in California and in another state, upon your death it may be necessary to have a Probate proceeding in California, and an *ancillary* (secondary) Probate proceeding in the state where the property is located. This can double the cost of Probate. Still another problem with out of state property is the matter of taxes. Some states have an Inheritance or Transfer Tax that may be due in the state where the property is located as well as in California. It may be necessary to file a tax return in two states. In addition to increased taxes, this can significantly increase the cost of accounting fees.

If you own property in another state, it is important to consult with an attorney to learn the answers to all of these questions, namely:

> *Who will inherit my property under the laws of the state where it is located?*
>
> *Will a Probate procedure be necessary to transfer that property to my beneficiaries?*
>
> *What taxes will need to be paid in that state?*

If you find that Probate will be necessary to transfer real property that you own in California or elsewhere, you may decide that the cost of Probate is too expensive. You may be tempted to go for the quick fix of having the deed to the property changed so that you are joint owners with the intended beneficiary of the property; or you may decide to transfer the property to your intended beneficiary and keep a Life Estate for yourself.

This will avoid Probate, but it may not be the best Estate Plan because you will not have maximum control over the property during your lifetime. If you hold real property as a Joint Tenant or as a Life Tenant, you will not be able to sell that property during your lifetime without getting permission from your beneficiary. And if the beneficiary gives permission and the property is sold, the beneficiary will have the legal right to share in the proceeds of the sale.

You may be thinking "I can make my son joint owner of my home and avoid any need for Probate. I trust him to do what I want with the property. If I decide to sell, I know he won't ask for any part of the proceeds regardless of his legal right to those funds."

And all that may be true, but it may cost you more in taxes to sell your property than if you kept the property in your name only.

Under today's law, you can sell your home without paying a Capital Gains Tax, provided you lived there for 2 of the prior 5 years and the Capital Gains on the sale is not greater than $250,000 ($500,000 if married). If you sell your home after making the Life Estate transfer (or making your child a Joint Tenant), then unless your child occupies the home as his primary residence, his share of the property is subject to a Capital Gains Tax.

If your son does not take his share of the proceeds, then why should he pay any Capital Gains Tax?

In such case, you'll be the one to pay the tax on your son's share of the proceeds.

Is there a better way to avoid Probate?

Maybe. Read on.

How To Avoid Probate   3

TRUE OR FALSE?

(   ) If you have a Will, then Probate will be necessary.

(   ) Probate will be necessary if you don't have a Will.

(   ) Probate is necessary if you own property that is worth more than $100,000.

If you answered false to all of the above, you are either a lawyer, or you carefully read the last chapter.

All of these sentences are false because all of your property may pass to your beneficiaries automatically, without the need for Probate, such as property held jointly or in a Pay-On-Death account. The point we were trying to make is:

> Whether Probate is necessary has nothing to do with whether there is a Will, or even how much money is involved. The determining factor is how the property is titled (owned).

There are three basic ways to title property:

      ✧ in your name only

      ✧ jointly with another

      ✧ in trust for another

Chapter 1 examined the pros and cons of holding property in your name only, with the biggest "con" being that Probate may be necessary.

In Chapter 2 we noted that holding property jointly with another solved the Probate problem, but at the sacrifice of the control and protection offered by keeping property in your name only. In this Chapter we examine another option which may be the solution to these problems, namely the REVOCABLE LIVING TRUST (also known as an *Inter Vivos Trust*).

A Revocable Living Trust is designed to care for your property during your lifetime and then to distribute your property once you die without the need for Probate. You may have been encouraged to set up such a Trust by your financial planner, attorney, or accountant. Even people of modest means are being encouraged to use a Trust as the basis of their Estate Plan. But Trusts also have their benefits and drawbacks. Before getting into that, let's first discuss what a Trust is and how it works.

HOW A TRUST IS CREATED

To create a **Revocable Living Trust**, an attorney prepares a Trust Agreement in accordance with the client's needs and desires. The "Agreement" refers to the fact that the person creating the Trust (the *Settlor* or *Trustor*) is contracting with someone to be the **Trustee** (manager) of property placed in the Trust. By signing the Trust Agreement, the Trustee agrees to manage the Trust property according to the directions given in the Trust Agreement.

If the Settlor places property into the Trust, he is also referred to as the *Grantor*. We will refer to the Revocable Living Trust as the "Living Trust" or just the "Trust" and the person who sets up and funds the Trust as the "Settlor." Usually the Settlor appoints himself as initial Trustee so that he is in total control of property that he places into the Trust. In that case, he signs the Trust Agreement as the Settlor and also as the Trustee who agrees to follow the terms of the Trust Agreement. The Trust Agreement also appoints a **Successor Trustee** to take over the management of the Trust property should the Trustee resign, become disabled or die.

Once the Trust document is properly signed, the Settlor can transfer property into the Trust. The Settlor does this by changing the name on the account from his individual name to his name as Trustee. For example, if Susan Clark sets up a Trust naming herself as Trustee, and she wants to put her bank account into the Trust, all she need do is instruct the bank to change the name on the account from Susan Clark to Susan Clark, Trustee.

If Susan wants to put real property that she owns into the Trust, she can have her attorney or a title insurance company prepare and record a new deed with the owner of the property identified as Susan Clark, Trustee:

SUSAN CLARK, TRUSTEE OF THE SUSAN CLARK
REVOCABLE LIVING TRUST
UNDER AGREEMENT DATED OCTOBER 5, 2006.

The Trust Agreement states how property placed into the Trust is to be managed during Susan's lifetime. Susan, as Trustee, controls the Trust property. For example, monies she keeps in a Trust bank account can be withdrawn or added to in the same manner as if the account were in her name only.

During her lifetime, Susan is free to *amend* (i.e.change the terms) of her Trust or even terminate (i.e., revoke) the Trust altogether and have the Trust property placed back into her own name. If Susan does not revoke the Trust during her lifetime, once she dies, the Trust becomes irrevocable. Her Successor Trustee is required to follow the terms of the Trust Agreement as it is written. If the Trust says to give the Trust property to certain beneficiaries, the Successor Trustee will do so; and in most cases without the need for Probate. If the Trust directs the Successor Trustee to continue to hold property in Trust and use the money to take care of a member of Susan's family, the Successor Trustee will use the Trust funds to care for the family member in the manner described in the Trust Agreement.

The Successor Trustee must also follow California statutes relating to the administration of the Trust. For example, within 60 days, the Successor Trustee must inform all of the beneficiaries, in writing, that he is now administering the Trust, and upon request, must provide the beneficiary with a copy of the Trust (Prob. 16061.7).

THE PROS AND CONS OF A TRUST

A Living Trust has many good features.

☆ AVOID PROBATE

As discussed in Chapter 1, Probate can be time consuming and expensive. Both the Personal Representative and his attorney are entitled to payment for their services. These fees can be significant. It may be necessary to hire accountants and appraisers, as well. If you have property in two states, then two Probate procedures may be necessary (one in each state) and that could have the effect of doubling the cost of Probate. If the Trust is properly drafted and your property placed into the Trust, there should be no need for Probate. Upon your death, your Successor Trustee can transfer property, in this or any other state, to the beneficiary of your Trust.

☆ AVOID A CHALLENGE TO YOUR ESTATE PLAN

A Trust operates much like a Will because it provides for the distribution of your Estate when you die. Unlike a Will, it is not subject to Probate, so no Court is charged with the duty of "proving" that your Trust is valid. Even though no Court needs to prove that the Trust is valid, it can still be challenged. Once you are deceased, your Successor Trustee must notify all of your *heirs* (i.e., next of kin as determined by the California Laws of Intestate Succession) of the existence of your Trust, and provide them with a copy of the Trust, if requested.

Once your heirs and the beneficiaries of your Trust are notified, each has 120 days from the date of the notice, or 60 days from receipt of the Trust document (whichever is later) to bring a Court action to challenge the Trust (Prob. 16061.7).

☆ PRIVACY

Your Trust is a private document. Unless someone decides to challenge the terms of your Trust, no one but your next of kin and beneficiaries of your Trust need ever read it. When opening a Trust account, the bank might ask to see your Trust, but under California law you can present the bank with a *Certificate of Trust* instead of giving them a copy of the Trust. The Certificate of Trust gives basic information relating to the Trust, including the date of execution of the Trust; the Trust identification number; the identity of the Settlor, current Trustee, beneficiaries of the Trust, etc. Your attorney can prepare a Certificate of Trust at the same time he prepares the Trust. He will include all of the items of information required by California statute (Prob. 18100.5).

If you have a Will, once it is admitted to Probate it becomes part of the Court records. Anyone can examine the Court records, read your Will and see who you did (or did not) provide for. Other Probate documents such as the inventory of your Probate Estate, creditor's claims, etc. are also open to public scrutiny. In some states, Court records are now available on the Internet!

LEASE SAFE DEPOSIT BOX AS TRUSTEE

Under California law, if you hold a safe deposit box in your name only, once the lessor (usually a bank) learns of your death, access to the box is restricted. Anyone who finds the key to your safe deposit box has the right to enter it for the limited purpose of removing your burial instructions, Will or Trust (Prob. 331).

The lessor will allow access to the safe deposit, provided it is under the supervision of one of its officers or employees. The officer or employee will allow the person entering the box to make an inventory of its contents. The decedent's Will or Trust may be removed after the lessor makes a copy of the documents. The lessor has the right to charge a reasonable fee to copy these documents.

Whoever removes the Will must deliver it to Clerk of the Superior Court in the county where the decedent lived. He must also mail or deliver a copy of the Will to the person named as Executor of the Will (Prob. 331, 7051).

One of the benefits of having a Living Trust, is that you can lease the safe deposit box in your name as Trustee. You can have an agreement with the bank that upon your death or disability, your Successor Trustee has full authority to enter the box and remove any and all of the items from that box.

By leasing the safe deposit box in your capacity as Trustee, you can avoid having the bank officer, or anyone other than your Successor Trustee, look at the contents of your safe deposit box.

☆ CARE FOR FAMILY MEMBER

You can make provision in your Trust to care for a minor child or family member after you die. If your family member is immature or a born spender, and you are concerned that he may spend, within months, what it took you a lifetime to earn, you can have your attorney prepare a Trust that will spread the inheritance over an extended period of time.

Your Trust can direct the Trustee to give a certain amount of money every 5 or 10 years; for example you can direct the Trustee to give part of the gift when the beneficiary reaches 25, another amount when he reaches 35, and then 45, etc.

If your beneficiary has a creditor problem, you can set up a *Spendthrift Trust*. You can direct your Successor Trustee to use the Trust funds for your beneficiary's health care, education, and living expenses, and nothing else. Creditors of the beneficiary will not be able to collect a debt or a money judgement from the income of the Trust, provided the Trust document states that the Trust income may not be transferred voluntarily or involuntarily (Prob. 15300). An important exception is money owed by the beneficiary for alimony or child support. A beneficiary of a Trust who is entitled to receive either principal or income from the Trust must make support payments as ordered by the Court (Prob. 15305).

NO CREDITOR PROTECTION FOR SETTLOR
Although you can set up a Spendthrift Trust for the benefit of a family member, you cannot set one up for yourself. Property you place in your Revocable Living Trust is freely accessible to you. It is likewise accessible to your creditors both before and after your death. If you die owing money, your creditors can have a Personal Representative appointed to locate funds to pay those debts. The Personal Representative can require that the your Trust property be used to pay for those debts (Civ. Proc. 695.030).

✩✩ AVOID THE NEED FOR A CONSERVATOR

Once you have a Trust, you do not need to worry about who will take care of your property should you become disabled or too aged to handle your finances. The person you appointed as Successor Trustee will take over the care of the Trust property if you are unable to do so. If you do not have a Trust, and become incapacitated, a Court may need to appoint a Conservator to care for your property. The cost to establish and maintain the conservatorship is charged to you. As we will see in Chapter 9, such legal procedures can be expensive; and once established cannot be terminated unless you are restored to health or die (Prob. 1863).

With all these perks, you may be ready to call your attorney to make an appointment to set up a Trust, but before doing so there are a few things you need to consider.

THE CONS

⊠ COMPLEXITY

A Trust is a fairly complex document, often more than 20 pages long. It needs to be that long because you are establishing a vehicle for taking care of your property during your lifetime, as well as after your death. Your Trust may be written in "legalese," so it may take you considerable time and effort to understand it.

It is important to have your Trust document prepared by an attorney who has the patience to work with you until you fully understand each paragraph of the document and are satisfied that what it states is what you really want.

⊠ COST

Because of the thoroughness of the document and the fact that it is custom designed for you, a Trust will cost much more to draft than a simple Will. In addition to the initial cost of the Trust, it can be expensive to maintain the Trust should you become disabled or die. Your Successor Trustee has the right to charge for his duties as Trustee, as well as to charge for any specialized services performed. A financial institution can charge to serve as Successor Trustee, and also charge to manage the Trust portfolio. If you decide to have a financial institution serve as Trustee, then it is important that you compare the fee schedules of different institutions.

Should you choose an attorney to be your Successor Trustee, the attorney has the right to charge to manage the Trust, and also to charge for any legal work he performs. However, under California law, unless the attorney is related to you by blood or marriage, he will need to get the permission of the beneficiaries of your Trust for this dual compensation. In fact, if your Successor Trustee hires an attorney who is one of his close relatives (child, spouse, sibling, parent) he will need to get the beneficiaries' approval before paying attorney fees to his relative. If the beneficiaries do not agree to such compensation, the attorney/Trustee can petition the Probate Court for approval of his attorney fees (Prob. 15687).

You may decide to appoint your spouse or a family member as Successor Trustee, who may want little, or no, compensation. Regardless of who you choose to be Successor Trustee, you need to come to a fee agreement. The agreement can be for a set amount or a percentage of the value of the Trust, or other method to be used to determine his compensation.

If you choose a professional (attorney, accountant, financial planner, etc.) your agreement needs to include fees for work that may be done in his professional capacity. The fee agreement should be in writing and signed by you and your Successor Trustee. The fee agreement can be included in the Trust document with a provision that whoever accepts the job of Successor Trustee, agrees to accept the fee as provided in the Trust document (Prob. 15680).

If you make no provision for fees , your Successor Trustee the right to take a reasonable fee from the Trust property. If the beneficiaries of the Trust do not think the fee reasonable, they can ask the Court to set the fee. But that will probably trigger a legal battle. It is better that you set the fee. Hopefully, that will head off unnecessary legal fees.

☆ ⊠ THE TRUST IS LEGALLY ENFORCEABLE

Any beneficiary of the Trust can petition the Superior Court to settle a dispute arising out of the administration of the Trust. For example, if the Trustee is abusing his power or not accounting for Trust funds, the beneficiaries can ask the Court to have the Trustee removed (Prob. 17200).

We gave this section a cross and a star, because the right to have a Trust enforced or administered by a court is a double edged sword. It is great to have the Court protect the rights of your beneficiaries, but the cost of a Court battle could be greater than using Probate to transfer your Estate. Worse yet, your beneficiaries are at a disadvantage because the Trustee can charge the legal expenses to your Trust, while the beneficiaries must pay for their legal battles out of their own pocket. Even if the beneficiaries win the argument, the Trustee's legal fees are paid from the Trust, so there is just that much less for the beneficiaries to inherit.

The Court can require your Trustee to be personally liable for his legal costs, but that only happens if the Trustee acted illegally or unreasonably.

⊠   YOU MAY NEED YOUR SPOUSE/RDP'S PERMISSION
     TO TRANSFER PROPERTY INTO YOUR TRUST

Most couples prepare a Trust as part of their overall Estate Plan. Sometimes a married person or a Registered Domestic Partner has a Trust that was established prior to the marriage, or he may decide to create a Trust to care for children from a previous marriage. The Settlor is free to place any of his Separate Property and his half of the couple's Community Property into his Trust but he may not place his Spouse/RDP's half of the Community Property into the Trust (or anywhere else not accessible to his Spouse/RDP) without the written consent of his Spouse/RDP, or a signed waiver of his right to that property (Fam. 1100, Prob. 147).

If you are married and make a transfer of Community Property into your Trust without permission from your Spouse/RDP and that transfer results in your Spouse/RDP being deprived of his half interest in the Community Property, your Spouse/RDP has the right to petition (ask) the Court to undo the transfer and return his share of the Community Property. Your Spouse/RDP can petition the Probate Court at any time before or after your death. However, if your Spouse/RDP knows of the transfer and does nothing for three years, the Court could find that your Spouse/RDP failed to assert his rights in a timely manner and refuse to grant the petition (Fam. 1101).

⊠ PROBATE MIGHT STILL BE NECESSARY

The Trust only works for those items that you place in the Trust. If you own property in your name only, then upon your death, a Probate procedure might be necessary in order to transfer the property to your beneficiary. For example, if you purchase a security in your name only, without a "Transfer On Death" designation to a beneficiary or to your Trust, then a Probate procedure may be necessary to determine who should inherit the security.

The attorney who prepares the Trust usually creates a safety net for such situations. He prepares a Will for you to sign at the same time you sign the Trust. The Will makes your Trust the beneficiary of your Probate Estate. If you own anything in your name only, should a Probate procedure be necessary, the Will directs your Personal Representative to make that asset part of your Trust by transferring the asset to your Successor Trustee. Your Successor Trustee will add that asset to your Trust (Prob. 6300).

The Will prepared by the attorney is called a **Pour Over Will** because it is designed to "pour" any asset titled in your name only, into the Trust. Having a Pour Over Will ensures that your property will go to the beneficiaries named in your Trust. But the downside of holding property in your name only is that a full Probate procedure may be necessary just to get that asset into your Trust. If avoiding Probate is your goal, holding property, in your name only, defeats that goal.

You can ensure that a Probate procedure will not be necessary by transferring your assets into your Trust during your lifetime, but if you neglect to put something into your Trust, the Pour Over Will stands by to transfer that asset into your Trust.

TAXES AND YOUR TRUST

Putting property into a Revocable Living Trust does not shield that property from taxes. All of the property held in a Revocable Living Trust is taxed as if the Settlor were holding that property in his own name. If the property earns income, income taxes will be due, and at the same rate as the Settlor would have paid if he had no Trust. Once the Settlor dies, both the federal and state government have the right to impose an *Estate Tax* on property transferred to a beneficiary as a result of the death.

All the property owned as of the date of death becomes the decedent's *Taxable Estate.* This includes *real property* (residential lots, condominiums, etc.) and *personal property* (cars, life insurance policies, business interests, securities, IRA accounts, etc.). It includes property held in the decedent's name alone, as well as property that he held jointly or in Trust. It also includes gifts given by the decedent during his lifetime that exceeded the *Annual Gift Tax Exclusion.* Up until the year 2002 that value was $10,000 per person, per year. The Annual Gift Tax Exclusion was adjusted for inflation in 2002 to $11,000 and again in 2006 to $12,000 (26 U.S.C. 2503(b)). For most of us, this is not a concern because no federal Estate Tax need be paid unless the decedent's Taxable Estate exceeds the federal *Estate Tax Exclusion* amount. That value is currently two million dollars and is scheduled to go even higher.

YEAR	ESTATE TAX EXCLUSION AMOUNT
2006-2008	$2,000,000
2009	$3,500,000

The California Estate Tax was repealed as of January 1, 2005. The federal Estate Tax is scheduled to be phased out in the year 2010, but reinstated in the year 2011 with an Estate Tax Exclusion Amount of $1,000,000 — unless lawmakers change the tax law once again.

A TRUST TO REDUCE ESTATE TAXES

Under current law, Estates of those who die in 2010 are exempt from federal Estate Taxes, but in 2011, the Estate Tax is scheduled to be reinstated and Estates worth more than $1,000,000 will once again be subject to a sizeable Estate Tax. A couple with an Estate in excess of a million dollars can reduce the risk of an Estate Tax by setting up "His and Her" Trusts, so that each person can take advantage of his own Exclusion Amount.

For example, if a husband and wife own two million dollars, they can separate their funds into two Trusts each valued at one million dollars. The Trusts can be set up so that a surviving spouse can use the income from the deceased partner's Trust for living expenses. In this way, their standard of living need not be reduced by separating their funds into two Trusts.

If they do not wish to separate funds, they can set up a single Joint Trust that separates into two Trusts once one partner dies. Again, the surviving spouse is free to use the income from both Trusts. Once both partners are deceased, the beneficiaries of their respective Trusts will inherit the funds, hopefully with no Estate Tax due.

If the couple make no Trust provision, and they hold their property jointly, the last to die will own the two million dollars with only one Estate Tax Exclusion available. If lawmakers do not change the tax law, and the surviving spouse dies in 2011, or later, everything over one million dollars will be subject to federal Estate Taxes. A Revocable Living Trust is a relatively simple way for a married couple to reduce, if not eliminate, the need to pay Estate Taxes. However, there is still the problem of the federal Gift Tax and the Capital Gains Tax.

THE UN-UNIFIED GIFT TAX

As explained, up to 2002, the federal Annual Gift Tax Exclusion was $10,000. It increased to $11,000 in 2002, and then to $12,000 in 2006. The IRS keeps a running count of amounts you give to someone that exceed the Annual Gift Tax Exclusion that is effective in the year of the donation.

Although you are required to report a gift that exceeds the Annual Gift Tax Exclusion, no tax need be paid unless that running total is more than the federal lifetime Gift Tax Exclusion. That amount is currently one million dollars. If your running total does not exceed the Gift Tax Exclusion amount during your lifetime, once you die, the cumulative value of gifts you reported to the IRS will be added to your Taxable Estate.

Until the Estate Tax law was changed, the Gift and Estate Tax were unified. No Gift Tax needed to be paid unless the total value of the taxable gifts exceeded the federal Estate Tax Exclusion amount. In 2004 that changed. The Estate Tax Exclusion amount went up to $1,500,000, but the amount for the Gift Tax Exclusion remained at $1,000,000, so they now are no longer unified.

To summarize:
If you make a gift to anyone that is greater than the Annual Gift Tax Exclusion for that year, you must report the gift to the IRS. The IRS keeps a running count of gifts you made in excess of the Annual Gift Tax Exclusion. In 2004, if that sum exceeds $1,000,000, you will pay a Gift Tax on any amount that you give that is over the Annual Gift Tax Exclusion. The Estate Tax is scheduled to be repealed in 2010, but not the Gift Tax.

California does not have a Gift Tax at this time.

The current federal Estate tax is scheduled to be phased out in the year 2010, but a new Capital Gains Tax is scheduled for 2010 that may prove even more costly than the Estate Tax. The new Capital Gains Tax is related to the way inherited property is evaluated by the federal government. Real and personal property is inherited at a "stepped-up" basis, meaning that if the decedent's property increased in value from the time he acquired it, the beneficiary inherits the property at its fair market value as of the decedent's date of death. For example, if the decedent bought stock for $20,000 and it is worth $50,000 as of his date of death, the beneficiary will take a step-up in basis of $30,000; i.e. the beneficiary inherits the stock at the current $50,000 value. If the beneficiary sells the stock for $50,000, he pays no Capital Gains Tax. If the beneficiary holds onto the stock and later sells it for $60,000, the beneficiary will pay a Capital Gains Tax only on the $10,000 increase in value since the decedent's death.

Up to 2009, there is no limit to the amount a beneficiary can take as a step-up in basis. But in 2010 caps are set in place. The decedent's Estate will be allowed a 1.3 million dollar step-up in basis, plus another 3 million for property passing to the surviving spouse (26 U.S.C. 1022(b)). The new law could result in significant Capital Gains taxes that the beneficiary must pay. For example, suppose in 2010 you inherit a business from your father that he purchased for $100,000 and it is now worth 2 million dollars. There is a capital gain of 1.9 million dollars, but you are allowed a step-up in basis of only 1.3 million. If you sell it for 2 million dollars $600,000 of your inheritance will be subject to a Capital Gains tax.

We will discuss methods of reducing the Gift Tax and the Capital Gains Tax in Chapter 7.

MAYBE A WILL IS BEST AFTER ALL

Although many methods can be used to transfer property without the need for Probate, it may be each method has a downside that is objectionable to you. Maybe you don't have enough money at this time to warrant the cost of setting up a Trust. Holding property jointly with another may raise issues of security and independence. Holding property so that it goes directly to a few beneficiaries in a Pay-On-Death account may not be as flexible as you wish. This may be the case if you want to give gifts to several charities or to a minor child.

For example, you can hold all your property so that it goes directly to your son without the need for Probate. If you ask him to use some of the money for your grandchild's education, it may be that your grandchild gets none of the money because your son is sued or falls upon hard times. If you keep your property in your name only and leave a Will giving a certain amount of money to your grandchild, the child will know exactly how much money you left and the purpose of that gift.

After taking into account all the pros and cons of avoiding Probate, you may well opt for a Will and a Probate procedure. If you make such a decision, it is important to keep in mind that Estate Planning is not an "all or nothing" choice. You can arrange your Estate so that certain items pass automatically to your intended beneficiary, and other items can be left in your name only, to be distributed as part of a Probate procedure. By arranging your finances in this manner, you can reduce the value of your Probate Estate, and that in turn should reduce the cost of Probate.

In the next chapter, we discuss the Will as an Estate Planning tool.

Those of you who have a Will may be thinking that there is no reason to read the Chapter, but does your Will:

- Make provision for the amount to be paid to your Personal Representative?

- Make gifts of your personal property? (jewelry, car, etc.)

- Name a Guardian to care for your minor child?

- Make adjustment for gifts or loans that you gave to the beneficiaries of your Will?

- Give specific instructions about how your bills and taxes are to be paid; i.e., which of your beneficiaries will have his inheritance reduced in order to pay your debts and taxes?

Has your Will been prepared so that it will be difficult for anyone to challenge it?

Have you stored your Will so that it is safe AND easily accessible to you during your lifetime and to your Personal Representative after your death?

If you answered "Yes" to all of the above questions, then you can skip over to Chapter 5.

Your Will – Your Way 4

Many people decide that the Will is the best route to go but do not act upon it, thinking it unnecessary to prepare a Will until they are very old and about to die. But according to reports published by the National Center for Health Statistics (a division of the U.S. Department of Health and Human Services) 2 of every 10 people who die in any given year are under the age of 60. Twenty percent may seem like a small number until it hits close to home as it did with a young couple.

Alex and Cathy were an old-fashioned couple in a modern world. When they married, they knew they wanted a large family. There was no question that Cathy would stay home and raise the children while Alex went to work. Luckily he did very well as one of the managers of a string of restaurants. Better yet, he enjoyed his work. He loved to cook and would even take over the kitchen when he returned from work. That suited Cathy just fine because she had her hands full raising their three boys.

Cathy couldn't help thinking how lucky they were that morning as she fixed breakfast. A nice house. Healthy, if not rambunctious, boys. All in all, a comfortable marriage. Her only concern that day was the fact that Alex was flying off on a business trip. All this terrorist news made her nervous about flying. Alex reassured her that it was only an hour's flight, and besides he was flying the company plane and not a commercial airliner.

But it was not terrorists that brought down the plane, just a malfunctioning rudder.

THINGS A WILL CAN DO

Though we all agree that one never knows, still people put off making a Will, figuring that if they die before getting around to it, California law will take over and their property will be distributed in the manner that they would have wanted anyway. The problem with that logic is the complexity of the California Laws of Intestate Succession. It isn't too difficult to figure out who will inherit your property, if you are survived by a spouse, child, parent or sibling. But if none of these survive you, the ultimate beneficiary of your property may not be the person you would have chosen, had you taken the time to do so.

Even if you think you know who will inherit your property if you die without a Will, someone else may turn out to be the beneficiary of your Estate. Why chance having your property go to someone you may not even know or like? Best to prepare a Will and have your property inherited by the person of your choice.

Others think that it is not necessary to have a Will because they have arranged their finances so that all of their property will be inherited without the need for Probate. But money could come into your Estate after your death. This could happen in any number of ways from winning the lottery and dying (of happiness, no doubt) to receiving insurance funds after your death. For example, if you die in a house fire, the company that insures your home may need to pay for damages done to the property. In such case, the funds will need to be paid to your Estate. A Personal Representative may need to be appointed and the insurance funds distributed according to the Laws of Intestate Succession. If you die without a Will, your Estate may be distributed differently than you would have wished. And there are other important reasons to make a Will.

🗐 APPOINT PERSONAL REPRESENTATIVE

The Court will give top priority to the person you name as Personal Representative of your Will. Without a Will, the Court will use the order of priority as given in California statute (Prob. 8461). The statute lists some 18 classes of people who have priority in serving as your Personal Representative. Your Spouse/RDP has top priority followed in order by your adult child(ren), grandchild(ren), other descendants, parent, sibling, descendants of a sibling, (nieces, nephews, etc.) grandparent, descendants of grandparents (i.e., your aunts, uncles, cousins) etc. If two or more with the same priority want the job and cannot come to an agreement, it will be up to the Court to decide who should serve.

🗐 SET PERSONAL REPRESENTATIVE'S FEE

Once you decide on a Personal Representative, you need to check with that person to be sure that he is willing to serve in that capacity. And if so, then you should come to an understanding about how much compensation he will receive to settle your Estate. If you do not make provision for his fee, he will be entitled to receive the amount as stated under California law (Prob. 10800). As explained on page 27, that fee can be substantial.

You can put the amount of agreed compensation in your Will; however your Personal Representative can reject that amount and ask for the amount allowed under law (Prob. 10804) To avoid the problem, have your attorney draft an Agreement that you and your Personal Representative sign and incorporate into your Will. Having a separate fee Agreement will not stop your Personal Representative from asking for more money, but with such an Agreement, the Court will not agree to the increase unless something unusual occurs (such as a law suit) causing much more work than an ordinary Probate proceeding.

You also need to keep in mind that the Pesonal Representative's fee is just to administer the Estate. It does not include payment for professional work he may do while settling the Estate. For example, if you appoint your attorney as Personal Representative, he can agree to the fee stated in the Will for his work as Personal Representative, and then ask the Court to be paid for his work as attorney for the Estate. California law allows him to be paid attorney fees in addition to his fees as Personal Representative, provided he asks the Court, in advance, for attorney fees (Prob. 10804).

The same proble can arise with any professional. If you appoint your accountant to serve as Personal Representative, he may seek compensation for his work as Personal Representative and also for any accounting work he does such as preparing and filing tax returns; preparing an inventory and doing an accounting for the beneficiaries. A financial planner who serves as Personal Representative may be compensated for his management of the Estate property (buying and selling securities, taking care of rental property, etc.) in addition to his fee to administer the Estate.

But the main problem with appointing a professional as your Personal Representative is the same as appointing a professional to serve as the Successor Trustee of your Trust; namely, that it creates a potential conflict of interest. The professional can use his position as Personal Representative to generate fees that might have been avoided had someone else settled the Estate.

When choosing a Personal Representative, consider the relationship of the Personal Representative to the beneficiaries and determine whether it would be better to appoint a non-professional for the job.

⬛ MAKE GIFTS OF YOUR PERSONAL PROPERTY

Another benefit to making a Will is that you can make provision for who will get your personal property (computers, antiques, securities, boats, snowmobiles etc.). When making a Will consider making provision for your car. If you make a *specific gift* i.e. a gift to a named beneficiary of your Will, it will be relatively simple for your Personal Representative to transfer the car to your beneficiary. If you do not make a specific gift of your car, your Personal Representative will decide what to do with it. He may decide to sell it and include the proceeds of the sale in the Estate funds to be distributed as part of the Probate Estate; or he can give the car to one beneficiary of your Estate as part of that beneficiary's share of the Estate.

GIFTS OF PERSONAL ITEMS

Many who have lost someone close to them report that the distribution of small personal items caused the greatest conflict. If you arrange your finances so that no Probate procedure is necessary, your next of kin will need to decide among themselves how to distribute your *personal effects* (clothing, books, music collection, etc.). Without guidance from you, and no Personal Representative with authority to make decisions, there could be disagreement and hard feelings over items of little monetary value, but much sentimental value. If you make a Will, you can include a list of gifts of personal effects in your Will and your Personal Representative will distribute those gifts according to your list. Of course, it is not possible to make a list of each and every item you own; but you can instruct your Personal Representative to allow certain family members to take their choice of items not mentioned in your Will. If two or more family members want the same item, instruct your Personal Representative to use an appropriate lottery system (coin toss, high card in a cut of a deck of cards, etc.) to decide who "wins."

CAUTION YOU CAN'T GIVE WHAT YOU DON'T HAVE

You need to give considerable thought whenever you make a specific gift to someone. It could be that you no longer own the item at the time of your death. This could happen with property or money. For example, suppose you leave all of your Estate to your son, with a specific gift of $10,000 to each of your three grandchildren. Your son is the **residuary beneficiary** of the Probate Estate, meaning he gets whatever is left once all of the bills are paid and all of the specific gifts made. If the cost of your last illness leaves your Probate Estate with only $30,000 to distribute, would you want the grandchildren to get their gifts and your son nothing? The simple solution is to make all of them residuary beneficiaries by leaving each a percent of your Estate. For example, instead of making a specific gift to each grandchild you could leave 70% to your son and 10% to each grandchild.

NON-PROBATE ASSETS
Property held in a Pay-On-Death Account, a Totten Trust Account, the proceeds of a life insurance policy, Trust property, Joint Property With Right of Survivorship and IRA accounts are all *non-Probate assets* because they will be inherited by your named beneficiary without the need for Probate. You are free to change the beneficiary of a non-Probate asset during your lifetime, but once you are deceased, the gift is made. You cannot change the beneficiary of such gift in your Will because you have, in effect, already made a gift of that asset (Prob. 5302, 5303, 5304).

Unless you named your Estate as the beneficiary of a non-Probate asset, it should not even be mentioned in your Will. To do so might cause your Will to be challenged by whoever was named as the beneficiary of the non-Probate asset.

MAKE ADJUSTMENT FOR PRIOR GIFTS

With a Will, you can make adjustments for gifts or loans given during your lifetime. For example, if you have loaned money to a family member and do not expect to be repaid, you can deduct the loan from that person's inheritance. Of course, it may be that you are not concerned with inequities. That was the case of an aged woman who had three children, Paul, Rita and Frank, her youngest. Frank always seemed to need some assistance from his mother. She often "loaned" him money that he never repaid.

Her other children were responsible and independent. Paul was married and had children of his own. He decided to purchase a house but was having trouble accumulating the down payment. His mother agreed to lend him the money. Paul and his wife offered to give his mother a mortgage on the property. The mother said a simple promissory note from Paul was sufficient, and she would have her attorney draft the note.

The attorney drafted the note but was concerned about the inequity. "You never made a Will. Were you to die, each of your children will inherit an equal amount of money. If Paul still owes money on this promissory note, he will either need to pay the balance to your Estate, or have it subtracted from the amount he inherits. All of the money you gave to Frank will not count towards his inheritance unless you leave a writing saying that the money you gave to Frank is an advancement of his inheritance, or you make a Will and make adjustment in the gift you give to Frank, or unless Frank acknowledges, in writing, that money you gave to him is to be deducted from his inheritance" (Prob. 6409).

"It's O.K." replied the mother "I love all my children equally . . . some are a little more equal than others."

CHOOSE A GUARDIAN FOR YOUR MINOR CHILD

If one parent dies, then it is the right, and duty, of the surviving parent to care for the child. But it could happen that both parents become incapacitated or die before the child is grown. If you have a minor child, you can use your Will to appoint someone to serve as the Guardian of the child in the event that both you and the other parent are deceased (Prob. 1500). You can even include a Trust in your Will, naming someone to serve as Trustee to care for property that you leave to your minor child. See Chapter 7 for more information about how to make provision for the care of your minor child in the event of your incapacity, or death.

MAKE PROVISION FOR PAYMENT OF DEBTS

Most Wills contain an instruction to the Personal Representative to ". . . pay all the expenses of my last illness, funeral expenses, costs of administration, taxes and just debts. . . "   Under California law, paying all of your debts does not include paying off a loan on a gift made to a beneficiary. For example, if you leave your car to a beneficiary, and you have a loan on the car, you need to specify whether you want the loan to be paid from your Probate Estate so that your beneficiary will inherit the car free and clear, or whether you want to have your benefi-ciary be responsible to pay off the loan. If you make no provision in your Will, your beneficiary will inherit the loan along with the car (Prob. 21131).

This same rule applies even if you do not make a specific gift of the item. For example, if there is a mortgage on your home, and you make no mention of who is to inherit the home, it will be inherited by your residuary beneficiaries who then become responsible to pay off the loan or make arrangements to refinance the property.

▤   MAKE PROVISION FOR PAYMENT OF TAXES

Taxes are another concern for those Estates large enough to file an Estate Taxes return. Federal law requires that Estate taxes be paid by the beneficiaries of the Estate in proportion to the value received, unless the decedent made some other arrangements to pay for the taxes . If you make no provision for the payment of taxes, whoever inherits your property will pay a percentage of the taxes based on the amount they receive.

The beneficiary must pay his share regardless of whether he inherits the property through a non-Probate transfer (joint owner, beneficiary of your Trust, beneficiary of a Pay On Death account, beneficiary of a life insurance policy, etc.) or as the beneficiary of your Probate Estate. If a beneficiary refuses to contribute his share of the taxes, under California law whoever is required to make payment (usually the surviving spouse or Personal Representative) can ask the Court to order the beneficiary to contribute his share of the taxes (26 U.S.C. 6324 (a)(2), Prob. 20110, 20111, 20116).

If this is not as you wish you can direct your Personal Representative to pay all of your taxes from your Probate Estate. If you do so, beneficiaries of a specific gift, and those who inherit property from a non-Probate transfer will not contribute to the payment of your taxes. All of your taxes will be paid from your Probate Estate. This means that the amount that your residuary beneficiaries receive will be reduced by the amount of taxes paid.

PREPARING YOUR WILL

After reading the past few pages you may be thinking that everyone should have a Will. And we would agree with your conclusion. Regardless of whether you arrange for all of your property to pass directly without the need for Probate, and regardless of whether you have a Trust, it is important that you have a Will for all of the reasons just stated.

In the state of California, you can prepare a Will in your own hand, without the assistance of an attorney. Such a Will is called a **holographic** Will. Many states have laws that prohibit the Probate Court from accepting an unwitnessed holographic Will. California allows a holographic Will (witnessed or unwitnessed) to be admitted to Probate provided the signature and the material parts of the Will (the date, and the "who" gets "what") are in the Will maker's own hand (Prob. 6111).

But the problem with a holographic Will is its authenticity. If no one sees you sign the Will, how do they know you actually wrote it out? It could be a forgery, or maybe someone was forcing you to sign it.

THE STATUTORY WILL
California statute has a statutory Will form. If you want to prepare a Will without the assistance of an attorney, it is best to use the California statutory Will form and have it signed and witnessed as described in the statute (Prob. 6240). Probate section 6200 through 6243 explain the meaning of legal terms used in the statutory Will. Before drafting your Will it is important to take the time to read through these sections. You can find these statutes at your local county law library or at the California statute Web site. http://www.leginfo.ca.gov/

CAN YOUR WILL BE CHALLENGED?

There are any number of reasons that people can use to challenge your Will. We have already mentioned that a holographic Will is easy to challenge. Someone can say that you didn't sign the Will — that it was a forgery. Or maybe they will say that you didn't know what you were doing when you signed the Will.

Having two witnesses usually solves the problem; but if either witness is a beneficiary of your will, it will be presumed that the witness got that gift by using duress, menace, fraud or undue influence (Prob. 6112). Although the law presumes the gift was made because of improper actions on the part of the witness, the witness will get the gift unless someone challenges the Will and the Court hears evidence to prove that such was in fact the case.

Even if you sign the Will in the presence of two disinterested witnesses, it could be that the Will is challenged because someone is accused of pressuring you into giving him most if not all of your property. California courts have ruled that to prove **undue influence** whoever makes the challenge needs to prove that there was a confidential relationship between the Will maker and the beneficiary (close relative, spiritual advisor, attorney, doctor, financial advisor, etc.) AND the beneficiary actively worked to get the Will maker to sign the Will (*Estate of Callahan*, 67 Cal.2d 609 (1967); 423 P.2d 963).

There are other grounds on which to challenge a Will. To understand what challenges may be successful, we need to know what the state of California considers to be a valid Will.

In the state of California, a Will is valid if at the time the decedent made the Will:

> ➢ he was 18 years of age or older - and -
> ➢ he was not being unduly influenced by anyone - and -
> ➢ he was of sound mind.

A Will maker is considered to be of sound mind at the time he made the Will if:

- ☑ he knew what he was doing (namely making a Will); and
- ☑ he knew what property he had, and
- ☑ he remembered his family and how they would be affected by his Will, and
- ☑ he was not suffering from a delusional mental disorder affecting his ability to distribute his property (Prob. 6100, 6100.5, 6104)

HOW TO AVOID A CHALLENGE TO YOUR WILL

If you are concerned that someone will challenge your Will, then it is important that you consult with an attorney who is experienced in Estate Planning. You can meet with the attorney in the privacy of his office, and without anyone else present. Once the Will is prepared according to your direction, the attorney will supervise the signing of your Will. He will see to it that your Will is signed and witnessed in the presence of two disinterested witnesses — usually members of his staff.

Each witness will sign a paragraph that says they saw you sign the Will. Should anyone challenge the Will, your attorney and witnesses will be available to testify that you signed it of your own free Will and at the time you signed the Will you were competent and knew what you were doing.

You can even have your attorney include a **no contest** provision in your Will stating that if a beneficiary named in your Will challenges any provision in the Will, then he will inherit none of your Probate Estate. Such a provision is called an **In Terrorem Clause** because it is designed to cause fear (if not terror) in the heart of your beneficiary.

Many states will not enforce such a clause, because they want people to have the right to challenge a Will, and let the Court decide whether that challenge is proper. But California courts have upheld such provisions. The Court in a 1988 case stated "No contest clauses are valid in California and are favored by the public policies of discouraging litigation and giving effect to the purposes expressed by the testator" (*Estate of Ferber*, 66 Cal.App.4th 233 (1998), 77 Cal Rptr.2d 744).

The Estate of Ferber is an interesting case to read because of the comprehensive In Terrorem Clause that Mr. Ferber included in his Will. If you want to include an In Terrorem Clause in your Will, you may want to read this case, not only to read the Clause, but also, to see how the Court interpreted this Will provision.

STORING YOUR WILL

Once you sign your Will, you may wonder where to store it. If an attorney prepared your Will, he may suggest that he place it in his vault for safekeeping. By doing so, he ensures that your heirs will need to contact him as soon as you die. Once the attorney is notified of your death he will forward the Will to the Clerk of the Superior Court. California law prohibits the attorney (or anyone else) from charging a fee to deliver the Will to the court (Prob. 8200).

Asking the attorney to forward the Will to the Court does not obligate the beneficiaries of your Estate to employ the attorney should Probate be necessary. By storing your Will the attorney is assured of meeting your beneficiaries and having an opportunity for future employment.

But there are problems with such an arrangement. The Will could be lost or mistaken for another Will. That happened in at least one case. That happened in at least one case. The attorney prepared aWill for two people with the same name and similar family circumstances. When one person died the attorney submitted the wrong Will to Probate. Luckily the error was quickly discovered. The decedent had a distinctive signature. The family challenged the Will based on the unfamiliar signature and the way the property was to be distributed. They knew the decedent would never have distributed his property in the manner stated in the Will.

If you decide to allow your attorney to store the Will, you need assurance that the attorney will be responsible for the document.

You should get a receipt and something in writing that says:

⇨ The attorney accepts full responsibility for storage of the Will. Should it be lost or damaged, he will replace the document at no cost to you; and if you are deceased, he will, at no cost to your beneficiaries, present sufficient evidence to the Court to accept a valid copy of the Will into Probate.

⇨ There will be no charge to you, or your heirs, for the storage and retrieval of the document.

⇨ Should he sell his practice, retire, or die, he or the successor to his practice, will return the original document to you.

If you prepared your Will without benefit of legal counsel, you need to store your Will in a secure place such as a safe deposit box. You can keep the document in a fireproof safe deposit box within your home; and give a duplicate key to the person you chose to be your Personal Representative.

THE SAFE DEPOSIT BOX, SAFE BUT . . .

You might consider placing your document in a safe deposit box that you lease at a bank. The only problem with the bank safe deposit box is convenient access. If you hold a safe deposit box in your name only, should you die, the bank will restrict access to the box. Under California law, the bank may allow anyone who has the key to your safe deposit box to inspect its contents, provided they do so under the supervision of an officer or employee of the company (Prob. 331).

If your Will is there, they can forward it to the Probate Court. The bank will not allow anything else to be removed without Court authority. Once a Personal Representative is appointed by the Court, he will have such authority. He will be able to take possession of the contents of your safe deposit box. If you arranged your finances to avoid Probate, it is self defeating to have entry to a safe deposit box trigger a Probate procedure.

For those who are happily married, the solution to the roblem, may be to lease the box jointly with your Spouse/RDP such that each of you has free access to the box. However, this may not be the best choice if you think your Spouse/RDP will be unhappy with certain provisions made in your Will. Some Wills never see the light of day for this reason. In such case, it may be better to keep the safe deposit box in your name only so that an official of the bank will forward your Will to the Court.

As explained in Chapter 3, those who have a Trust can solve the problem by giving their Successor Trustee joint access to the safe deposit box.

If you are single and do not have a Trust, you can lease the box jointly with a trusted family member. Of course, if privacy and security are important to you, then that may outweigh any concern for the convenience of your beneficiaries.

Regardless of where you choose to store your Will, let your Personal Representative know that you have a Will and how to retrieve it in the event of your death.

I thought you said a Will is not enough

After reading this chapter, you may be thinking that the book is poorly named. After all, look at all the good things a Will can do:

* choose the person you want to settle your Estate
* arrange to have your Personal Representative settle your Estate for a reasonable fee
* give your personal items, including your car, to the person of your choice
* choose a Guardian for your child
* discourage a challenge to your Will.

But that is not all there is to an Estate Plan. A Will cares for your property when you are deceased, but it cannot provide for the care of your property in the event you become disabled. A complete Estate Plan provides for the care of your property during your lifetime and for the care of your person as well.

In these days of extended old age, many of us will need assistance with our health care and/or finances as we age. It is important to arrange to have someone manage finances and make medical decisions in the event that we are too aged or too ill to do so ourselves. These topics are covered in Chapters 8 and 9.

And a Will may be effective to transfer all that you own upon your death, but it cannot help your family pay for your debts. It may be that you have so many debts that your family is left with little or nothing. A complete Estate Plan provides for the financial well being of your family once you are deceased; and that is the topic of the next chapter.

Arranging To Pay Bills 5

You can think of your Estate Plan as being composed of two separate parts, a Lifetime Plan and an Inheritance Plan. Your Lifetime Plan provides for the care of your property during your lifetime, with the goal being maximum control and protection. Your Inheritance Plan provides for the inheritance of your property, with the goal being minimum cost and hassle to your beneficiaries. You could consider your Estate Plan to be a master plan that balances the goals of the Lifetime Plan with those of the Inheritance Plan.

When people consider their Inheritance Plan, they are mostly concerned about giving their possessions away. Many do not take into account how the bills they have accumulated will be paid once they are deceased, or even who will be responsible for paying those bills. Most of us do not worry about providing for the payment of our debts, thinking "I'll have that paid off long before I die." But with easily available credit, many are maintaining a high debt balance as a way of life. Paying off all of their loans is not a priority. Many will live their lives without ever being free of debt.

This does not imply that people do not know how to manage their funds. For many people (and corporations), it makes good sense to use other people's money to carry on business. In fact, great debt is a badge of honor for the wealthy. If a bank will lend you a million dollars, it means you have the means to repay that amount. Banks will not lend much money to those with few assets. Rich or poor, we all need to think about how our debts will be paid once we are gone.

WHO IS RESPONSIBLE TO PAY DEBTS?

Suppose you die without funds, and owing money. Does the debt die with you or is someone else responsible to pay what you owe? If you are married, the first person the creditor will look to, is your spouse. To understand the basis of this expectation, you need to know a bit of the history of our legal system.

Our laws are derived from the English Common Law. Under English Common law, a single woman had the right to own property in her own name and also the right to contract to buy or sell property. When a woman married, her legal identity merged with her spouse. She could not hold property free from her husband's claim or control. She could no longer enter into a contract without her husband's permission.

Once married, a woman became financially dependent on her husband. He, in turn, became legally responsible to provide his wife with basic necessities — food, clothing, shelter and medical services. If anyone provided basic necessities to his wife, then, regardless of whether the husband agreed to be responsible for the debt, he became obliged to pay for them. This law was called the DOCTRINE OF NECESSARIES.

In the United States, a series of Married Women's Rights Acts were passed giving a married woman the right to own property. The California law gives a married woman the same right to contract, own property and run a business in the same manner as any single woman (Fam. 721).

As Married Women's Rights laws were passed, states had to decide whether the Doctrine of Necessaries still applied— especially in light of the equal protection under the law. Specifically, if a husband is responsible to pay for his wife's necessities, shouldn't his wife be responsible to pay for his necessities?

Some states decided that the law was obsolete and that neither husband nor wife should be responsible for the other's debts, unless they contracted or agreed to do so. Other states decided that each partner is responsible to provide basic necessities for his spouse. California took the latter approach. Anyone who provides necessities for a married person in this state has the right to demand payment from the spouse — whether or not the spouse agreed to be personally liable to pay for the necessities (Fam. 914).

In 2005, the California legislature extended all of the rights and responsibilities of a married couple to Registered Domestic Partners, so Registered Domestic Partners are each liable to pay for the necessities of their partner (Fam. 297.5).

NO RESPONSIBILITY FOR SUPPORT IF SEPARATED

As explained in Chapter 1, money earned when the couple is living separately is Separate Property. Neither party is responsible to support the other while they are separated, unless the Spouse/RDP is required to do so under a support agreement or Court order (Fam. 771, 4302).

Even though the parties are not responsible to support each other while they are living separately, still if one partner is unable to pay for his common necessities, his creditor has the right to demand payment for those basic necessities from the other partner (Fam. 914).

COMMUNITY DEBT VS. SEPARATE DEBT

A *Community Debt* is a debt which both parties agreed to pay, or a debt incurred for the benfit of the family. All of the couple's property (Community or Separate) is available to pay for a Community Debt. A *Separate Debt* is a money owed by one party prior to the marriage, or a liablility incurred by one partner only, that is not for the benefit of the family. The debtor must use his Separate Property to pay for his Separate Debt. However, if that is not enough, all of the couple's Community Property can be used to pay for the debt. The Separate Property of the non-debtor Spouse/RDP is not available to pay for the Separate Debt of the debtor Spouse/RDP (Civ. Proc. 695.020, Fam. 1000).

LIABILITY AFTER DEATH

The rules governing monies to be used to pay the debts of a deceased Spouse/RDP are complex and beyond the scope of this book (see Prob. 11444). But, in general, all of the couple's Community Property is available to pay a Community Debt. If the decedent left a Separate Debt, it needs to be paid from his Separate Property. If there is not enough Separate Property to pay the debt, the decedent's share of their Community Property is available to pay the debt. That share is available even if the surviving Spouse/RDP now owns the property without any need for Probate. For example, suppose the couple acquired an expensive painting during their union. That painting now belongs to the surviving Spouse/RDP, but the decedent's creditor can demand that the surviving Spouse/RDP use the decedent's half of the value of the painting to satisfy that debt.

Which brings us to the question of whether the painting really is Community Property.

If the surviving Spouse/RDP can prove that the painting was purchased with money owned prior to their union, it is Separate Property and is not available to pay the debt. But if the painting was purchased with money earned during the marriage, it is Community Property and half of the value of the painting will go toward payment of the decedent's Separate Debt.

This example illustrates the need to keep a record that identifies Separate Property. It may not be an issue where all of the property owned by the couple is Community Property; but it is a different matter should there be a significant difference in the amount each person brings to the marriage, or receives as a gift or inheritance during the marriage.

You may be thinking that it is easy enough to identify Separate Property by titling property in one name only. But if one party buys a car or real property and does not put the name of the Spouse/RDP on the title to the property, it does not necessarily mean that the property is Separate Property. It could be Community Property if it was purchased with monies earned by one of the partners during their union. To identify Separate Property, there needs to be a paper trail showing that the car or residence was purchased with money owned by the buyer prior to the union, or from a gift or an inheritance.

Your attorney can help you set up a record that can be quickly produced should a creditor demand payment for your spouse's debts. That record is especially important should one of you die without a Will. As explained in Chapter 1, the Laws of Intestate Succession apply to the decedent's half of the Community Property, and all of his Separate Property. Having a record that identifies Community Property and Separate property will make it easier to Probate the Estate.

JOINT DEBTS

A *joint debt* is a debt that two or more people are responsible to pay. Usually the contract or promissory note signed by the borrowers makes them *jointly and severally liable* for the debt. This means they both agree to pay the debt and each of them, individually, agrees to pay the debt.

A joint debt can also be in the form of monies owed by one person with payment guaranteed by another person. If the person who owes the money does not pay, the *guarantor* (the person who guaranteed payment) is responsible to pay the debt.

Should you die, your hospital bills, nursing home bills, funeral expenses, legal fees for the Probate of your Estate, are all debts of your Estate. They are not joint debts unless someone guaranteed payment for the monies owed. Hospital and nursing home bills are considered to be necessities, so if you are married and there are insufficient funds in your Estate to pay for these bills, your surviving Spouse/RDP is responsible for payment, regardless of whether your Spouse/RDP agreed to be jointly liable for the debt.

JOINT PROPERTY BUT NO JOINT DEBT
Suppose you have a credit card in your name only, and you have a joint bank account with your son. Should you die, can the credit card company require that half of the joint funds be set aside to pay the debt?

The answer to this question depends on how the joint account is titled. If the account was set up as Tenants In Common, each of you own half the account.

Upon your death, your son continues to own his half of the account. The credit card company has the right to demand that your half of the account be used to pay your credit card debt.

If the account was held as Joint Tenants With Right of Survivorship, upon your death, your son owns the account 100%. California courts have ruled that the surviving joint owner of an account that was set up with right of survivorship owns the property as of the date of death. Your creditors cannot require payment from an account that belongs to your son only (*Ziegler v. Bonnell* (1942) 52 Cal.App.2d 217, 126 P.2d 118).

The same principal applies to property owned Jointly With Right of Survivorship by a married couple. If the couple own property (bank account, securities or real property) jointly, once one of them dies, the other is the sole owner of that property. It becomes the Separate Property of the surviving Spouse/RDP. But as explained in Chapter 2, the downside is that only the decedent's half takes a step-up in basis.

If you are married and your property has appreciated significantly in value and you don't anticipate a problem with creditors, you may want to hold your property as Community Property With Right of Survivorship. Should either of you die, the surviving spouse will inherit the property at its market value as of the date of death and can immediately sell the property with no concern about paying a Capital Gains Tax (Civ. 682.1).

PAYING FOR CREDIT CARD DEBT

Most of us are wise enough not to hold a credit card jointly with a child, but holding a credit card jointly with a Spouse/RDP is commonplace, especially if the card is being used to pay for necessities. If you hold a credit card with your Spouse/RDP and you are concerned that it might be a struggle to pay it off should one of you die, consider purchasing credit card insurance to cover the debt.

Many credit card companies offer insurance policies and include the premium as part of the monthly payment. It benefits the credit card company to offer life insurance as part of the credit package, because they are assured of prompt payment should the borrower die.

In these days of high credit card interest rates, you might be struggling to pay your monthly credit charge. Adding still another charge to the account may not be an option, regardless of the security offered to your spouse. In such case, a better route might be for you to remove your name from the account and open a new account in your name only. This is especially important if you are using your credit card to pay for your business expenses, and not family necessities. Your surviving Spouse/RDP is not responsible to use his/her Separate Property to pay for your business debts unless your spouse agreed to do so.

Still another reason not to hold a joint credit card is that each of you can establish your own line of credit in the event one of you retires or is out of work. Should the breadwinner of the family die, it may be difficult for the surviving spouse to establish credit if the Spouse/RDP is retired and/or has no recent work record. It is easier for an unemployed Spouse/RDP to establish a line of credit when he/she is married to someone who is working.

OTHER TYPES OF LOAN INSURANCE

Many mortgage companies offer mortgage insurance to their borrowers. Those who have a relatively low mortgage rate might consider having mortgage insurance on the life of the primary wage earner of the family. Even those with a higher rate might want such make the effort to purchase mortgage insurance if they are raising children. With such insurance, the family can inherit the homestead free of debt. The monthly insurance charge may be a small price to pay to ensure that the children can continue to live in their own home until they are grown.

Car loan insurance is still another thing to consider. If a married couple purchases (or leases) a car, and one of them dies, it may be a struggle for the other to pay off the loan. That was the case with Eva and Howard. Both had to work to support their three children. They owned two well used cars. It seemed that one car or the other was always in the shop. When they saw a *NO INTEREST* advertisement for a new car, they decided the offer was too good to pass up.

The monthly payments were high, but it was their only luxury. With both their salaries, they were able to make the payments. When Howard had his first heart attack, he was out of work for several weeks so they struggled to keep the payments current. Howard worked in construction, and was anxious to return to work. The doctors advised that such work might be too strenuous for his weakened heart. Construction work was all Howard knew, and the pay was good, so he ignored the warning and went back to his old job.

The second heart attack was fatal, leaving Eva as the sole means of support for her family.

With Howard gone there was no need for two cars. Eva could not afford the payments on the new car anyway, so she decided to sell it. Unfortunately, what she could get for the car was significantly less than the balance owed. Once she fell behind in payments she decided to surrender the car rather than have them repossess it. She was sure they would understand, considering all that she had been through these past several months, not to mention that she was a widow with three small children.

They didn't understand.

The company took the car and then sued for the balance of monies owed. The judge was sympathetic, but under the law there is no "life is tough" defense. He ruled that Eva had to pay the monies owed; and, as per the terms of the loan agreement, she even had to pay the fees for the company's attorney and all court costs. What an emotional and financial nightmare!

The pity was, it all could have been avoided, had they worked payment of debts into their Estate Plan. Howard was the primary driver of the new car and the primary wage earner. All he had to do was put the loan in his name only, and take out loan insurance. Eva would have inherited the car, debt free. She could have kept it or sold it as she saw fit.

PURCHASING LIFE INSURANCE

The good part of purchasing loan insurance — be it credit card insurance, mortgage insurance or car insurance, is that you may be able to purchase the policy without taking a medical examination. The down side is that companies generally do not offer such insurance to those over the age of 65; and for those under 65 the cost of the insurance is a factor. It usually costs more to purchase loan insurance than a life insurance policy. Those in fairly good health need to comparison shop. If it is your goal to have insurance cover all of your outstanding debts, then the cost of a single life insurance policy may be much less than purchasing several loan insurance policies.

The Estate Planning strategy of purchasing life insurance to pay off all of your loans works best if you are married and your spouse is jointly liable for your debts. If you name your Spouse/RDP as beneficiary of the life insurance policy, (s)he can use the life insurance funds to pay off all monies owed — but (s)he is not required to do so. Under California law, your Spouse/RDP may keep as much of the life insurance proceeds as is reasonably necessary for the support of himself and his dependents (Civ. Proc. 704.100).

With or without debt, you may be wondering about life insurance — should you have it? How much is enough? The answer to these questions depends on the "sleep at night" factor, namely how much insurance do you need so that you won't worry about insurance coverage when you go to sleep at night? It is often more an emotional than a financial issue.

Some people have an "every man for himself" attitude and are content to have no life insurance at all. When they die, whatever they have, they have. And that is what their heirs will inherit. Others worry about how their loved ones will manage if they are not around to support them, and decide to purchase enough insurance to maintain their dependents in their accustomed life style.

The same person may have different thoughts about insurance coverage as circumstances change — from no coverage in his bachelor days to more-than-enough coverage in his child rearing days to just-enough-to-bury-me in his senior years.

Insurance companies recognize that people's needs change over the years. Many companies offer flexible insurance coverage. As with any consumer item, it is a good idea to shop around. In addition to the problem of how much life insurance to carry, there is the concern of how the monies will be spent. Leaving a large sum of money to a person who is less than prudent, may lead to a spending spree.

ANNUITIES TO SPREAD THE INHERITANCE

Most people go through their inheritance within two years. For many, the reason the money is gone so soon, is that there just wasn't much money to inherit in the first place. But for others, it's a spending frenzy.

People's spending habits remain much the same throughout their lifetime. Some people are born squirrels, always saving for the winter. For others, it's Earn-A-Penny Spend-A-Penny.

Most of us fall somewhere in between. We are not extravagant in our spending habits, yet it is a struggle to save. But why should we struggle to purchase an insurance policy if the intended beneficiary will spend it all in a few months?

If you want to leave life insurance proceeds to someone you love, but the intended beneficiary is immature, or a born spendthrift, then a simple solution may be to purchase an *Annuity* with payments spread out over time, instead of a life insurance policy with a single lump sum payment. You can purchase an Annuity so that upon your death the *Annuitant* receives his inheritance in monthly payments or quarterly or yearly. The proceeds of the policy will be exempt from your beneficiary's creditors, but only to the extent reasonably necessary for his support and that of his dependents (Civ. Proc. 704.100).

Some insurance companies allow a beneficiary/Annuitant to decide whether he wants to take the insurance proceeds as a single lump sum, or as an Annuity. Before purchasing the policy, you need to verify that this option will not be available to your beneficiary.

The next question to consider is whether you can leave other property to your family free of the claims of your creditors. We explained earlier that if you are married, all of your Separate Property and your half of the Community Property is available to pay your debts. Your Spouse/RDP is responsible to pay for your necessities, but not for any other debt that you may owe, unless (s)he agreed to be liable.

Even though you may die with more debts than money, there are still things that can be inherited by your beneficiaries free from the claims of your creditors.

SOME THINGS ARE CREDITOR PROOF

There are certain items that can be inherited by your beneficiaries free of the claims of your creditors.

✧ RETIREMENT PLANS ✧

Self-employed retirement plans and Individual Retirement Annuities or Accounts ("IRA") provided for in the Internal Revenue Code of 1986, as amended, are exempt from the claims of creditors to the extent that the amount held in these retirement plans do not exceed the maximum amounts exempt from federal income taxes under that Code (Civ. Proc. 704.115).

Money received by the beneficiaries of these plans are exempt from the claims of the decedent's creditors, with the following exceptions:

BACK ALIMONY OR SUPPORT

A Court can order that pension funds be used to pay back alimony or support (Civ. Proc. 706.052, 703.070).

NOT EXEMPT FROM TAXES

In general, income taxes are not paid when money is placed in a retirement plan. Taxes are paid when the monies are withdrawn from the account regardless of whether the monies are withdrawn by the retiree or the person he named as beneficiary of the retirement plan.

✧ EXEMPTIONS FOR SURVIVING SPOUSE/RDP ✧

There are several items that your surviving Spouse/RDP and/or minor children may take free from the claims of any of your creditors.

✧ EXEMPT PERSONAL PROPERTY

Your surviving Spouse/RDP and/or minor child can ask the Court to allow them to keep any of your property that was exempt from the enforcement of a money judgment during your lifetime. This includes:

⇨ up to $2,775 of value in one motor vehicle

⇨ up to $1,150 in jewelry

⇨ up to $1,750 in tools or books used for work

⇨ any award granted to you under the crime victim's reparation law

⇨ up to $17,425 of monies due to you because of personal bodily injury

⇨ household furnishings, appliances, books, musical instruments, etc. provided any particular item is not greater than $450 in value

These exemptions do not apply to a creditor who is owed money on the property. For example, if you owe $10,000 on your car, and it is worth $11,000, only $1,000 of the value of the car is exempt (Civ. Proc. 703.010, 703.140, Prob. 6510).

✧ FAMILY ALLOWANCE

Those who are dependent on you for their support (child, Spouse/RDP, parent of decedent) are entitled to a reasonable **Family Allowance** for their maintenance, during the time it takes to Probate your Estate. The Court will determine how much money the family member is to receive. In general, the judge will grant a Family Allowance only to those who do not have a reasonable income from other sources (Prob. 6540).

If there is not enough in your Estate to pay all of your creditors, the Court will limit the time that a family member can be supported to one year from the day the Personal Representative is given authority to administer the Estate (Probate 6543).

THE HOMESTEAD EXEMPTION

California homeowners are entitled to creditor protection for their **homestead**, i.e., their principal residence. The amount of protection varies with your circumstances. Up to $150,000 of the equity that you have in your homestead is protected if:

⇨ you or your spouse are 65 or older - or -

⇨ you are 55 or older with a gross annual income of $15,000 or less; or if married, your combined income is $20,000 or less - or -

⇨ you are receiving social security disability benefits.

If none of the above apply, but you are living with a spouse or family member who is not an owner of the residence, then $75,000 is protected.

In all other cases, $50,000 of the equity in your homestead is creditor proof (Civ. Proc. 704.730, 704.995). This does not mean that your creditors cannot force the sale of your home. If you have a mortgage on your home and you do not keep up your payments, the lender can go to Court and foreclose against the property; i.e., sell your home to repay the debt. Creditors other than a mortgagee, cannot force the sale unless the monies owed are greater than the exemption value. For example, suppose you are 50 years old and single. If your home is worth $150,000 and you have a $100,000 mortgage, your creditors cannot force the sale of your home because your mortgagee would get the first $100,000 and you would get the rest. But suppose your house was worth $200,000, the creditor could foreclose. The bank would get its $100,000, you would get the next $50,000 and the rest of the sale price of your home would be available to pay the money you owe. If no bid is offered in excess of the homestead exemption and mortgage, the creditor will not be entitled to recover his costs Civ. Proc. 704.840).

HOMESTEAD PROTECTION FOR YOUR BENEFICIARIES

Your **Homestead Exemption** continues for the benefit of your Spouse/RDP or any other family member who lived with you and who owned the property jointly with you. Even if your home is in your name only, the homestead is protected from your creditors, provided you leave an interest in the property to your Spouse/RDP or to a family member who lived with you (Civ. Proc. 704.995).

As explained, if you owe more money than is allowed under your Homestead Exemption, your creditors can still force the sale of your home after you are deceased, but if you have a Spouse/RDP or minor child they can't do so until 60 days from the date the inventory of your Probate Estate is filed with the Court, or later, if the Court so orders (Prob. 6500).

If you do not own your homestead jointly with your Spouse/RDP and you do not leave the property to your Spouse/RDP, he/she is still entitled to inherit up to $17,425 of value in the homestead free from the claims of your creditors (Civ. Proc. 703.140, Prob. 6510).

✧ WRONGFUL DEATH AWARD ✧

Your family has the right to bring a law suit if you die because of the wrongful act of another. The amount awarded to your Spouse/RDP or to a dependent relative is exempt from the claims of creditors to the extent reasonably necessary for their support. If your family member has a judgment against him, the wrongful death award can be given in periodic payments. The payments are protected provided those monies are necessary for the support of your family member (Civ. Proc. 667.7, 704.140, 704.150).

AN ESTATE PLAN FOR THE BANKRUPT

You may think the above title to be an oxymoron (a contradiction in terms). If a person is bankrupt, why plan for an Estate he doesn't have? But facts are, that people who file for bankruptcy are often quite wealthy and that is their downfall. Because they have substantial income or property, banks and people are willing to lend them money. If more money is borrowed than can be repaid, the unhappy result is bankruptcy. In the event you are concerned about meeting your responsibilities as parent or spouse, yet you enjoy a life style of financial brinksmanship, then consider investing in items that are "creditor proof."

That's exactly what Alan decided to do. Alan was astute, well aware of his strengths and weaknesses. He enjoyed his work and knew he had the capacity to earn large sums of money. But he also knew he was a gambler. Not the Las Vegas type, but a gambler in business ventures. "No risk, no gain" was one of his favorite sayings.

If you charted Alan's net worth over the years it would look like the peaks and valleys of the NASDAQ. Lots of high highs and low lows. Unfortunately, he married a woman who did not share his adventurous spirit. His wife became increasingly intolerant of their financial instability. She came to realize that this was his life style and things would never change. "All gamblers die broke," she said as she walked out the door with their 12 year old daughter in tow.

That, and the fact that he had to declare bankruptcy, brought Alan up short; and he began to be concerned about his future and that of his family.

Alan talked things over with his bankruptcy attorney "I am a good businessman, but not a clairvoyant. There was no way to predict the turn of events that led to this situation. But I know I will bounce back, and it will just be a matter of time before I earn my next fortune. I also know that I am an entrepreneur and not a 9 to 5 type guy so this could happen again. What concerns me is how to provide some security for my child in case something happens to me before she is grown."

"There are few items in California that are creditor proof. Your Homestead Exemption of $75,000 will extend to your daughter if she is living with you and you leave your home to her. You could put money into a federal retirement plan such as an IRA or Keogh account, and your daughter can inherit that free of your debts." (Civ. Proc. 704.115, 704.995).

Alan didn't think that would work. "I am my own boss, but I don't have the self discipline to put money aside each month for my retirement."

The attorney suggested "You could purchase a life insurance policy and make her the beneficiary of the policy. She will be allowed to keep as much of the proceeds of the policy as is necessary for her support. And you could set up a joint account, so that if you die she will own the money in the account" (Civ. Proc. 704.100).

Alan didn't think much of those suggestions "Couldn't my creditors force me to give them the cash value of any insurance policy I own? And couldn't they force me to use the monies in any account that I own to pay for my debts?"

102 A Will Is Not Enough In California

"Sure, but up to $9,700 of the cash value of your life insurance policies is creditor proof. And if you have money in the account when you die, your daughter would get it."

Alan was annoyed "You're saying that here in California, all that I can protect for my daughter is money we share in a joint bank account? What about all those millionaires who protect their money in offshore Trusts? If I really hit it big, why can't I do that?"

"You could, but there are many drawbacks. Just to set up an Offshore Trust costs tens of thousands of dollars, not to mention how much it would cost just to maintain the Trust."

Alan said "Yes, but if I had millions of dollars that would not be a problem."

"True, but there are other considerations. Once you put your money into the Trust, you are essentially giving up control of that money."

Alan was skeptical "Oh come now. Why would anyone put his money where he can't get to it?"

The attorney explained "The Trust can be set up so that funds are available for whatever the millionaire wants. Usually funds are made available to support his family. Trust funds can be used to maintain the family home or yacht. Monies from the Trust can be used to pay for travel or for an expensive vacation. And of course the Trust would provide for the transfer of the property to the millionaire's beneficiaries, once the millionaire dies.

What the millionaire can't do is be the Trustee of the Trust, because if he were, he would have control over the money, and his creditors could take legal action here in the United States to force him to use his Trustee powers to use that money to pay his creditors."

"How can they force the issue? Why couldn't he, as Trustee, just refuse?"

"Remember, that as long as the millionaire is a citizen of the United States, and he is physically present in the states, he is subject to the laws of this country. If a creditor goes to Court and wins, the U. S. Judge could order the millionaire, as Trustee, to use Trust funds to pay that debt. If the millionaire-Trustee refused, the Judge could put him in jail for contempt of Court. No, for an Offshore Trust to work, the Trust must be a foreign Trust, that is, drafted according to the laws of a foreign country, Trust property must be located outside of the United States, and the Trustee cannot be a citizen of the United States."

Alan said "Well I guess the millionaire might have a relative who is not a U.S. citizen to manage the Trust."

The attorney agreed "Yes, or he could use a financial institution that does not do business in the U.S., to manage the funds. But there are other problems with an Offshore Trust. There's the safety factor. Trust funds are kept outside of the United States. If the funds are kept in a foreign bank and the country suffers an economic collapse, then those funds could be lost."

Alan wondered "Isn't that much the same risk as money in a U.S. bank? Only $100,000 of the cash in a U. S. bank account is insured. If the bank fails, any money in that bank over $100,000 could be lost."

The attorney disagreed "Our U.S government is stable, and we trust that they will regulate U.S. banks and keep our money safe. But that is not the case with other small countries. The government of a small country could collapse and the banks along with it."

"But why keep money in a bank? Most millionaires have their funds invested in stocks and bonds, or in real estate."

The attorney agreed "True, but real estate could be risky. If your Trust contains real property located within the United States, your creditor could go to a U.S. court and take that property."

Alan wondered "Couldn't the creditor take the overseas property as well?"

"He could, but it would be hard. For one thing he would need to find the property. And the Trustee is not about to tell him where it is, unless the creditor sues, and the laws of that foreign country require the Trustee to tell. Even if the creditor locates Trust property, whether it is stocks, bonds, or real estate, most Offshore Trusts are established in countries that are not creditor friendly. For example, if you set up an Offshore Trust in the Cook Islands, they will not accept a judgment that a creditor won in the United States. The creditor will need to employ a Cook Islands attorney to sue you all over again in the Cook Islands. That's expensive. And the Cook Islands have a higher standard of proof. Here in the U.S., all your creditor need do is show that you owe the money *by a preponderance of the evidence*. That's lawyer talk for "the jury must be more than 50% sure you owe the money.""

"In the Cook Islands, the creditor's attorney must prove you owe the money *beyond a reasonable doubt* (Cook Islands, International Trusts Act of 1984 Section 13B(1)). That standard is the one we use here in the U.S. for criminal cases. In addition, the foreign country usually has a short Statute of Limitations, so if your creditor does not sue you in that country within that period of time, he cannot sue you at all."

Alan said "I can see why Offshore Trusts are so popular."

The attorney cautioned "But there are other problems. The U.S. considers transfers into and/or out of the Trust to be taxable. The IRS requires special tax returns to be filed for all foreign Trusts. In addition, the IRS looks closely at Offshore Trusts to determine whether they are fraudulent transfers, designed to avoid U.S. income taxes or U.S. Estate taxes. The IRS wants to be sure that the creditor the millionaire is avoiding isn't Uncle Sam!"

Alan said "Yes, but if you pay your taxes, that shouldn't be a problem. If I ever get to the point where I am that wealthy, I'll come back to discuss setting up an Offshore Trust."

The attorney refused "No, I'm just a country lawyer. If you want to go that route, you need a specialist — someone who has overseas connections, and who has experience in writing such Trusts. If you are serious about setting up an Offshore Trust, let me know and I will recommend someone to you."

"O.K. I will."

The attorney offered a final word of caution "If you are able to accumulate a significant amount of money, don't risk it all in a business venture. Limit the amount of money you can lose to just the money that you invest in business. Keep your personal funds separate and protected from your business debts. If you want to start a business, make sure that you cannot be personally liable for your business debts. You can avoid personal liability by forming a corporation, or a Limited Partnership, or a Limited Liability Company.** Stay away from a sole proprietorship or a business partnership."

** These topics are discussed in the next chapter.

Your Business Estate Plan 6

It would take a very thick book to do justice to the topic of Business Estate Planning. Estate Planning issues must be discussed for each type of business:

CONTROL How to control and protect your business during your lifetime.

BENEFICIARY How to be sure your business goes to the beneficiary of your choice.

COST How to transfer your business to your beneficiary quickly and at lowest cost.

With just one chapter to devote to the topic, we can only provide the reader with an overview of the subject. Hopefully, the overview will give the reader some ideas that can later be pursued with an attorney.

We have written this chapter for the reader who listed a business value as part of his net worth on page 4. People who are self employed, but who do not think of themselves as owners of a business, may profit from the information covered in this chapter, as well.

This chapter should also be of interest to someone who has the possibility of inheriting a business interest, such as the child of a small business owner, or perhaps the spouse of someone who is self employed. Even those who are thinking of starting a business, may find it worthwhile to take a few minutes to read this chapter.

Those who have no present business interest may want to skip this chapter and go on to Chapter 7.

Your business is your property, and as such it is included as part of your overall Estate Plan. But owning a business isn't as simple as just holding title to a tangible item such as a car or parcel of real estate. For example, if you own a business in your name only, i.e. as a **sole proprietor**, there may be no single document that indicates ownership of your business property. If you are doing business under a name other than your own, you may have registered a Trademark or Service Mark with the California Secretary of State. The *Certificate of Registration* issued by the Secretary of State may identify you as the owner of the business, but it does not identify your business property (Bus. & Prof. 14230, 14240).

You could own a truck, computer, copier or other expensive business equipment. Title to that property is probably in your personal name. Your business bank account may be in your name only, or in the name of the business with you alone as signatory on the account. Charge cards and business loans are either in your name only, or in the name of your company with your name as guarantor.

If you want to leave your business to your son, how do you do it? Do you leave him the equipment used in the business? If you are doing business under your own name and not a registered Trademark or Service Mark, how do you give him that name? And how do you handle business related loans? If you leave him the business, will he agree to be responsible for any outstanding business debt?

In addition to providing for the transfer of your business, you need to make provision for its operation in the event of your incapacity or death. If you do not make such provision, a Court may need to make that decision for you. In particular, if you become incapacitated, it may be necessary to have a Court appoint a Conservator to operate your business. If you die, and have not provided for the transfer or continued operation of the business, your Personal Representative may operate the business for up to six months. After that he will need Court permission to operate the business until it can be transferred to the proper beneficiary (Prob. 9760).

Partnerships can be even more complicated, unless there is a written partnership agreement that says how the business is to be transferred in the event that one of the partners dies. Even the transfer of a corporation can be a major headache if there are several shareholders and no shareholders' agreement to say how shares should be transferred in the event of the death of a shareholder.

For these reasons, it is important to think about an Estate Plan for your business. You need to ask yourself:

How can I have maximum protection and control over my business during my lifetime?

How can I ensure that my business continues to operate in the event of my incapacity?

How can I structure my business so that it can be transferred quickly and at minimum cost to my beneficiaries?

We will examine each type of business ownership as it relates to these questions.

WHAT'S THE BEST TYPE OF BUSINESS OWNERSHIP?

Those who read the first five chapters know us well enough not to expect a definitive answer to the above question. Our job, as we see it, is to explain the rules of the game (i.e., California law) to the reader. Once you know how things work in California, you can make an informed decision as to the type of business ownership that best accomplishes your goal.

SOLE PROPRIETORSHIP
Maximum control — Maximum liability

You are the boss if you do business in your name only, but you take full personal responsibility for any loss suffered by the company; and as explained, you may need to consult with an attorney if you want to make arrangements for someone to take over your business should you become incapacitated or die.

Because of this personal liability issue, many people think it best to form a corporation as soon as they start up the business. That may not be the best strategy. It takes money to form a corporation. You may need to pay an attorney to set up the corporation. You will need to pay a filing fee to file the Articles of Incorporation with the California Secretary of State. Each year you need to file an annual report with the Corporations Unit of the Secretary of State and pay an annual filing fee (Corp. 200, Corp. 1502).

And there may be additional accounting fees. Each year you will need to file separate corporate income tax returns; one for the state and one for the IRS.

You do not need to pay filing fees to the Secretary of State to form a sole proprietorship, and you do not need to file separate income tax returns. You can include your business income as part of your personal income tax return and not go through the cost and hassle of filing a separate corporate return.

Another reason to start business as a sole proprietorship is the risk of failure. Although every new business owner thinks his venture must surely culminate in riches, research conducted by the Brandow Company shows that only 55% of new businesses get to celebrate their third birthday (see their data at **www.brandow.com**). You can always form a corporation should your business succeed. If the business does not succeed, then at least you didn't waste time, effort and money to form a corporation.

But What About My Personal Liability?

Many people seek to limit their personal liability by forming a corporation, however, that doesn't always work in the real world. For example, if you wish to rent a store front or office space, an experienced landlord will allow you to lease the space in the corporate name, but he will require you to sign as a guarantor. Should the business fail, he will have the right to sue you, personally, for the full value of the lease. Once you have established a successful business, the landlord may agree to just hold the business liable; and in that case having a corporation instead of a sole proprietorship will limit your personal liability.

Regardless of what form of business ownership you choose, you can be held personally liable for any fraudulent or negligent act that you commit. The way to avoid personal liability for fraudulent acts is not to willfully (deliberately) deceive or cheat anyone.

Most of us are honest folk, but negligence is another matter. We all make mistakes. The way to limit your liability for negligence is to purchase insurance that provides protection for mistakes and accidents. For example, if you open a title insurance business, you can purchase an Errors and Omissions insurance policy to cover a loss caused by a mistake you might make in a title search. If you have a business involving the care of a person (adult or child day care center, nurse practitioner, etc.), it is important to have coverage for an injury to a client due to accident or negligence.

If you have a business location (a storefront or office) consider purchasing a comprehensive business insurance policy to cover injury to anyone who visits your business, as well as damages to the premises. For example, if you open a flower shop you can get insurance to cover an injury to a customer who slips and falls. The same policy can cover vandalism to your shop, such as a broken plate glass window. You can be compensated for loss should a storm cause the electricity to go out and your shipment of fresh cut flowers wilt for lack of refrigeration.

The purpose of any business insurance policy is to shift the risk of a business loss from your pocket to that of the insurance company.

And the downside is . . .

The problem with insurance is the greater the risk, the greater the cost. We all would like 100% insurance coverage, but few of us can afford the premium. What holds true for life insurance holds true for business insurance. The right amount of insurance coverage for you is the amount that allows you to sleep at night.

A business partnership is much like a marriage. You can both start out with the best of intentions, only to find that you are hopelessly incompatible. The break-up of a business partnership can be just as bitter and hotly contested as the breakup of a marriage. A properly drafted Partnership Agreement is a must — not only to set the terms of a dissolution, but to clearly state what is expected of each partner; i.e., how much each will contribute to the business venture in terms of effort or financing.

The Partnership Agreement should cover what will happen to the partner's share in the event of his incapacity or death. Most Partnership Agreements provide for an appraisal of the business and the buy out of the deceased (or disabled) partner's share. The Partnership Agreement may need to be backed up with financing. For example, you could sign a Partnership Agreement that requires the company to buy out your partnership interest should you become disabled or die. But what good is the Agreement if there is not enough cash in the company to pay for the buy out?

You will have better protection if the Partnership Agreement requires the company to maintain disability and life insurance to pay for the buy out. Many insurance companies offer Key man insurance. The policy is designed to compensate the company for the loss of someone who is essential to the continuation of the business. If sufficient insurance is purchased, the proceeds of the policy can be used to cover any loss suffered by the company and to buy out the share of the company that was owned by the deceased or disabled partner.

The sole proprietorship and the partnership are the earliest type of business organization. California laws governing these types of business organizations have their roots in English Common Law. Common law requires the sole proprietor and each business partner to take full personal responsibility for the debts of the company. As people became ever more litigious (lawyer talk for "sue happy") businessmen sought to limit their liability and prevailed on the legislature to create a form of business ownership to limit that liability.

Legislatures in each state responded to that need by giving businessmen the right to create a company (the corporation) with an identity separate from the owners of the business. By doing business as a corporation, the businessman's liability is limited to the money he invests in the company. A person can sue the corporation for business debts, but not the owners of the corporation.

This does not mean that a corporate owner can use the corporation to do things that are fraudulent. If he does, he can be held personally liable. The owner of the corporation cannot use the corporation as a "veil" to cover his wrongdoing. California courts have "pierced the corporate veil" and held shareholders, officers and directors personally liable whenever they decided that justice would be served by holding the people and not just the corporation accountable for their acts. The Supreme Court of California ruled that "... it is an issue of whether in the particular case presented ... justice and equity can best be accomplished and fraud and unfairness defeated by a disregard of the distinct entity of the corporate form." The Supreme Court of California (*Mesler v. Bragg Management Co.*, 39 Cal.3d 290 (1985); 702 P.2d 601)

Whoever forms a corporation (the *incorporator*) has maximum control over the corporation. He decides how the company will operate by having the Articles of Incorporation and the company By-laws prepared according to his specifications. He can keep full control of the company as the only shareholder, or he can distribute shares and give up as much control as he wishes. Transferring corporate ownership is simple. It is a matter of signing a stock certificate transferring the shares of stock in the company. You can have a Transfer On Death designation to a named beneficiary.

If you own shares of stock in your name only, without a TOD designation, your Personal Representative will transfer the shares to the proper beneficiary. But keeping shares in your name only may not be the best way to go if you own a majority of shares and operate the business yourself. If Probate is necessary, it may take several months before the shares are transferred to the proper beneficiary, meanwhile, someone needs to continue to operate the business. If you do not leave directions for the continuation of the business, the Personal Representative (or the Probate Court) may decide it is best to just sell the company and give the proceeds of the sale to your beneficiaries.

The better route is to have your attorney prepare a Revocable Living Trust and transfer the shares into the Trust. The Trust document can give your Successor Trustee specific instructions about how the business is to be managed or transferred should you become incapacitated or die. Still another important benefit is to avoid the need to Probate what may be your only valuable asset.

THE LIMITED PARTNERSHIP

Just as a sole proprietor can limit his liability by forming a corporation, the partners of a general partnership can limit their liability by converting the partnership to a *Limited Partnership*. As with the corporation, the Limited Partnership is a creation of the legislature and is regulated by California law. The name of the Limited Partnership must identify it as a limited partnership or contain the initials "LP." A Certificate of Limited Partnership must be filed with the California Secretary of State (Corp. 15612, 15621).

The structure of a Limited Partnership differs from a general partnership. In a general partnership, each partner has full authority to conduct business on behalf of the partnership. Each partner is personally liable for monies owed by the partnership, regardless of whether that partner actually incurred the debt. The Limited Partnership has *General Partners* and *Limited Partners*. Only a General Partner has authority to conduct partnership business. A Limited Partner has no control over the management of the company and has no personal liability for company debts (Corp. 15632, 15643). However, the General Partner and the Limited Partnership itself can be sued for monies owed.

But even a General Partner can avoid personal liability by forming a corporation, and then letting the corporation serve as the sole General Partner. An unpaid creditor of the Limited Partnership can sue the corporate General Partner, but not the shareholders of the corporation. Liability can be limited to the amount of money invested in the business venture. None of the owners will have personal liability. Of course, as with the corporation, all parties can be held personally liable for fraudulent or criminal acts performed in their partnership capacity.

The astute reader might be wondering "Why would any-one form a corporation (and pay all of the costs to set up the corporation) and then make the corporation the General Partner of a Limited Partnership (after paying all that money to set up the Partnership)? If limited business liability is the goal, why not just form a corporation?"

Answers to those questions are many and in fact, far removed from the original goal of limiting the business risk of the partners to just the money they invested in the business. The Limited Partnership can be used as a means of transferring a family business to the children with some significant tax benefits. For example, suppose Mom & Pop run a small, highly profitable, rapidly expanding, gourmet chocolate shop. They have two children, both in college. Right now, the business is worth about $500,000, but they figure that by the time they retire, the business could be worth millions. If their children inherit the business at that time, there could be significant Estate Taxes due. Also, because they are making lots of money right now, they are paying very high income taxes.

Both problems can be solved with a Family Limited Partnership. Mom and Pop can be the General Partners of the company and retain total control. They can make each child a Limited Partner by transferring shares of the business worth less than the Annual Gift Tax Exclusion. The Exclusion for the year 2006 is $12,000, so together Mom and Pop can gift shares of the partnership up to $24,000 per child, per year. By gifting a percentage of the business each year, the parents can eventually transfer all of the business to the children. When the parents die, there will be no Gift or Estate Tax because the children already own the business. Of course there is still the problem of the Capital Gains Tax should the children decide to sell the business.

Regardless of how much of the company they give away, Mom and Pop can keep total control of the company because they are General Partners. When the parents are ready to retire, one or both of the children can take over as General Partner — but if making chocolate is not their thing, the parents can arrange to have a corporation manage the Limited Partnership and the children continue to receive income as limited partners. As for the current income tax problem, the children, as limited partners, are entitled to receive income from the business. Income paid to the children and their parents is generally taxed at a lower rate than the taxes to just Mom and Pop. For example, suppose the company earns $100,000. Mom and Pop will pay a high rate of income tax if they are the only two partners in the company. If the children become partners, each partner can earn $25,000 and the overall bill for income taxes will be smaller.

Still another important advantage of the Family Limited Partnership over the corporation is creditor protection for the children's partnership interest. For example, suppose one of the children becomes a dentist, gets sued for malpractice, and loses the case. If Mom and Pop had incorporated the business and given the children most of the shares of stock in the company, the creditor could take the shares to satisfy the judgment. The creditor could wind up owning the company! Not so, with a Limited Partnership interest. A judge may order that the income from the Limited Partnership be used to pay the judgment, but he cannot order the Partnership share itself to be given to the creditor unless the Limited Partnership Agreement allows for such transfer or all General Partners and a majority in interest of Limited Partners agree (Corp. 15672, 15673, 15674). Not likely with Mom and Pop as General Partners. They might even decide to use company income to pay themselves salary and not distribute anything to the hapless creditor!

We used an actual business as an example to explain how the Limited Partnership worked. It didn't take Estate Planning attorneys long to figure out that the "family business" could be just income producing items (such as stocks and bonds) that Mom and Pop placed into the Limited Partnership. The family "business" could be just the business of earning income. In other words, the Family Limited Partnership (or even a Family Partnership) could just be a type of an Estate Plan created solely for the purpose of transferring assets to the children to avoid paying Estate Taxes, and to pay less in income taxes.

It didn't take the IRS long to challenge this method of Estate Planning. A series of IRS rulings and court cases followed, with the main issue being whether a bona fide business partnership existed.

There is a common sense rule of evidence that says "If it looks like a duck and walks like a duck, and quacks like a duck, it must be a duck." In 1946 the Supreme Court decided that whether a family partnership is really a business partnership for tax purposes, should be determined on a case by case basis; and that the IRS should use the "walk and quack" test. Only the justices said this in proper legal terms. They said to determine whether a partnership exists depends on ". . .whether the partners really and truly intended to join together for the purpose of carrying on a business and sharing in the profits or losses or both. And their intention in this respect is a question of fact, to be determined from testimony disclosed by their agreement, considered as a whole, and by their conduct in execution of its provisions" (*Commissioner v. Tower*, 327 U.S. 280 (1946)).

THE LIMITED LIABILITY COMPANY

The IRS continues to take a close look at family partnerships, and will challenge any tax break if the family partnership (limited or not) does not meet the basic requirement of being a bona fide business partnership. Perhaps in response to IRS challenges, in the 1990s each of the 50 states, and even the District of Columbia, passed laws enabling residents of their state to form a new business entity called a *Limited Liability Company* ("LLC" or "L.L.C.") (Corp. 17052).

A California LLC is formed by filing Articles of Organization with the California Secretary of State. It is not required to be a profit making venture. It can be formed to engage in any lawful business activity, except banking and insurance business (Corp. 17002, 17050).

The LLC combines the better features of the Limited Partnership and the Corporation. Like the corporation, it can be formed by one or more people. The members of the LLC must enter into an *Operating Agreement* that states how company business is to be conducted.

The LLC can be run by a manager (who is not a member of the company) or it can be run by a member or members of the company. As with a corporation, all members have limited liability, regardless of whether that member happens to be managing the company. As with a Limited Partnership, a creditor cannot take possession or control of a share of the company owned by a member. The most the creditor can do is get a court to assign income generated by that share to the creditor (Corp. 17101, 17158).

Now Mom and Pop can form a LLC, give away some or all of the shares of the company during their lifetime, and still keep control of the company, and with no more personal liability than a non-managing member of the Limited Liability Company.

Transfers into the Limited Liability Company can be made so that there are no Estate or Gift Tax consequences. Income can be distributed to the children, or not, as Mom and Pop see fit.

The skeptic is probably thinking "Maximum control, limited liability, easily transferred to my beneficiaries, no Estate Tax. This is too good to be true. There must be a catch somewhere."

And so there is. It's called the Capital Gains Tax. If you transfer property during your lifetime, that property is valued by the IRS as of the date of transfer. If you gift a share of the Limited Liability Company during your lifetime, your beneficiary will take your basis in the property (i.e., the value that you paid for your interest in the Company). If you sell the share to your beneficiar*y, his basis is the fair market value of the share as of the date of purchase. Either way, once the beneficiary decides to sell the property, there may be a significant Capital Gains Tax due.

An experienced Estate Planning attorney should be able to suggest any number of ways to solve the problem, including purchasing life insurance to pay the tax.

INSURANCE TO PAY DEBTS AND TAXES

Regardless of what form of business ownership you have, you need to think about what will happen to your business in the event of your incapacity or death. And in particular, how company debts will be paid. If your business is highly leveraged (business talk for "owes lots of money"), you also need to consider how those loans will be paid should you become disabled or die. One solution is to purchase Key man insurance. As explained earlier, Key man insurance is protection for the company against the loss of a valuable employee. The company purchases the policy and the proceeds are paid to the company to compensate it for the loss; but ultimately the policy benefits those who inherit the business.

Taxes are still another concern. Your business may be worth millions on paper, and your Estate Taxes will be based on that value. Your heirs might be forced to sell the company just to pay the taxes, but without your leadership they may get only a fraction of the value of the company.

Even if the federal government decides to eliminate federal Estate Taxes, the state of California, or any other state where you have a business location, may decide to levy an Estate or Inheritance Tax.

And there is still the problem of the Capital Gains Tax. No one in Congress is talking about doing away with the Capital Gains Tax — and that tax could be sizeable. One solution to the problem of an unknown Estate Tax and/or Capital Gains Tax is to purchase life insurance that can be used to pay for any Estate Tax that may be due upon your death and any Capital Gains Tax that may be due when your beneficiary sells the property he inherits.

That may sound like a good, simple, solution, but you need to think things through before calling your insurance agent. The first question being:

How much insurance should I purchase?

That is a tough question. If you are in good health, who knows what will happen before you die. Will your business increase in value or go bust? Will the federal government really do away with Estate Taxes or will they do nothing and allow the tax to be reinstated in 2011?

The last question is particularly troublesome. Under today's tax law, if you purchase a life insurance policy, or even control the benefits of the policy, all of the proceeds of the policy will be counted as part of your taxable Estate. You may be buying insurance just to pay more in taxes to Uncle Sam.

You don't need a soothsayer or psychic to solve the problem. A financial planner with access to computer generated models can predict your life expectancy, how much your business will be worth when you retire and even the probability that the economy will require Estate Taxes to be reinstated!

Suppose your financial planner predicts that Estate Taxes will be reinstated and that your heirs will probably need to pay one million dollars in federal and state Estate Taxes. If you purchase a million dollar insurance policy, the proceeds of the policy will be included in your Estate. If there is an Estate Tax of 40% your heirs will net only $600,000 of the million dollar policy, with the rest going to pay for Estate Taxes on the policy itself. Your heirs will need to come up with an additional $400,000 to make up for the original million dollars predicted as being necessary to pay your Estate Taxes. A solution to this dilemma is the **IRREVOCABLE LIFE INSURANCE TRUST.**

THE IRREVOCABLE LIFE INSURANCE TRUST

An ***Irrevocable Life Insurance Trust*** can be designed to provide money to pay any tax that may be due after your death. To be sure that the IRS does not count the proceeds of the Trust as part of your taxable Estate the Trust must meet the following requirements:

⇨ The Trust must be irrevocable.

⇨ You cannot be Trustee.

The Trust can be set up for the benefit of your child. In such case, the child can be Trustee of the Trust. The child, as Trustee, will purchase an insurance policy on your life. You may need to file a Gift Tax return if you give your child a large sum of money to purchase the policy. It is better to have the child purchase a policy that is paid in quarterly or annual premiums instead of a single lump sum payment. You can give the child an amount each year up to the Annual Gift Tax Exclusion ($12,000 in the year 2006) to pay for the premium. If you are married, you and your spouse can gift up to $24,000 per year without the need to file a Gift Tax return.

As tax laws change, the child/Trustee can use as much of the gift as is needed to purchase sufficient insurance to cover the taxes. The Trust can be set up to cover Estate taxes or Capital Gains taxes, or both. For example, the Trustee can purchase an insurance policy that pays a million dollars upon your death. Those insurance funds can be used to pay your Estate taxes. Should it happen that no Estate taxes are due, the Trustee can keep the monies invested until the business is sold. The Trust funds can be used to pay any Capital Gains Tax that may be due at that time. If monies are left over once all taxes are paid, they can be distributed to the named beneficiaries of the Trust.

Your attorney can design an Irrevocable Insurance Trust in any number of ways to meet the special needs of you and your family. For example, an Irrevocable Insurance Trust can be set up to solve problems described in the last Chapter. Alan wanted to leave insurance proceeds for his child but was concerned that the cash value of the policy could be taken by his creditors. A properly drafted Irrevocable Insurance Trust can solve such problem, because the Trust, and not Alan, is the owner of the policy.

Of course, it costs significant money to set up and maintain an Irrevocable Insurance Trust. Those who do not have concerns about creditors may wonder whether it's necessary to go through all that cost and bother if there will be no more Estate Taxes in the future. After all a simple life insurance policy can cover any Capital Gains Tax that may be due. But, as explained, the tax law as passed in 2001 reinstates the federal Estate Tax in 2011. If lawmakers take no further action, the Estate of anyone who dies on January 1, 2011, and thereafter is subject to a federal Estate Tax for an Estate over one million dollars.

Someone with an active imagination could envision the following scenario:

It is New Year's eve, 2010. A 97 year old lies sleeping, at his home, surrounded by his four grandchildren who are his sole heirs.

"He looks so peaceful."

"Yes. Surprising, considering that he has terminal cancer, failing kidneys and heart. His doctor says he can't last more than a few days. The doctor left a supply of morphine so that we can keep Gramps comfortable over the New Year's holiday. The doctor gave him a shot just before he left."

"The doctor said not to give Gramps another shot unless he was in pain. His heart is in such a weakened condition, he could easily overdose on morphine."

"Yes, of course."

"Too bad he didn't get a chance to do some Estate Planning before he had that stroke last year. "

"I thought his attorney took care of all that."

"His attorney suggested he set up an Irrevocable Insurance Trust to pay for any Estate Tax, but Gramps felt sure that Congress would pass a law that would permanently repeal the Estate Tax."

"I can't imagine Gramps coming to that conclusion. The economy is down and the government needs to raise taxes. It is easier for legislators to leave the law as written back in 2001, than take some affirmative action."

"Gramps was always a sharp business man, but in his later years his mind wasn't as clear as when he earned his five million dollars."

"Is that what we are going to inherit?"

"Not unless he dies before midnight. After midnight the Estate Tax is reinstated, and at a rate of 45%. we'll be lucky to come away with half a mill each."

"Gramps moved. I think he may be in pain."

"Yes, he does look uncomfortable."

"It isn't right to let him suffer like this."

"Yes, of course."

Continuing To Care 7

There are any number of reasons that people give for wanting to continue on with their lives. For the lucky ones, their main reason for living is that they are having a great time and don't want it to end. For many, it is more a sense of responsibility. During child rearing years the concern of the parent is what will happen to the child should the parent suddenly die. Once a child is grown, the roles often reverse, and it is the child worrying about what will happen to his parent if the child were not present to see to the care of the aging parent. Even pet lovers worry about what will happen to their pet should the owner no longer be around.

There is little that can be done to prepare those who depend on you for the loss of your companionship and emotional support; but there are many things you can do to provide financial support for those who rely on you. Even people of modest means can make financial provision so their loved ones will have an easy transition from being dependent to becoming self sufficient.

This chapter explains the many simple, and relatively inexpensive, things you can do to provide care for your loved ones should you not be present to do so yourself.

It doesn't happen very often, but both parents could die or become incapacitated before their child reaches adulthood. Most parents don't want to think about, much less prepare for such a happening. But in this age of postponing parenthood, many parents are in their fifties and sixties and still raising children. The probability of a life threatening illness increases with age, so parents need to understand the importance of planning ahead.

Parents with dangerous occupations also need to provide for the care of their minor child in the event of the disability or death of both parents. It is surprising to think of how many of us are employed in high risk occupations. Construction workers, military personnel, firemen, state and federal law enforcement agents, and in this day and age, even postal workers face hazards on a daily basis.

Regardless of the parent's age or occupation, planning for the care of a minor child should be part of every parent's Estate Plan, not only because it is the responsible thing to do, but also because it is relatively simple and inexpensive to do.

A child must be cared for in two ways, the **person** of the child and the **property** of the child. To care for the person of the child, someone must be in charge of the child's everyday living, not only food and shelter but also to provide social, ethical and religious training. Someone must have legal authority to make medical decisions and see to the child's education. To care for the child's property, someone must be responsible to see that monies left to the child are used for the care of the child and that anything left over is preserved until the child becomes an adult.

A Guardian will need to be appointed to care for the person and property of the child in the event that both parents become incapacitated or die before the child is grown.

USING A WILL TO APPOINT A GUARDIAN

As explained in Chapter 4, each parent can use his Will to appoint someone to serve as Guardian of their minor child in the event that both parents die before the child is grown.

It is a good idea for both parents to name the same person to serve as Guardian. If the child's parents appoint different people for the job, and then die simultaneously, it will be up to a judge to decide who is best suited to be Guardian. If they do not die simultaneously, the Court will give top priority to the person named in the Will of the last parent to die (Prob. 1500, 1514).

One problem with using a Will to appoint someone to be your child's Guardian, is that for the appointment to be effective, the Will must be admitted to Probate; i.e., the Court must determine that the Will is valid; and the person you chose as Guardian needs to file a petition to be appointed as the child's Guardian. It might take several weeks before that person has the legal authority to care for the child.

A better approach may be to have your attorney prepare a separate document expressing your choice of Guardian in the event that you and the other parent are both deceased, or for some reason unable to care for the child. That document can be presented to the Court as part of a petition asking the Court to appoint a Guardian of the person or property of your child (Prob. 1502).

The person you name as Guardian must be both willing and able to assume the job, so you need to check with that person before making the appointment.

THE BEST CHOICE OF GUARDIAN

Many parents never get around to appointing a Guardian for their minor child because they cannot come to an agreement as to the best choice of Guardian. "I think my mother should be Guardian. After all she raised me, and I turned out fine" can signal the opening salvo of a lengthy, and often unresolved battle.

Not being able to agree on a choice of Guardian should not discourage you from appointing the person of your choice either as part of your Will or in a separate writing. The thing to keep in mind is that the Guardian of your choice will take over only if the other parent is deceased or incapacitated. Even if you both die simultaneously, and you each name someone different to serve as Guardian, your choice of Guardian will at least be brought to the attention of the Court.

It is important that the person you choose to serve as Guardian be compatible with the child. If your choice of Guardian is not that of the child's, the child can object to the appointment. If the child is old enough to form an intelligent preference, the Court will seriously consider the child's choice of Guardian and then appoint a Guardian based on the what the Court determines to be in the child's best interest (Prob. 1514).

As any parent is well aware, it is expensive to raise a child. The person you consider to be the best choice to serve as Guardian might not be able to do so unless you leave sufficient monies to pay for the care of the child. If you have limited finances, consider purchasing term insurance on your life and/or on the life of the other parent of the child. A *term life insurance policy* insures your life for a certain period of time. You can limit the term until the child is grown. The cost of the policy is relatively inexpensive because it has no cash surrender value and no money is paid unless the insured person dies during the term of the policy. If you can only afford one policy, insure the life of the parent who contributes most to the support of the child.

Some companies offer a combination of term life and disability insurance, in the event that the bread-winner becomes disabled and unable to work. As with any other purchase, it is important to comparison shop to obtain the best price for the coverage.

If you are married, you may want to name your spouse as the beneficiary of the term insurance policy with your child as an alternate beneficiary. Married or single, you can name your minor child as the primary beneficiary of the policy. Under California law, the insurance company may give amounts up to $5,000 to the child by transferring the funds to an adult member of the minor's family. The company is required to seek Court permission before transferring funds that exceed that amount (Prob. 3401).

If the insurance proceeds are significant in value, the Court will probably require that a Guardian of the property be appointed to protect the funds until the child reaches 18.

We discussed the ways parents can control who is appointed to serve as the Guardian of their minor child should both parents be incapacitated or deceased. Guardianship is a necessity in such cases. But if at least one of the parents is able to care for the person of the child, it may be wise to avoid the need for the Court to appoint a Guardian for property left to the child.

Even if the surviving parent is appointed to serve as Guardian, the amount you leave to the child will be reduced by the cost of establishing and maintaining the guardianship. An attorney needs to be employed to establish the guardianship. Within ninety days of his appointment, the Guardian must file an inventory with the Court. Not less than once every two years, he must provide an accounting to the Court (Prob. 2610, 2620). If property left to the child is significant, the Guardian may need to employ a financial advisor to manage the funds and an accountant to file reports with the Court. With permission from the Court, the Guardian and the people he employs to help him (including his attorney) are paid for their services from the child's property (Prob. 2430).

Money left for the child may be significantly reduced by the cost of caring for the property. This can be avoided by leaving property to the child in such a manner, that will make it unnecessary for the Court to appoint a Guardian of the property of the child. One way to do so is to include a Trust for the child as part of your Will. Another is to set up a Revocable Living Trust that includes provisions for the care of the child. If you have limited finances, a good alternative is to appoint someone to serve as Custodian of the gift under the CALIFORNIA UNIFORM TRANSFERS TO MINORS ACT.

THE UNIFORM TRANSFERS TO MINORS ACT

The **California Uniform Transfers to Minors Act** is designed to protect gifts made to a minor by appointing someone to be the **Custodian** of a gift until the child is an adult. For example, you can make a minor child the beneficiary of your life insurance policy, and name a trusted relative or friend or even a financial institution to be the Custodian of the gift. Should you die while the child is a minor, the insurance company will give the proceeds of the policy to the person you named as Custodian to hold until the child is an adult.

You can make a gift to a minor in your Will. You can appoint your Personal Representative (or anyone else) as Custodian of the gift (Prob. 3903). For example:

I give the sum of $100,000 to _____(name)
as custodian for _____ (name of minor)
under the California Uniform Transfers to Minors Act.

THE LIFETIME GIFT

You can even use the Uniform Transfers to Minors Law to make a gift during your lifetime of items such as shares in a corporation or a limited partnership interest. You can nominate yourself as Custodian of the gift, or you can name another person to serve as Custodian. Once the lifetime gift is made it becomes irrevocable, so this method is not appropriate unless you are sure that you want the child to have the gift once he is grown (Prob. 3904, 3909).

In general, the Custodian must distribute the gift when the child reaches 18; however, you can specify that a lifetime gift be given at a later age — up to age 25. You can specify that a gift made by Will be distributed at any time after 18 and up to the child's 26th birthday. If you make no mention of age, the Custodian will distribute the gift on the child's 18th birthday (Prob. 3920, 3920.5).

MANAGING THE PROPERTY

Under California law, while the Custodian is in possession of the gift, he can use as much of the gift as he thinks advisable for the benefit of the child. He can pay monies directly to the child, or use the funds for the child's benefit. In making the distribution he is not obliged to take into account that someone else has a duty to support the child — even if the Custodian is the child's parent and it is his own responsibility to support the child (Prob. 3912).

The Custodian can do the opposite and distribute nothing. He can refuse to use any of the monies for the child and just keep the funds invested until the funds are distributed when the child is an adult. In such case, the child's parent or guardian (or even the child once he is 14) can ask a Court to order that the monies be used for the care of the child. (Prob. 3914). The judge will determine what is in the child's best interest and then rule on the matter.

Hopefully, the Custodian will give a regular accounting to the child's parent or guardian. If not, any member of the child's family, or the child once he reaches 14, can ask the Court to order a full accounting of the custodial property (Prob. 3919).

As with any type of Estate Plan, you need to examine all aspects of the transfer to see if there is anything that may be objectionable to you.

THE CUSTODIAN'S FEE

The law requires the Custodian to invest and manage the property in a responsible, prudent manner. The Custodian is entitled to be paid for his effort. If the gift is sizeable, his fee can be sizeable. Before appointing a person or a financial institution as Custodian, it is best to come to a written agreement about how the property will be managed and the charge for doing so (Prob. 3915).

NO GROUP GIFT

You cannot make a single gift to more than one child under the Uniform Transfers To Minors Act. For example, if you want to make a single gift of real property to two or more minor children, you need to do so by another method, such as creating a Trust for the children (Prob. 3910).

THE COST OF PROBATE

As discussed, you can include a gift to a minor in your Will by naming a Custodian for the gift. As with any gift made under a Will, a Probate procedure will be necessary to distribute the gift to the Custodian. If you are trying to avoid Probate, this may not be the best way to go. If your gift is significant, the better route is to set up a Revocable Living Trust. You can manage the Trust while you are able. Should you become incapacitated or die before the child is grown your Successor Trustee will take over. Unlike the Uniform Gift to Minors, you can direct the Trustee to give the gift to the child at any age you think proper.

Which brings us to another problem, namely, that there is no flexibility as to the final distribution of a gift made under the Uniform Transfers to Minors Act.

MANDATORY DISTRIBUTION

A Custodian appointed under the Uniform Transfers To Minors Act must distribute the gift by the child's 18th birthday. That can be extended to 25 if you make the gift part or your Will or age 26, for a lifetime gift (Prob. 3920, 3920.5). The gift must be made regardless of whether the child is mature enough to handle the money in a responsible manner. A sizeable gift to an immature beneficiary is not the best Estate Plan.

Perhaps the reason that the story of Cinderella has such universal appeal is that many stepchildren, at one point or another, feel left out. The law seems to reinforce that perception. Unless a married person makes provision otherwise, a spouse has priority over the child in health matters both before and after death. If a married person is too ill to make medical decisions, the doctors will turn to the spouse for directions. Should a married person die, the decedent's Spouse/RDP, and not the child, has authority to agree to an anatomical gift (Health & Safety 7151).

If a married couple hold all of their property jointly, that property will go to the surviving spouse and not to the child of the deceased parent. This might not be a problem if the surviving spouse is the natural parent of the child. It could be a major problem if the natural parent dies first. The stepchild of the surviving parent may be left with nothing.

In such situations, the stepparent comes across as villain, but it is the parent, and not the stepparent, who decides whether the child will inherit property belonging to the natural parent. Too often the stepchild is left out by default, i.e., the natural parent doesn't give the matter any thought, or perhaps the natural parent is confident that the stepparent will do "what's right."

That was the case with Walter. He always wanted to be a father, so he was pleased when Todd was born just before the first anniversary of Walter's marriage to Nancy. Twin girls were born just 15 months later. Unfortunately the twins' birth was premature, causing them to have medical and developmental problems. Nancy had her hands full just caring for the three children, so it was up to Walter to support the family.

Walter was up to the job. He was both conscientious and ambitious. He started his own interior decorating business, complete with a retail sales storefront to sell fabrics, and an upholstery shop in the rear of the store. With hard work and long hours, he was able to make a comfortable living. But the strain of raising a family and running a business took its toll, both on him and the marriage. At 40, he felt like an old man.

All that changed when he hired Annie to manage the retail part of his business. Her energy and sunny disposition were just what the business (and Walter) needed.

Walter's divorce from Nancy was amicable. Walter was a loving father who took his responsibilities seriously. He was generous when it came to supporting the children. Walter had only finished high school, and he wanted more for his son. He encouraged Todd to do well in school so that he could go on to college, and maybe become a doctor or lawyer. The twins had developmental problems; but Walter encouraged them to reach their maximum potential. It was his goal to help them become self sufficient.

Annie got along very well with her stepchildren. She had no trouble with Walter's desire to support the children and give them a good start in life. Even though they held all of their money in a joint account, she never questioned any expense made on behalf of the children.

Walter never gave much thought to an Estate Plan. After all, he was healthy, and in the prime of his earning capacity. He often said that he was fortunate to have married two wonderful women. If he had a dark thought, it soon passed, rationalizing that if something happened to him, Annie would take care of the children.

But she didn't.

Walter died in one of those freak accidents. He was trimming the branches from his tree with an electric saw and accidentally touched an overhead wire. All he owned was tied up in the business that he held jointly with Annie. Annie felt that she was a major factor in the success of that business. Why should she share any of her hard earned money with Nancy? As for the children, it was Nancy's job to raise them. After all they were Nancy's children, and not Annie's children. If it was a struggle to support the children, then that was Nancy's problem!

A better argument (but one she didn't raise) was that Walter really wanted Annie to inherit everything. If he wanted to provide for his children, he could have done so in any number of different ways, beginning with his marriage to Annie:

✍ He could have insisted on a Premarital Agreement that could have provided for certain funds to be kept separate for the benefit of his children.

✍ He could have signed a partnership agreement with Annie that would have given his share of the business to his children, in the event of his death.

✍ If he didn't want to negotiate with Annie about a premarital or partnership agreement, he could have had his attorney prepare a Trust that would have cared for his children until they were old enough to be on their own.

✍ If nothing else, he could have purchased a life insurance policy with the children as beneficiaries of the policy.

THE SECOND MARRIAGE TRUST

Walter's situation is not unique. Second marriages are commonplace in America. Many who are widowed or divorced, remarry. If children are involved, the parent may have divided loyalties. The parent may want to provide income to the child until the child completes his education, and then leave whatever is left of his Estate to his surviving spouse. More often it is the other way around. The parent wants to be sure that the surviving spouse has sufficient income to support his/her current life-style, but once the surviving spouse dies, the parent wants all that remains to go to his children. A properly drafted Trust can provide for the care of a spouse and child in whatever way the Settlor of the Trust thinks best.

That was the case with an elderly widower who married a pretty girl less than half his age. Their Premarital Agreement made it clear that all his property would go to his son from his first marriage. Surprisingly, the marriage turned out well. So well that the couple had two daughters. The husband decided to divide his Estate equally between his three children and to provide for the care of his wife until the youngest child was grown.

His attorney suggested a Trust. "You can be Trustee during your lifetime. Once you die, your Successor Trustee can immediately distribute one-third of the Trust to your son who is now 55. No sense to keep him waiting. The rest of your money can remain in your Trust. Income from the Trust can be used to support your wife and children until the youngest is 25. Then, whatever remains in the Trust can be distributed equally to your daughters."

"Good idea" said the elderly gentlemen, with a smile "Just make sure it is revocable during my lifetime. Who knows what adventures I might be up to in the future?"

It isn't just stepchildren who can be left out if no provision is made. Even a child from a long-standing marriage can be cut off against the wishes of a parent. A parent may assume that all of their children will be treated equally when both parents are gone, but if all their property is held jointly, the last parent to die is the one who gets to decide "who gets what." Too often, the wishes of the deceased parent are ignored.

That was the case with Joan. She was married to Herb for over forty years. He was the breadwinner, but he was content to let Joan handle all of the finances. Joan wanted to be sure that each of their three daughters would always have a decent place to live. They purchased a three story house and each of the daughters moved into a different floor of the home. It was the parent's intent that once they were both gone, the daughters would inherit and occupy the building. The couple owned everything jointly, so when Joan died, all of their property, including the home, was owned by Herb.

The grief suffered by Herbert at his wife's death was more than he could manage. He alternated between sadness, despair and anger.

His middle daughter took the brunt of his anger. Their relationship had always been strained. She felt she could never live up to her father's expectations. She was not the cute baby of the family as was her younger sister. She was not the eldest daughter who always seemed to make her Dad proud. He always made her feel that she was a disappointment to him. Once her mother died, she had no one left to buffer the relationship with her father.

Soon after Joan's death, Herb had an attorney draft a Will leaving all property to his eldest and youngest daughter. None of the children knew what he had done.

Herbert decided to take a trip to Europe to try to escape the pain of his mourning. When he was in France, he suffered a heart attack and died. He died within six months of Joan's death. If he had returned from Europe, he may have reconciled with his daughter, but as it happened, there was no time for them to develop a better relationship.

With both their parents gone, the eldest and youngest daughter decided to sell the home. The youngest sister offered some of the proceeds to the middle daughter. She refused the offer with unkind words. In her mind, being offered less than her one-third share meant that her sisters approved of their father's action. It was as if she were being disinherited all over again.

It was unfortunate that Joan's best plans were thwarted. They didn't have to be. She and Herbert could have kept a Life Estate in the property with the remainder going to all three girls. That would have ensured that each daughter received an equal inheritance. More importantly, the family would not have been torn by the hurt and anger that was more a product of a husband's grief rather than the absence of a father's love.

Still another way to solve the problem is to set up a Family Trust so that the beneficiaries of the Trust cannot be changed unless both parents agree to the change. Family assets are placed in the Trust with the parents as co-Trustees. When one parent dies, the Trust becomes irrevocable. The Trust income goes to the surviving parent. Once the parent dies, whatever remains in the Trust is distributed in the manner as was agreed by both parents.

The caregiver of someone who is incapacitated, or developmentally disabled needs to, as part of his Estate Plan, provide for the care of the incapacitated person as well as himself. Should the caregiver become disabled or die, someone will need to take over and make medical decisions for the incapacitated person and see to it that he is properly housed and fed.

An aging parent of a developmentally disabled adult child may worry about how the child will manage without the parent to oversee his care. An aged Spouse/RDP, caring for his incapacitated partner, may be concerned about who will take over should his Spouse/RDP die first. Often a family member will agree to take responsibility for the care of an incapacitated person; but perhaps no one wants the job. If there are large sums of money involved it may be the opposite case, too many people may want to be in control. One family member may want the incapacitated child or spouse to remain at home with the assistance of a home health care worker. Another may think the best place is an assisted living facility with 24 hour care. The caregiver may be concerned that a tug-of-war will erupt once he dies.

In such case, the caregiver should consult with an attorney to ensure future care for the incapacitated person. The attorney may suggest that a conservatorship be set up with the caregiver and his choice of successor caregiver serving as Joint-Conservators (Prob. 1811). The Joint Conservator can take full responsibility for the job should the caregiver become disabled or die. Once the conservatorship is in place, the Court will continue to supervise the care of the disabled adult until he is restored to capacity or dies.

MANAGEMENT OF COMMUNITY PROPERTY

Regardless of who is appointed as Conservator, the Spouse/RDP of the incapacitated person is solely responsible for the care and management of Community Property owned by the couple. If the caregiver Spouse/RDP wishes to buy or sell property and the signature of the incapacitated Spouse/RDP is needed, the Conservator will need to sign the document. In general, the Conservator will seek Court approval before signing the document (Prob. 3051, 3071).

APPOINTING THE CONSERVATOR

One of the problems associated with setting up a conservatorship is the cost of the procedure. It may cost hundreds, if not thousands, of dollars to set up and maintain the conservatorship. If the incapacitated person is without funds, the caregiver can ask Legal Aid or Legal Services for assistance. See page xii for information about finding the nearest Legal Aid or Legal Services office.

Those who have adequate funds may hesitate to go through the effort and expense to set up a conservatorship if it may not be needed for years to come. An alternative is for the caregiver to make provision in his Will for the appointment of a Conservator. Under California law the parent of a disabled child or the Spouse/RDP of an incapacitated person may use his Will to appoint a Conservator of the person or property of the incapacitated person (Prob. 1811). Once the caregiver is deceased and the Will admitted to Probate, whoever is named in the Will will have priority in the appointment of a Conservator of the person and/or property of the incapacitated person.

A TRUST FOR THE DISABLED

Government assistance is available to provide medical and custodial care for those who are disabled and without the means to care for themselves. Both state and federal government provide such assistance with programs such as Social Security disability benefits and Medicaid. The family often supplements the government program by providing for the incapacitated person's *special needs* or *supplemental needs* such as hobbies, special education, outings to a movie or a sports event — things that give the incapacitated person some quality of life. This is not a problem while family members are alive and able to provide for the incapacitated person. The worry is how to continue that care should the provider die.

To be eligible for government assistance programs the incapacitated person must essentially be without funds. Family members fear that leaving money to the incapacitated person in a Will or Trust will disqualify him from receiving government assistance. Parents of a disabled child may decide to solve the problem by leaving the money to a sibling or other family member with verbal instructions to take care of the child once the parent is deceased.

Of course, the problem with that approach is that once the funds are left to the family member, they become his property. Property of the family member is available to his creditors. The funds could be lost in a divorce, or the family member could die and the funds inherited by someone who is not willing to care for the disabled child.

A better solution is to have an experienced Elder Law attorney set up a **Supplemental Needs Trust.** The Trust can be funded by the parent during his lifetime, or after his death by making the Trust the beneficiary of his Will or Trust. It can also be funded by a life insurance policy on the life of the parent. The parent can purchase the policy and name the Supplemental Needs Trust as the beneficiary of the insurance funds.

The Trustee of the Supplemental Needs Trust can use the monies in the Trust to provide for the child's supplemental or special needs during his lifetime. The Trust Agreement can provide that upon the death of the incapacitated person, whatever remains in the Trust be distributed to whomever the parent names as the remainder beneficiary of the Trust.

 NOT RECOMMENDED FOR DISABLED SPOUSE

The Trust we just described is appropriate for a disabled child, who has no funds of his own. The Trust is funded with monies owned by a parent and not the child. This Trust may not be the way to go if the disabled person is married and the Trust is funded by monies owned by the well spouse or his disabled spouse. When determining Medicaid eligibility, the federal government considers monies owned by both the husband and wife. If a Trust is set up using money owned by either of them, the government will consider the Trust funds to be available to pay for the care of the disabled spouse (42 U.S.C.1382c(a)(3), 1396p(d)(4)(A)).

In Chapters 9 and 10 we discuss different ways a married couple can arrange their finances to provide for their health care without jeopardizing their right to qualify for medical assistance.

CARING FOR YOUR PET

A woman died at peace,
leaving her fortune
and care of her cat to her niece.
Alas, the fortune and the cat
Soon disappeared after that.

You could leave money to someone with the understanding that the person will take care of your pet, but the moral of the above limerick is that just leaving money will not guarantee care for your pet. The better route is to have your attorney prepare a Will that includes specific instructions and funds to provide for the care of your pet during its lifetime. Those with a Trust can include a similar provision as part of the Trust. The provision for your pet should include directions saying how the remaining funds are to be distributed after the death of the pet.

A TRUST TO CARE FOR YOUR PET

If you are financially able and have several pets, you may want to set up a special Trust for the care of your pets upon your death or incapacity (Prob. 15212). The person you name as Trustee will be charged with the duty to use Trust funds to pay for the care of those animals who survive you. You also need to name a residuary beneficiary (a person or perhaps a charitable organization) to receive whatever remains in the Trust once all of the animals are deceased. Animal support groups, such as the Humane Society, have people who will care for the pet of a deceased owner. You might consider appointing such group as the remainder beneficiary of the Trust in exchange for the lifetime care of your pet(s).

Still another alternative is to ask a fellow pet lover to care for the animal. If no one among your circle of family and friends is able to do so, then ask your pet's veterinarian to consider starting an "Orphaned Pet Service" to assist in finding new homes for pets who lose their owners. It is good public relations and a potential source of income. If this is agreeable to the Veterinarian, you can make arrangements in your Will to pay the Vet to care for the pet until a suitable family can be found. This is a more humane approach than the, all too common practice of putting a pet "to sleep" rather than have the pet suffer the loss of its master. And in at least one case, that reasoning backfired.

Eleanor always had a pet in the house. After her husband died, her two poodles were her constant companions. When Eleanor became ill with cancer, she worried about what would happen to her "buddies" without her to care for them. She finally decided it best to have her family put them to sleep when she died.

Eleanor endured surgery, chemotherapy, radiation therapy, and even some holistic remedies, but she continued to go downhill. Eleanor's family came in to visit her at the hospital to say their last good-byes. She was so ill, she didn't even recognize them. No one thought she could last the day. Because the family was from out of state, and time short, they decided to put the pets to sleep so that when she died, they need only take care of the funeral arrangements.

To everyone's surprise, Eleanor rallied. She lived two more long, lonely years.

She often said she wished they had put her to sleep instead of her buddies.

THE CHARITABLE TRUST

We explained how a Trust can be set up to care for a pet and whatever is left over (the remainder) given to a charitable organization. There are other kinds of charitable trusts that can be set up to benefit the giver as well as the receiver. For example, suppose you own stock which has appreciated substantially over the years, but pays few dividends. This hasn't been a problem in the past because you earned a good income. But now you wish to retire, and will need additional income. You would like to cash in the stock and invest the funds in something that can supplement your retirement income, but your accountant says that a significant portion of the value of the stock will go to Uncle Sam as payment for the Capital Gains Tax.

By now you know that a clever Estate Planning attorney will have any number of ways to solve the problem. The dialogue with your attorney might go something like this:

ATTORNEY: "Do you have a favorite charity?"

"Yes, why do you ask?"

ATTORNEY: "You can set up a Charitable Remainder Trust and donate the stock to that charity by depositing the stock in the Trust. Charities don't pay taxes, so the stock can be sold and the proceeds invested in property that produces a good income. In return for the donation, you can receive an income for the next 20 years or you can receive a monthly Annuity based on your life expectancy."

"What's in it for the charity?"

ATTORNEY: "The charity gets whatever is left after paying you the Annuity."

"Yes, but suppose I die next year, and my wife is left without the securities and no income."

ATTORNEY: "No problem. If you decide on a 20 year Annuity, you can name your wife or any other beneficiary to receive the balance of the Annuity. If you wish, you can have an Annuity based on your life expectancy and that of your spouse. If you predecease your spouse, then the income continues until she dies."

"It seems to me that if the Annuity is based on my life expectancy AND my wife's life expectancy, there won't be much left for the charity."

ATTORNEY: "How much is left for the charity depends on the value of the gift and the cost of the Annuity. The cost of the Annuity depends on the combined life expectancy of you and your wife. I think the best way to understand this plan is for you to look at actual numbers. There are any number of ways to set up a Charitable Remainder Trust. I can explain each option to you. For each option, I will give you the cost of setting up the program, the amount of money you will get, and how much money will actually go to your favorite charity. Of course it must be an IRS approved charity. Once you see the numbers you can make an informed decision as to whether you want to sell the stock and pay the Capital Gains Tax, or set up a Charitable Trust and receive an income."

"Good idea."

Historically, Estate Planning for the wealthy was all about the Estate Tax. Estate Planning attorneys would spend their time dreaming up different ways to reduce Estate Taxes for their wealthy clients. The IRS would spend their time examining and challenging any Estate plan that appeared too innovative. It seems likely that by 2010 the federal Estate Tax will be a memory. Is the game over?

Hardly. As explained in Chapter 3, instead of paying an Estate Tax, the child who inherits property that has appreciated more than 1.3 million dollars will pay a Capital Gains Tax on the excess when he sells the property. In a way, that makes sense. A major criticism of the Estate Tax was that it had to be paid within nine months of the date of death. That created a hardship for those inheriting property with a high market value but with no cash to pay taxes on that value.

Critics of the Estate Tax often cited the example of the cash poor farm located on valuable land. Once the owner of the farm died, the family would be forced to sell the farm just to pay Estate Taxes. By substituting the Capital Gains Tax for the Estate Tax, that problem is eliminated. No tax is due until the beneficiary sells the property. Theoretically, the family farm can now be inherited generation to generation without a tax consequence.

But there are few family farms in today's economy. Future heirs are more likely to inherit highly appreciated real property or securities that they will want to sell. And when they do, they may need to pay a significant Capital Gains Tax.

The new game for Estate Planning attorneys will be to devise an Estate Plan that will reduce the Capital Gains Tax. The IRS will, no doubt, enjoy challenging those plans.

One tried (and legal) method of reducing the Capital Gains Tax is the Charitable Remainder Trust as was just discussed. It doesn't take a crystal ball to see that this could well be the basis of future Estate Plans, so we will take a few more pages to describe the pros and cons of the Trust.

THE CHARITABLE REMAINDER ANNUITY TRUST

A **Charitable Remainder Annuity Trust** is a Trust that is established according to the Internal Revenue Code (26 U.S.C. 664). Charities do not pay taxes, so property donated to the Trust can be sold by the Trustee free of the Capital Gains Tax. Money from the sale is invested so that it provides an income (an *Annuity*) to the beneficiary (the *Annuitant*) for a fixed period of time, say 20 years, or for the Annuitant's lifetime as computed by actuarial tables (i.e., life expectancy tables). The charity receives whatever is left (the *remainder*) after payment of the Annuity. How much income the donor will receive and how much the charity will receive, is agreed upon at the time the Trust is set up.

The Trust can be set up in any number of ways depending on the goal of the *donor* (the person making the gift). In the example just given, the goal of the donor was to convert non-income producing property to income producing property without paying a high Capital Gains Tax. A wealthy donor may be more concerned about his child paying a high Capital Gains Tax should the child inherit highly appreciated property.

For example, suppose you bought acreage in northern California that appreciated significantly over the years and is now worth over a million dollars. You have been putting off selling the property because of the Capital Gains Tax. But it has been a burden to you. It produces no income and you need to pay property taxes each year. You did not mind the sacrifice because you figured that your son would inherit the property at a step-up in basis. But now with the new tax law, by the time you die, the property may be worth three million dollars. He is only allowed a 1.3 million dollar step up in basis, so your son may need to pay a significant Capital Gains Tax when he sells the property.

Setting up a Charitable Remainder Annuity Trust solves the problem of the Capital Gains Tax. The land is transferred to the Charitable Trust. Charities pay no tax, so the Trustee can sell the land and the full market value of the property will be available for investment.

The Trust could be set up with you receiving an income for life, and your son receiving the Annuity after your death. The only problem with this arrangement is that your son is significantly younger than you are. There may not be much left to benefit the charity if they must wait for both of you to die. The solution is to have the Annuity based on your life only and then use part of the income that you receive to purchase a three million dollar insurance policy on your life with your son as beneficiary. The three million dollars is the estimated value of the land that your son would have inherited at your death. But with this arrangement he will inherit the insurance proceeds free of any Capital Gains Tax.

The astute reader (and probably one with an accounting background) will say "Aha, you may have avoided the Capital Gains Tax, but the Estate Tax Exclusion value does not increase to 3.5 million dollars until the year 2009. The three million dollar life insurance policy counts as part of your Taxable Estate, so if you die before 2009, your son will pay an Estate Tax! "

And of course our clever imaginary attorney has a solution in the form of an Irrevocable Insurance Trust. You can set up an Irrevocable Trust so that the Trust owns the insurance policy and not you. The insurance policy is not included in your taxable Estate, so your son pays no Estate Tax. See the end of Chapter 6 for an explanation of how the Irrevocable Insurance Trust works.

As with any Estate Plan you need to consider the downside, and the Charitable Remainder Annuity Trust is no exception.

⌧   ATTORNEY FEES

It may cost significant attorney fees to set up the Trust. Some charities may offer to have their attorney prepare the Trust at no cost to you, or perhaps they offer a "standard" Trust document that their attorney prepared. But using the charity's Trust document represents a conflict of interest. Their Trust was prepared by an attorney for the greatest benefit to his client (that's the charity, not you).

It is important that you employ your own attorney to represent you. He knows the extent of your Estate and he understands what you wish to accomplish.

⊠ THE COMPLEXITY OF THE PLAN

A Charitable Remainder Annuity Trust is a sophisticated Estate Planning tool designed to benefit the well-to-do donor and an IRS approved charity. There are any number of ways to set up the plan. It is important to have an attorney who will take the time to explore different plans until you decide upon the best plan for you.

⊠ THE TRUST IS IRREVOCABLE

Once established, the Trust is not revocable, so it is important to understand all of the aspects of the Trust. In particular, you need to know how much it will cost in attorney's fees to set up the Trust, how much income you will receive, and over what period of time. The income you receive as an Annuitant is taxable to you. You need to consider that while taxes may change over the years, the terms of the Trust cannot be changed. Have your attorney, accountant or financial planner give you an educated guess as to what you might expect in terms of future income tax liability.

Although future income tax payments may be uncertain, the power of the Charitable Remainder Trust is the tax benefit to the donor at the time the Trust is set up.

☑ NO CAPITAL GAINS TAX

Had you sold the property and invested the money yourself, you would have paid a Capital Gains Tax. That tax could have been substantial, depending on the tax rate in effect at the time of the transfer. By gifting the property, the full value of the land can be used to produce investment income.

☑ NO PROPERTY TAX

Once your property is transferred into the Trust, you will no longer need to pay annual property taxes.

☑   NO GIFT TAX

The property you transfer into the Trust is a gift to a charity and as such is not included in the sum total of taxable gifts that you give during your lifetime.

☑   INCOME TAX DEDUCTION

Because you are making a charitable donation, you should be able to take a charitable deduction on your income tax return in the year of the donation.

There are other "perks" in addition to the tax benefits:

☑   NO PROBATE EXPENSE

It might take an expensive and time consuming Probate procedure to transfer the property to a beneficiary upon your death. By transferring the property to the Trust during your lifetime, you avoid the need for a Probate procedure to transfer the property after your death.

☑   GIVE WHEN NEEDED INSTEAD OF LATER

A Charitable Remainder Annuity Trust can be set up in any number of different ways to accommodate your Estate Plan. For example, if you are not in need of a present income, but expect that you will spend significant sums on your child's education, you can set up a 20 year Annuity with your child as the Annuitant. This will get the child through college and probably be a great help should the child decide to start a family. Why have the child inherit property in later, high earning years rather than in the early, high expense/low income years?

☑ CREDITOR PROTECTION

If you keep the land and are sued, you could lose it to pay your creditors. If a beneficiary inherits the land, it could be lost to his/her creditors. But once the property is transferred to the Trust, the gift is made. Neither your creditors nor your beneficiary's creditors can gain access to the Trust funds. The most a creditor can do is seek payment from the money that is received as an income.

☑ GOOD DEED

If you are concerned that your son will be tagged with a Capital Gains Tax once you die, it means that your property has appreciated more than 1.3 million dollars, and you are fortunate indeed. By setting up a Charitable Trust, you are making a donation to the charity of your choice. You are sharing your good fortune with others. You can consider this as "giving back" to the community, or just plain doing a good deed.

BECOME A PHILANTHROPIST

Instead of giving the property to an established charity, you can become a philanthropist and set up your own Charitable foundation. The foundation can be in the form of an IRS approved Charitable Trust. You can be the Trustee of the Charitable Trust and your child the Successor Trustee. The Trust can be set up according to your specific charitable purposes. You can use the Trust to benefit a single cause or several worthy projects. This can be an exciting adventure for those with ample resources and a community spirit.

An Estate Plan For Your Person

The law makes a distinction between your property (what you own) and your person (your body). We have been discussing how to set up an Estate Plan for your property with the goal of maximum control over your Estate during your lifetime, and minimum cost and hassle to your heirs once you die. An Estate Plan for your person is just as important as an Estate Plan for your property. The goals are much the same. Maximum control over your body during your lifetime. Minimum cost and hassle to your family for your final disposition.

You may think it strange to speak of planning for maximum control of your body during your lifetime. After all, it's your body. Who else but you has any right to control what you do with your body? That may be true so long as you have capacity, but should you become seriously ill, you may be unable to express your wishes about the care you wish to receive. If you do not have an Estate Plan in place for your person, then your next of kin, or maybe the state of California may make health decisions for you.

The same applies to the final disposition of your body. If you don't make burial and funeral arrangements, then someone will need to make these decisions for you.

As this chapter will show, it is relatively simple and inexpensive to set up an Estate Plan for your Person.

People with a large family often arrange for a family burial site. Over the years deceased family members come to occupy a space in that site, but others may have been buried elsewhere. Surviving family members often lose track of the number of spaces left. If this is the case with your family, you need to take inventory of the number of spaces available and who in the family expects to use those spaces.

It is important to keep in touch with the cemetery and let them know if there is a change in the expected occupant of the burial site.

OUT OF STATE BURIAL SITE

It may be that the family burial site is not in the state of California. In such case, it is important to consider the cost of transporting the body from California to the out-of-state cemetery. That cost can be substantial, in some cases doubling the cost of the burial. If there is no emotional attachment to the out-of-state burial site, you may want to consider assigning the burial site to a family member who lives closer to the site and making your own burial arrangements here in California.

It is important to make your own burial arrangements. Even if you don't particularly care where you are buried, it may be very important to your family. That is often the case in second marriages. If you have children from a first marriage, they may want their parents to be "reunited in death." Your current spouse may not take kindly to having you buried with your former spouse. This might result in hard feelings, if not an out-and-out battle.

The same problem can arise with those in a gay relationship. The decedent's family might not have acknowledged the relationship. The family might decide to have the decedent buried in the family plot and exclude the gay partner from participating in the burial arrangements.

You can head off disputes about your final resting place, by making your own burial arrangements. If you do not do so, the person with authority to decide the matter for you is determined by California statute (Health & Safety 7100). Under California law, the person with priority to decide your final disposition is as follows:

1st   the person you appointed to serve as your Health Care Agent under a Power of Attorney

2nd   your Spouse/RDP

3rd   your parent(s)

4th   a majority of your adult children

5th   a majority of your adult siblings

6th   your next of kin as determined by the Laws of Intestate Succession.

ARRANGING FOR CREMATION

Increasingly people are opting for cremation. The reasons for choosing cremation are varied, but for many, it is a matter of finances. The cost of cremation is approximately one-sixth that of an ordinary funeral and burial. A major saving is the cost of the casket. A casket is not necessary for the cremation. An alternate container of fiberboard or similar materials, can be used to transport the body. Embalming is not necessary either, unless there is to be a funeral with a viewing.

Federal law prohibits a funeral director from telling you that a casket or embalming is necessary for a direct (immediate) cremation (16 Code of Federal Regulations ("CFR") 453.3 (b)(1)(ii)).

For those who are considering cremation, there are a few things to consider.

THE PACEMAKER

Cremating a body with a pacemaker or any radiation producing device can cause damage to the cremation chamber and/or to the person performing the cremation. If you have such an electronic aid, it will need to be removed prior to the cremation. You might check with the cremation service to determine the cost of having the pacemaker removed.

A pacemaker can be donated for use in animals with a medical need for the device. If you are interested in making such donation, you can ask your local veterinarian to refer you to an animal clinic that performs the procedure, and then arrange to have it removed prior to your burial or cremation.

THE OVERWEIGHT

Cremation technology has kept up with the expanding waist line of our population. Most Cremation Services can accommodate a body weighing up to 400 pounds. But if you are extremely obese, you need to ask the cremation service whether their facility is large enough. If you cannot locate a crematory that can accommodate your weight, you will need to make burial arrangements.

WHAT TO DO WITH THE ASHES

In addition to planning for the procedure, you need to give your family some guidance as to where to place the ashes. Some cemeteries allow an urn containing the cremated remains of a family member to be placed in an occupied family plot. Similarly, some cemeteries will allow the cremated remains to be placed in the space in a mausoleum that is currently occupied by a member of the decedent's family. If you intend to be cremated and all your family spaces are occupied you may want to call the cemetery and ask them to explain their policy as it relates to the burial of urns in occupied sites.

If burial in the family site is not an option, you will need to arrange for a separate burial space. Many cemeteries have a separate building called a *columbarium*, which is especially designed to store urns. You can purchase a storage place for the urn in the same manner as the purchase of a burial space in a cemetery.

If you wish to have your *cremains* (cremated remains) scattered, you need to let your next of kin know where and how this is to be done. If you want your ashes spread out to sea, your family will need to arrange to have a boat go out at least three nautical miles, because federal law prohibits ashes from being scattered any closer than that distance from land (40 CFR 229.1).

Cremains can be scattered in a lake or stream provided such scattering is at least 500 yards from shoreline (Health & Safety 7117).

THE MILITARY BURIAL

If you are an honorably discharged veteran or the spouse of such veteran, you have the right to be buried in a Veterans National Cemetery. If your Veteran spouse was buried in a Veterans National Cemetery, you have the right to be buried in that same grave site unless soil conditions require a separate burial site.

You can get information about burial at a Veterans National Cemetery by calling the Veteran's Administration at (800) 827-1000, or visiting their Web site.

 VA CEMETERY WEB SITE
http://www.cem.va.gov

The site has information on the following topics:
  ➢ National and Military Cemeteries
  ➢ Burial, Headstones and Markers
  ➢ State Cemetery Grants Program

You cannot reserve a grave site in advance, so your family will need to make arrangements and establish your eligibility to be buried in a Veterans National Cemetery. At that time, they will need to provide the following information:
  ➢ your rank, serial, social security and VA claim numbers
  ➢ the branch of service in which you served, the date and place of your entry into and separation from the service
  ➢ a copy of your official military discharge document bearing an official seal or a DD 214 form.

If you wish to be buried in a national cemetery, you need to make all of these items readily accessible to your family.

In addition to making arrangements for a burial space or for a cremation, consider purchasing a *Preneed Funeral Arrangement*. It will be easier on your family emotionally and financially if you make your own funeral plan.

Federal law requires that you receive a general price list at the beginning of any discussion for the purchase of funeral services (16 CFR 453.2). Once you decide upon a plan, the seller should give you a contract that states the prices charged for *services* (embalming, viewing, transportation, etc.) and *merchandise purchased* (casket, urn, acknowledgment cards, register books, clothing, etc.) and *cash advance items*, i.e., things paid for by the funeral director and then reimbursed back to him. This includes paying for death certificates, arranging to have the obituary printed, payment for religious services, etc. (16 CFR 453.5).

Even though the seller gives you a "standard" contract, it does not mean that it cannot be changed. If you are not satisfied with the way a certain section of the contract reads, attach an addendum to the contract that explains, in plain English, your understanding of that passage. If you are concerned about something that is not mentioned in the contract, insist the contract be amended to include that item.

In particular, check to see whether the contract answers the following questions:

Does the contract cover all costs?
The contract should contain an itemized list stating exactly what goods and services are included in the sales price.

Your contract may include an allowance towards cash advance items such as the printing of the obituary or payment to the clergy, or your contract may provide that payment be made at the time of the funeral. Your contract should state that the amount charged by the funeral director for a cash advance item be no more than the amount paid by the director for that item.

Is the price guaranteed?

Some Preneed Funeral Arrangements have a fixed price for the goods and services you choose, meaning that the funeral director will provide the goods and services at the same price as agreed at the time of the contract. It is important that your contract state that the person or company who is selling you the Funeral Arrangement is the same person or company who will actually provide those goods and services. If not, you need to have the provider of the goods and services sign the contract saying that he agrees to be bound by the terms of your agreement. If the seller says that it is not necessary for the provider to sign your contract because he and the provider have a separate written agreement, have that agreement attached to your contract.

You might opt for a Preneed Funeral Arrangement that is not a fixed price. The company can charge additional monies for the plan that you have chosen upon your death. In these days of inflation and increasing life expectancy, it is important that your contract clearly state how the price will be determined when the contract is finally put into effect.

How are the contract funds protected?

California laws are designed to protect the purchaser of a Preneed Funeral Arrangement. If you pay cash for your Preneed Arrangement, the funds must, within 30 days, be placed in a Trust account in a bank or trust company authorized by the state of California to serve as Trustee (Bus. & Prof. 7736, 7737). Have the contract state that you will be furnished with proof of deposit within 30 days; and that they will notify you, in writing, should they change the bank or trust company.

The money in the account will belong to you during your lifetime, and will be paid to the funeral firm upon your death. But there are downsides to such plan.

TRUSTEE FEES

Monies earned on the Trust account can be used to pay a reasonable fee to the Trustee to administer the Trust. Under California law, the amount charged by the Trustee cannot exceed the amount of interest earned on the account (Bus. & Prof. 7735). Have your contract state how the Trustee's fee is to be computed.

INCOME IS TAXABLE

The money in the Trust account belongs to you until such time as it is used to pay for your funeral. Monies earned on the Trust account are taxable to you as income. Under California law, the Trustee may use the income from the account to pay those income taxes.

Your contract should state whether the Trustee will pay the tax on monies earned on the account, otherwise you may find yourself including the Trust income on your income tax return even though the taxes on the interest may have already been paid.

Is the funeral firm reputable?

All these protections don't do much good if you are not dealing with a reputable company. It is important to take the time to check up on whoever is selling you the contract. In California, anyone who offers Preneed Funeral contracts to the public must be licensed to do so. You can check to see if the seller is licensed by calling the California DEPARTMENT OF CONSUMER AFFAIRS. You may want to ask how long the firm has been in business and whether any complaints have been filed against them.

Can you cancel the contract?

California law gives you the right to cancel your Preneed Funeral contract and receive a refund of the monies in the Trust account, however, the funeral director has the right to charge up to 10% of the amount placed into the Trust account as a cancelation fee (Bus. & Prof. 7735).

FUNERAL PLANS FOR THOSE ON PUBLIC ASSISTANCE

People who are applying for, or receiving, Medicaid, Supplemental Security Income ("SSI") or other public assistance program have limits on the amount of assets that they own. If someone purchases a Preneed Funeral Arrangement, then the monies paid into the plan count as an asset because the purchaser of the plan can revoke the contract and get his money back. Understanding the problem, the California legislature included a provision in the law allowing for the conversion of a Preneed Funeral Arrangement to an irrevocable contract for those who need to apply for public assistance (Bus. & Prof. 7737).

If you are in the process of applying for a public assistance program, then before finalizing your funeral plan, it is prudent to check with your local DEPARTMENT OF HEALTH SERVICES to be sure that your plan will not affect your ability to qualify for the program.

Even if you are in good health at this time, it is prudent to have your contract provide that you can change your plan to one that is irrevocable if at any time you need to apply for a public assistance program. Check to see that your contract allows you to make such a change without any cost to you.

Suppose you die in another state or country?

Your contract should spell out what provision will be made in the event that you move to another state or die in another state or country. Many funeral firms are part of a national funeral service corporation with funeral firms located throughout the United States. You may be able to have the contract provide that there will be no additional charge if the contract is performed by one of the funeral firms owned by the parent company.

Can the plan be changed after your death?

It may happen that your heirs need to cancel the plan after your death because:

➢ your body is missing or cannot be recovered, or

➢ you were buried by another facility because no one knew that you had a Preneed contract, or

➢ you died in another country and were buried there.

Your contract should address these potential problems, and spell out how much money will be refunded and who is to receive the refund. You may also want to specify whether your heirs have the right to alter your funeral plans.

You may wonder why anyone would think of changing the decedent's funeral plan, but consider that in today's market, it is not uncommon for a Preneed Funeral Arrangement to cost several thousand dollars.

A top end funeral complete with solid bronze casket can cost upwards of $40,000. Some heirs might be motivated to save money by changing the plan to one of a lesser value.

That was the case with Lester. His mother, Mona, was a difficult woman with a personality that can only be described as "sour." Her husband deserted her after four years of marriage leaving her to raise Lester by herself. Once Lester was grown, Mona made it clear to him that she had done her job and now he was on his own. Lester could have used some help. He married and had three children. One of his children suffered with asthma and it was a constant struggle to keep up with the medical bills.

Mona believed in being good to herself. She did not intend to, nor did she, leave much money when she died. She knew that Lester would not be able to afford a "proper" burial for her, so she purchased a funeral plan and paid close to $23,000 for it. She was pleased when the funeral director told her that the monies would be kept safely in a Trust account until the time they were needed.

Lester was not familiar with California law, so when his mother died he asked an attorney at Legal Aid whether the Preneed Funeral Arrangement contract could be revoked or changed to some other arrangement — maybe cremation.

The attorney explained "I can appreciate how you feel, however under California law, once your mother died, her contract became irrevocable (Health & Safety 7100.1)."

The reader might be thinking "Revocable. Irrevocable. All this contract stuff is giving me a headache. Why can't I just set aside some money and let my kids figure it out?"

The problem with that approach is that the cost of your final illness may leave you with little or no funds for your burial. That could be a major problem for your family. The state of California will hold your family members personally responsible for the disposition of your body. As explained earlier, those family members include your surviving Spouse/RDP, adult children, parents, siblings and next of kin — in that order (Health & Safety 7100).

The state of California holds each family member responsible to dispose of your body. If no family member will take responsibility, the Coroner will arrange for the final disposition. If he does so, the state has the right to sue the family for three times the cost of the disposition AND charge them with a misdemeanor (Health & Safety 7103). If no family member can be found who lives within the state, the official in possession of the body will contact the State department and offer to have your body delivered to a school of medicine for the purpose of education or scientific research (Health & Safety 7203).

To avoid these problems, consider purchasing a life insurance policy to fund your funeral and burial, naming a trusted family members as the beneficiary of the policy. It is important that the person who is to receive the insurance funds understands why he is named as beneficiary of the policy. It isn't so much that a family member is not trustworthy as it is that they may not understand what you intended — especially in those cases where other funds are available to pay for the funeral.

Too often insurance funds are left to a child who refuses to contribute to the cost of the funeral saying "Dad wanted me to have this money. That's why he left it to me."

To avoid a misunderstanding, put it in writing. It need not be a formal contract. It could be something as simple as a letter to the insurance beneficiary, with copies to your next of kin as in the following example.

Dear Paul,

I purchased a $20,000 insurance policy today naming you as beneficiary of the policy. As we discussed this money is to be used to pay for the following:
- *my funeral, grave site and headstone*
- *perpetual care for my grave*
- *airfare for each of my grandchildren to attend the funeral*
- *dinner for the family after the wake*
- *lunch for the family after the funeral*

If there is any money left over, please accept it as my thanks for all the effort spent on my behalf.

Love,
Dad

P.S. I am sending a copy of this letter to your sister so that she will know that all arrangements have been made.

Whether or not you arrange to pay for your burial or funeral, let your next of kin know your feelings about your final disposition. If you wish to have a religious service, let your family know the type of service and where it is to be held. Tell your family where you wish to be buried, or if you intend to be cremated, where to place the ashes.

ANATOMICAL GIFTS

If you wish to make an anatomical gift, you can include it as part of your Will; but it may be some time before your Will is located. The better route is to make the donation by a separate writing. You can complete an *Organ Donor Card* when you renew your license or obtain a photo identification card ("ID") from the DEPARTMENT OF MOTOR VEHICLES. The Department will display a Donor dot on the front of you driver's license or photo ID (Veh. 12811). If you wish to make a donation but do not want to indicated that fact on your driver's license or photo ID, you can have your attorney prepare an Organ Donor Card to meet your special needs, or you can download a form to complete from the Internet.

 ORGAN DONOR PROGRAM
http://www.ordonorprogram.org

You can keep your Organ Donor Card at home with your important papers.

FACE TRANSPLANT
The Organ Donor Card allows you to give specific instructions about parts of the body that you do (or do not) wish to donate. In 2005, the first partial face transplant was performed in France. It was accompanied by a flurry of controversy regarding the use of the face of a donor without her prior written permission. It is important that you indicate on your Organ Donor Card whether you do, or do not, wish to make a donation of all, or part, of your face.

Regardless of whether you have an Organ Donor Card filed with the Department of Motor Vehicles, or whether you keep it at home, let your next of kin know that you wish to make a donation, if medically acceptable.

GIFT FOR EDUCATION AND RESEARCH

There is no age limit on organ and tissue donations, however doctors will probably not consider your body suitable for transplantation if you are of advanced age and in poor health. You can still donate your body to a school of medicine or dentistry for education and research. You can offer to release the body for study or research to a school of medicine at a university, such as:

University of California at San Diego School of Medicine La Jolla, CA 92093	(858) 534-4536
University of California, San Francisco State Curator for No. California San Francisco, CA 94143	(415) 476-1981
Western University of Health Sciences College of Osteopathic Medicine Pomona, CA 91766	(909) 469-5431

Schools will not accept a donation if the person was obese or died from a contagious disease, or a crushing injury, so you need to make alternate provision for such events. Schools generally pay for local transportation of the body to the school. But there could be substantial transportation costs should you die far from the school, so you need to give your family instructions about what to do should that happen.

If you do not wish to make an anatomical gift, let your family know how you feel. If you make no provision for a gift, and do not tell anyone how you feel about donating any or all of your body, the decision will be up to your family.

California statute (Health & Safety 7151) establishes an order of priority to authorize the donation:

1st   an Attorney-In-Fact, who you authorized under a Power of Attorney, to make such gift.

2nd   your Spouse/RDP

3rd   your adult son or daughter

4th   either of your parents

5th   an adult brother or sister

6th   a Court appointed Conservator or Guardian

If permission is obtained from a family member and there are others in the same or a higher priority, every effort must be made to contact those people and make them aware of the proposed gift. The anatomical gift cannot be made if someone with the same or higher priority objects to the gift. Similarly, the law prohibits the gift if you ever expressed an opposition to a donation.

AUTOPSIES

An autopsy is one of those things that most of us do not think about; reasoning that if it is needed, it will be carried out and, being dead, you will have no choice in the matter. But there are many times when an autopsy is optional. Sometimes a doctor is not sure of the cause of death, and asks the family to allow an autopsy. It may be in the family's best interest to consent to the procedure. The examination might reveal a genetic disorder, that could be treated if it later appears in another family member. An examination might reveal that death from a car "accident" could have been caused by a stroke or heart attack at the wheel. Perhaps the patient who died suddenly in a hospital was misdiagnosed. The nursing home resident could have died from negligence and not old age.

You may authorize an autopsy in your Will, but you may be long since buried before your Will is found. The better route is to give authorization in a separate document such as a **POWER OF ATTORNEY FOR HEALTH CARE**. If you do not authorize the procedure, you next of kin or anyone else who has the right to dispose of your body can agree to the procedure (Health & Safety 7113, Prob. 4683).

Your family may hesitate to allow the examination because of its cost. An autopsy can cost anywhere from several hundred to several thousand dollars. Most health insurance plans do not cover the cost of an autopsy, so whoever authorizes the procedure must arrange for payment. Still another reason people hesitate to order an autopsy is because they do not know whether you would have wanted a postmortem examination.

If you have strong feelings one way or another, let your family know how you feel about an optional autopsy.

Of course, there are problems with just telling someone how you feel about your burial arrangements, autopsies, and anatomical gifts:

YOU TELL THE WRONG PERSON
You may tell someone who does not have authority to carry out your wishes. That was the case with James. When his wife died, he moved to a retirement community where he lived for several years until his death. James had two sons who lived in different states. Although he loved his sons, he had difficulty talking to either of them about serious matters. It was easier for him to talk with his friends in the retirement community. They often spoke about dying and how they felt about different burial arrangements.

James would reminisce about his youth and growing up in a farming community in the plains state of Kansas. "I was happy and free. Out there you had room to breathe. It would be nice to be buried there — peaceful and spacious."

When he died, his friends told his sons about their father's desire to be buried in Kansas. They met the suggestion with scepticism and pragmatism:

"Dad didn't say anything like that to me."

"It would cost us double, if we had to arrange for burial in another state. I'm sure he didn't have that kind of expense in mind."

THE PERSON DOES NOT CARRY OUT YOUR WISHES
Sometimes the person you tell about the disposition of your body may not understand what you said or perhaps they hear only what they want to hear. Whether they follow your burial instructions or authorize an autopsy or anatomical gift may depend more about what costs are involved, and their own feelings, rather than what you may have wanted.

Even if you tell someone and trust that person to carry out your wishes, it could be that the person you confide in cannot carry out your instructions. For example, if you tell your spouse what arrangements to make, (s)he may become incapacitated or die before you do; or perhaps you both die together in a natural disaster or in a plane crash.

WHO WANTS TO TALK ABOUT IT?

For many people the main problem with telling someone what to do when you die is talking about your death. It may be an uncomfortable, if not unpleasant, subject for you to bring up, and for your family to discuss. If this is the case, consider putting the information in writing and give the instructions to the person who will have the job of carrying out your wishes.

Making provision for the disposition of your body is important, but it is more important to make sure that you are in control of the health care you receive should you become seriously ill. This is not a problem when you are well enough to make your own medical decisions; however it could happen that you are too ill to let people know what you want. The solution to the problem is appoint someone to serve as your HEALTH CARE AGENT with instructions about allowing medical treatment that you do, (or do not) want to receive, as well as instructions about the disposition of your body in the event you do not survive the illness.

You can appoint a Health Care Agent and give him authority to carry out your instructions by signing a DURABLE POWER OF ATTORNEY FOR HEALTH CARE.

You can have your attorney prepare a Durable Health Care Power of Attorney to meet your special needs or you can prepare one yourself using a form provided in California statute (Prob. 4701) called an ADVANCE HEALTH CARE DIRECTIVE. You can copy the form from your local law library, or you can download the form from the California Statute Web site. http://www.leginfo.ca.gov/calaw.html

THE ADVANCE HEALTH CARE DIRECTIVE

The statutory form of the California *Advance Health Care Directive* consists of three parts:

Part 1 contains a *Durable Power of Attorney for Health Care*. You can use this form to appoint a *Health Care Agent* and an Alternate Agent in the event your Health Care Agent is unable, or unwilling, to serve in that capacity.

Part 2 of the Advance Health Care Directive is entitled END-OF-LIFE DECISIONS. You can use this section to give directions to your health care providers (doctors, nurses, etc.) about whether life support systems should (or should not) be used in the event that you are dying and there is no hope for your recovery. Part 1 of the Directive gives your Agent authority to see that the directions you give in Part 2 are followed.

Part 3 of the Advance Health Care Directive contains a form that gives your Health Care Agent authority to carry out your wishes as to the final disposition of your body. You can give your Health Care Agent authority to make an anatomical gift, or if you wish, to refuse such donation. Similarly, you can authorize an autopsy, or you can direct your Agent to refuse the procedure, provided the autopsy is optional (Prob. 4701).

In 1996, the federal government passed the Health Insurance Portabiltiy and Accountability Act ("HIPAA"). The U.S. Department of Health and Human Service issued the Privacy Rule to implement HIPAA. The Privacy Rule restricts access to your medical records (45 CFR 164.524). The rule allows your Health Care Agent to access your medical records, however, it is a good idea to include a paragraph in Part 3 of your Health Care Directive referring to HIPAA and giving your Health Care Agent specific authority to access health information that may be protected under HIPAA.

California law allows you to register the name and telephone number of your Health Care Agent with the Secretary of State for use during an emergency (Prob. C 4800). You can obtain a registration form by calling (916) 652-3984 or by writing to:

Secretary of State, Special Filings Unit
P.O. Box 942877
Sacramento, CA 94277-0001

They will issue an *Adance Health Care Directive Registry Identification Card* that you can keep in your wallet.

Some readers may be thinking "My family will surely respect my wishes as to my final disposition. Why bother with an Advance Health Care Directive? I probably will never need anyone to assist me. And even if I did, my family will tell the doctor what I want."

That was George's thoughts exactly, even though his attorney advised him differently: "George, you are a man of substantial wealth. You made wise decision for the care of your finances in the event of your incapacity, but you should also make provision for someone to make your medical decisions in the event that you are too sick to make them yourself. This is easily done by signing an Advance Health Care Directive and appointing someone to be your Health Care Agent."

George said "My wife Loretta is a lovely lady, but she and my son from my first marriage are always at odds. If I choose one, the other would be hurt."

The attorney suggested "If you don't want to appoint a Health Care Agent, at least let people know what kind of medical treatment you want in the event that you are too ill to speak for yourself. For example, do you want intravenous feeding in the event that you are mortally ill with no hope of recovery?"

"You mean sign a Living Will?"

"Yes, it is referred to as the "End of Life Decision" section of the Advance Health Care Directive. You can complete just that part of the Advance Health Care Directive. If you do so, your doctors will know what type of medical care you wish in such a situation."

George said he would think about it. But he didn't.

The attorney's advice turned out to be prophetic. George suffered a stroke while driving. His injuries from the accident combined with the severity of the stroke made for a bleak prognosis. The doctors said George would die unless they put him on a ventilator and inserted a feeding tube. Even with life support systems, it was not expected that he would ever come out of the coma.

Loretta told the doctors "Let's try everything to keep him alive."

George's son did not see it that way.
"Why torture him with needles and tubes? Let him pass on peacefully."

George never signed a Living Will, so no one knew how he felt about artificial life support systems. He never appointed a Health Care Agent, so the doctors didn't know who George wanted to make his medical decisions.

Fearing that no matter what they did, one family member might be angry enough to file a law suit, the doctors requested that the matter be brought before the court, to let the judge decide the matter.

The judge decided that someone needed to be appointed as George's Conservator to make his medical decisions.

Loretta petitioned the court to be appointed as George's Conservator. So did his son. The court battle over who was to be George's Conservator was bitter (and expensive).

Before Loretta and George married they signed a Premarital Agreement. The Agreement provided for each to give up all rights to inherit property from the other. Loretta had little money of her own. The son accused Loretta of thinking of her own best interest and not that of his father. If George were to die, Loretta would be on her own.

Although George was a wealthy man, he was not overly generous with his son. His son was married and raising his own family. Without any help from his father, he struggled to support his family. Loretta accused the son of being anxious to get his substantial inheritance.

The judge ruled that each of the parties had a conflict of interest and could be prejudiced by his own circumstances. He appointed a professional, independent, Conservator to make medical decisions for George. The Conservator conferred with the doctors and determined that it was futile to continue life support systems.

George died.

A Health Care Estate Plan 9

We discussed an Estate Plan as it relates to the distribution or management of your Estate once you are deceased. In this age of extended life expectancy, a more pressing concern is how to manage and preserve your Estate in the event of a debilitating illness. As life expectancy increases, so does the percentage of the population who suffer incapacitating strokes, Alzheimer's disease or Parkinson's disease. It is estimated that more than half of the population who are 85 or older, have some degree of dementia. Your best Estate Plan could be sabotaged by a lengthy illness. In this chapter we will explore ways to pay for the health care that you may require as you age.

In addition to paying for your health care, you need to consider who will care for your finances and everyday physical needs in the event that you are too ill to do so yourself. A **Health Care Estate Plan** is a plan designed to care for your person and property in the event of an incapacitating illness. In the last chapter, we discussed how you can appoint a Health Care Agent to care for your person in the event of your incapacity. But there is still the problem of who will care for your property. In this chapter we will discuss how you can appoint someone to care for your property and manage your finances in the event of your incapacity.

The optimum way to provide for the care of your property in the event of your incapacity is to set up a Trust and appoint a Successor Trustee to care for your property in accordance with the directions you give in the Trust.

If you do not have sufficient assets to justify the cost of employing an attorney to draft a Trust, then there are other strategies, that you can use to solve the problem.

THE JOINT ACCOUNT

You can set up a joint checking account so that a trusted family member can write checks on the account. Of course there are all the inherent problems of a joint account that we discussed in the beginning of Chapter 2. You can avoid many of those problems by limiting the amount of money that can be accessed by the family member. For example, you can arrange your finances so that all of your bills are paid from a single checking account and your family member can access that account, only.

THE AGENCY ACCOUNT

If you set up a joint account, your family member will own whatever is in the account should your die. If this is not as you wish, you can sign a special Power of Attorney giving your family member (i.e. your "Agent") authority to conduct your business from this *Agency Account*. Your agreement with the bank can state that the authority of your Agent will continue even though you later may become disabled or incapacitated.

Your Agent may not use the account for his own benefit. California law requires him to keep records of all his transactions which he must, upon request, present to you or your legal representative (Prob. 5204). Upon your death your Agent may no longer access your account. But ultimately whoever you choose to be your Agent must be trust worthy because the bank is under no duty to stop him from writing checks on your account until the bank receives written notice of your death (Prob. 4304).

The joint or agency account solves the problem of how to pay your bills in the event you are temporarily ill. It does not solve the problem of how to manage your business affairs in the event of an extended illness. For example, suppose you have a stroke and can no longer be cared for at home. Should it be necessary for you to sell your home and move to an assisted living facility, no one will have the authority to sell the house for you. In such case, your friends or family members may be forced to ask the Court to appoint a Conservator to manage your finances, and if you did not appoint a Health Care Agent, to make your medical decisions as well.

Before doing so, the Court will need to be convinced that you are unable to do so yourself. The judge will have you examined to determine whether you are competent to manage your person and/or property. You will be charged for that examination. Determining whether you have capacity to take care of yourself can be an embarrassing, and demeaning experience. If you are sufficiently aware of the proceedings, you may want to employ an attorney to fight the matter (Prob. 1470, Welfare & Instit. 5352).

If the Court determines that you are incapacitated, he will appoint a Conservator of your person or property, or both. If a Conservator of your property is appointed, he will take possession of your property and file an inventory with the Court. The Court may require the Conservator to be bonded, and you will pay for that bond. The Conservator will need to account to the Court for any monies spent. He may need to employ an accountant to assist with the preparation of the inventory and accounting. He will need to employ an attorney to prepare reports to file with the Court (Prob. 2330, 2610, 2620).

The Conservator and his attorney are entitled to reasonable compensation for their services (Prob. 2640).

Court filing fees, examination fees, accounting fees, the cost of a bond, your attorney's fees, the Conservator's attorney fees, the Conservator's fees, all are paid from your Estate (that's your money!)

Conservatorship procedures are expensive to set up and maintain. Curious that so many people worry about how to avoid Probate, when the larger concern should be how to avoid Conservatorship. Consider that it is not all that hard to arrange your finances so that Probate is not necessary. The cost to administer your estate should be $0.

Even with a full Probate procedure, whatever it costs to Probate your Estate is a one-time expense. And Probate is a one-time procedure. Once monies are distributed to your beneficiaries, it is over. Not so if you become incapacitated. It can cost thousands of dollars to set up the Conservatorship; and more money to care for you and your property each year. And this expense continues, year after year, until you are returned to capacity, or die.

As with Probate it is not all that hard to avoid these unnecessary charges to your Estate. To avoid the need for a Conservator of your person, you can appoint a Health Care Agent to make your medical decisions should you be too ill to do so yourself. To avoid the need for a Guardian of your property, you can set up a Trust and appoint a Successor Trustee to care for your property in the event of your incapacity. For those of limited means, the **DURABLE POWER OF ATTORNEY** is the next best Estate plan.

A **Power of Attorney** is a legal document by which someone (the *Principal*) gives another (his *Agent* or *Attorney-In-Fact*) authority to do certain acts on behalf of the Principal. If you wish to have someone to be able to conduct business on your behalf in the event of your incapacity, you can make the Power of Attorney *durable* by including the phrase

> This power of attorney shall not be affected by the subsequent incapacity of the principal.

Those who have a Trust may be thinking that they have no need for a Power of Attorney because in the event of their incapacity, their Successor Trustee can take over and manage their property. But a Trust can only authorize a Successor Trustee to manage property that is in the Trust. Your Successor Trustee has no authority to do things for you personally, such as suing or defending a law suit on your behalf or applying for government benefits such as Medicaid or Social Security. You can give your Successor Trustee authority to do these important, personal, things for you by appointing him as your Attorney-In-Fact under a Durable Power of Attorney.

GENERAL VS. LIMITED POWER OF ATTORNEY

You can sign a Power of Attorney giving your Attorney-In-Fact broad general powers. With these powers your Attorney-In-Fact can do much the same with your property as you can. Instead of a General Power of Attorney, you can limit the things your Attorney-In-Fact can do with your property to just those things that you authorize in your Power of Attorney.

One power that should be specifically granted in your Power of Attorney, is the power to apply for medical assistance benefits in the event of your incapacity. In the next chapter we will be discussing the many things you can do to qualify for Medicaid. You need to give someone authority to take the necessary steps for you to become eligible for government benefits, in the event you are too ill to do so yourself. Even if you do not wish to give someone control over your finances at this time, you should give someone a Limited Power of Attorney with the power to apply for government benefits on your behalf.

Limited or General, the operative word in any Power of Attorney is POWER. Once your Attorney-In-Fact has authority to act, he essentially steps in your shoes and can do whatever you gave him authority to do. Your primary consideration in choosing an Attorney-In-Fact is trustworthiness. You need to choose someone who will follow your instructions and put the Power of Attorney to the use you intended. You need to choose someone, who, when using your Power of Attorney, will always put your interests ahead of his.

You may be less concerned with trustworthiness than the loss of independence. But the thing to keep in mind is that you still have the power to do all of the things you gave your Attorney-In-Fact authority to do. The only difference is that now, you both have the power to conduct your business transactions.

You can have your attorney prepare a Power of Attorney especially designed to meet your special needs or you can prepare your own power of attorney by using the form as set out in California Statute (Prob. 4401). You can copy the UNIFORM STATUTORY FORM POWER OF ATTORNEY at your local law library or you can download it from the California Statute Web site. http://www.leginfo.ca.gov

The statutory form gives you a choice of powers that you can grant to your Attorney-In-Fact.

_____ (A) Real property transactions,

_____ (B) Tangible personal property transactions.

_____ (C) Stock and Bond Transactions.

_____ (D) Commodity and option transactions.

_____ (E) Banking and other financial institution transactions.

_____ (F) Business operating transactions.

_____ (G) Insurance and annuity transactions.

_____ (H) Estate, trust, and other beneficiary transactions.

_____ (I) Claims and litigation.

_____ (J) Personal and family maintenance.

_____ (K) Social Security benefits, medicare, medicaid, or other governmental programs, or civil or military service.

_____ (L) Retirement plan transactions.

_____ (M) Tax matters.

_____ (N) ALL OF THE POWERS LISTED ABOVE.

You can give your Attorney-In-Fact authority to do any of these things by initialing that line; or you can give full authority by initialing (N), the last line.

 YOU MAY BE GIVING MORE POWER
THAN YOU WANTED TO GIVE

Each of the choices given is abridged. You need to read Probate Section 4400 through 4465 before initialling anything. Those sections explain exactly what authority you are giving to your Agent when you place your initial next to that choice. For example, if you initial (E) your Attorney-In-Fact can do any of your banking transactions, including writing checks on your account. If you initial (J) as well, your Attorney-In-Fact can write checks on your account to maintain the customary standard of living for you, your spouse, your children or anyone else who depends on you for support.

Probate statue 4460 explains all of the things you authorize your Attorney-In-Fact to do on your behalf when you initial (J):

⇨ pay for necessary medical, dental, surgical and custodial care

⇨ maintain or replace motor vehicles

⇨ pay for the usual vacation and travel expenses

⇨ pay for food, clothing, shelter, education, etc.

⇨ employ the normal domestic help

⇨ provide living quarters for you or family members by lease or purchase; including paying for the taxes and repair of their living quarters

⇨ continue to make contributions to your church, club, society or other order

⇨ open and maintain a charge account for you, your spouse, child, and anyone else you support.

Each of the other choices in the Uniform Statutory Form Power of Attorney gives your Attorney-In-Fact broad, general powers relating to that choice, so it is important to read each of the sections (4400 through 4465) before initialing any choice.

Those of you who sign a Power of Attorney for the sole purpose of avoiding a Conservatorship, may not want to give someone a Power of Attorney until it is needed. You may wish to conduct business on your own and not allow your Attorney-In-Fact to have any authority, until (and unless) you are too ill to manage your finances. But if you wait until that time you may be too ill to sign the document.

One possible solution is to sign the document and keep it in your possession until it is necessary for your Attorney-In-Fact to conduct business on your behalf.

An Attorney-In-Fact under a Power of Attorney cannot operate on behalf of the Principal, unless the Attorney-In-Fact has possession of the original Power of Attorney and presents it to whomever he wants to rely on that document. For example, if he wants to use the Power of Attorney to sell one of your securities, he will need to produce the original document, and proof of his identification (Prob. 4302). The securities broker may also ask him to sign an Affidavit (a written statement sworn to before a Notary Public) saying that the Power of Attorney is still in effect and that you did not revoke that Power of Attorney.

KEEP THE DOCUMENT IN YOUR POSSESSION

Before anyone (a bank, stockbroker, closing agent, etc.) will accept the Power of Attorney they will want to see the original document so that they are assured that your Attorney-In-Fact has authority to transact business on your behalf. If you keep the original document in your possession and do not give anyone a copy, your Attorney-In-Fact will not be able to act for you.

The only problem with this arrangement is that you need to arrange to make the document accessible to your Attorney-In-Fact in the event of your incapacity. If your Attorney-In-Fact is a trusted family member, you can tell him where you are storing the document with instructions to take possession of the Durable Power of Attorney in the event of your incapacity.

THE SPRINGING POWER OF ATTORNEY

A better solution may be to have your attorney draft a "springing" Durable Power of Attorney that is not operational until your family doctor and/or independent physician says that you are incapacitated and unable to manage your financial affairs.

Your Agent can hold the original document, but cannot use it until it "springs to life" when a doctor determines that you are too ill to care for your property. You can create a Springing Durable Power of Attorney by adding the following provision to the document

> This Durable Power of Attorney becomes operational only when my regularly attending physician and
> _____ (name of family member) sign an Affidavit stating that I am disabled or incapacitated.

If you sign a Springing Durable Power of Attorney, your Attorney-In-Fact can hold the original document, but he will not be able to use it until it "springs to life" once the Affidavit is signed (Prob. 4030, 4124, 4129).

USING THE POWER OF ATTORNEY FOR MEDICAL DECISIONS

Your attorney can design a Durable Power of Attorney, to meet your special needs. He can even include powers that relate to your health care. But as a practical matter, it may be better to have a separate Advance Health Care Directive. As explained in Chapter 8, an Advance Health Care Directive can be used to appoint a Health Care Agent and to give your Agent directions about the care you wish to receive in the event you are too ill to direct your medical treatment. There are other reasons to have a separate Advance Health Care Directive:

APPOINT DIFFERENT PEOPLE TO SERVE

You may want one person to serve as your Health Care Agent and another to serve as your Attorney-In-Fact. One family member may be an excellent choice to make your health care decisions, yet that person may not be the best person to make financial decisions on your behalf.

PRIVACY

Even if you want the same person to serve as your Health Care Agent and Attorney-In-Fact, there is still the matter of privacy. Your Health Care Agent will give a copy of your Advance Health Care Directive to your physician to be placed in your medical file. Your doctors have no need to know of your business dealings; and vice versa. To conduct business on your behalf your Attorney-In-Fact will need to give a copy of the Power of Attorney to your business associates (banks, stockbrokers, etc.). Your business associates have no need to know of your medical decisions.

ACCESS MEDICAL INFORMATION

As explained in the last chapter, under the Privacy Rule of HIPAA the person you appoint as your Health Care Agent under a Health Care Power of Attorney may access your medical records. However, in general, a Power of Attorey for finances is not sufficient to access your medical records under HIPAA. Read the summary of the HIPAA Privacy Rule for more information about who has the right to access your medical records. The summary appears at the U.S. Department of Health and Human Services Web site.
http://www.hhs.gov/hipaa

For privacy, and perhaps security reasons, consider having a separate Advance Health Care Directive and a separate Durable Power of Attorney rather than try to get it all into a single multi purpose document.

It is relatively simple and inexpensive to head off a conservatorship. All you need do is appoint an Attorney-In-Fact under a Durable Power of Attorney to manage your finances, and a Health Care Agent under an Advance Health Care Directive to make your medical care decisions. These documents authorize people of your choice to care for you and your property in the event of your incapacity. But, despite your best plans, something unusual could happen causing a Court to decide that you need a Conservator.

For example, suppose you disappear and cannot be found after a diligent search. It might be necessary to have a Court appoint a Conservator to manage your property in your absence. Or perhaps you develop an addiction or a mental illness causing self-destructive behavior. Your friends or family might decide that you are in need of protection and ask a Court to appoint a Conservator to care for your person; i.e., make your medical decisions and see to your everyday care (Prob. 1801, 1803, Welf. & Inst. 5350).

Although it may not be possible to avoid conservatorship all together, you can have a measure of control over your fate. You can use your Financial Power of Attorney to name someone to serve as the Conservator of your property in the event the Court finds it necessary to appoint one. And you can use the statutory form of the Advance Health Care Directive to appoint your Health Care Agent to serve as the Conservator of your person. You do not need to appoint the same person to serve as Conservator of your person and another to serve as Conservator of your property. However, should a Conservator of your person and property be necessary, it may cost you less to have one person serve in both capacities.

You can use the statutory form of Power of Attorney and Advance Health Care Directive to appoint someone to serve as your Conservator. However, if you are concerned about who will serve as your Conservator, it is best to have the document appointing the person of your choice drafted by an attorney. You can even have him include a list of those people who you do <u>not</u> wish to serve as your Conservator.

Should a conservatorship be necessary, the Court will want evidence that at the time you signed the document you were at least 18 years old and that you had sufficient mental capacity to make an intelligent choice of Conservator. Your attorney can have you sign the document in the presence of two credible witnesses (usually himself and a member of his office staff) who can testify that the document is a true expression of your wishes and that you knew exactly what you were doing when you signed the document.

If the judge is presented with a valid expression of your choice of Conservator, he will honor your wishes and appoint that person for the job — unless, for some reason, he finds that the person is unwilling or unable to serve in that capacity (Prob. 4126, 4701).

If two family members want to serve as your Conservator, the judge will give preference in the following order:

1st   your Spouse/RDP, or his/her choice of Conservator

2nd   your adult child or the child's choice of Conservator

3rd   your parent or the parent's choice of Conservator

4th   your brother or sister or your sibling's choice of Conservator (Prob. 1812).

Although the Court will give preference to those with top priority, the choice of Conservator is his (Prob. 1812). In making the selection, he will be guided by your best interests — meaning that he will chose the person he thinks will do the best job in caring for you.

If you do not express your choice of Conservator, it will be up to the judge to decide who is best suited for the job. But the problem with having the judge make the selection is that he knows little about those who come before his Court. Some people may look good on paper, but in fact may be a poor choice. For example, suppose a women is incapable of handling her finances and is in need of a Conservator of her property. If her son and daughter both want the job, the Court will consider their backgrounds and current commitments.

Suppose the son is a college graduate with a degree in business administration, and the daughter a homemaker with three small children, the judge might think the son a better choice. But it could be that the mother would never have chosen her son because of the many times she had to bail him out of debt.

Again, it is a matter of planning ahead, and being in charge of your own destiny, rather than leaving the choice up to a judge to decide.

The good news: You are going to live longer.

The bad news: It's going to cost you.

Scientists are doing a great job of prolonging life, but unless they find Ponce De Leon's fountain, the general population will continue to age. Along with age comes infirmities. Eyes fail. Hearing diminishes. Mobility declines. Digestive systems either speed up or slow down, all to the discomfort of the unhappy occupant of the body. It's all part of the "golden" years.

The pharmacology industry is well motivated to produce drugs that manage the ills associated with aging. Their research has led to a wealth of pharmaceutical products that do not cure, but do allow people to live in relative comfort into advanced age. The only problem is the cost of these drugs. Medicare covers the treatment of life-threatening brushes with heart disease, stroke, cancer and diabetes, but paying for maintenance medication is up to you. Even if you belong to a Medicare Prescription Drug Plan or have some other prescription insurance, you will need to contribute to the payment of your medication.

Medicare is also limited in long term nursing care coverage. The structure of Medicare has changed giving people the option of staying with the **Original Medicare Plan** or choosing a **Medicare Advantage Plan** such as a Medicare Health Maintenance Organization ("HMO"), or other Medicare Health Plans. Coverage depends on which plan is chosen. If you remain with the Original Medicare Plan you do not pay for the first 20 days of a stay in a skilled nursing facility (i.e., a nursing home). You pay up to $124** per day for days 21 through 100.

**This is the value for the year 2007. The federal government adjusts the amount each year.

Unless you have Medicare Supplemental Insurance coverage, it will cost you up to $9,920 for the next 80 days. After 100 days, you are on your own. A nursing home stay of one or two years can wipe out the life savings of most working people. Once savings are gone, the government provides care in the form of Medicaid coverage. If you have no assets to speak of, and a relatively low income, the cost of long-term nursing care is the least of your worries. Medicaid is available to take care of your medical and nursing care needs. And no need to worry if you are wealthy. You have enough money to pay for the care you might need. The rest of us need to think about ways to provide for long-term health care.

For those concerned about the loss of life savings because of illness, there is supplemental and/or long-term health care insurance. There are many different insurance plans available. You can call the National Association of Insurance Commissioners at (816) 783-8300 for information about long-term health care insurance.

THE CALIFORNIA PARTNERSHIP FOR LONG TERM CARE

The state of California has developed a plan for consumers, called the CALIFORNIA PARTNERSHIP FOR LONG TERM CARE. The "Partnership" refers to the fact that the California Department of Health Services is working with selected private insurance companies to provide quality long-term care insurance for California residents. The policy that is offered is called a *Partnership Policy*.

The policy must be approved by the Department of Health Services and it must pay for long-term care in the same way as any other high quality, long-term care policy.

The unique feature of the Partnership Policy is that each dollar of benefits paid by the policy enables the person who is insured under the policy to keep that same dollar amount as a non-countable asset in the event that person ever needs to apply for Medi-Cal benefits (Welf. & Inst. 2203).

To learn more about the Partnership Policy you can call (800) 227-3445 or visit the California Department of Health Services Web site.

 CALIFORNIA DEPARTMENT OF HEALTH SERVICES
http://www.dhs.ca.gov

LONG TERM INSURANCE FOR FEDERAL EMPLOYEES

The Long Term Care Security Act is designed to make long term care insurance available to federal employees, including postal workers, members of the uniformed services, civilian and military retirees, and their qualified relatives. You can call the Office of Personnel Management at (800) 582-3337 for information about the federal long term care insurance program or you can visit their Web site.

 OFFICE OF PERSONNEL MANAGEMENT
http://www.opm.gov/insure/ltc

The National Association Of Retired Federal Employees ("NARFE") was actively involved in developing the federal long term care insurance program. You can also get information about the program by calling the NARFE Legislative Hot-line toll-free (877) 217-8234 or by visiting their Web site.

 NATIONAL ASSOC. OF RETIRED FEDERAL EMPLOYEES
http://www.narfe.org

Long term care insurance sounds like the perfect solution, until you start examining the cost. The cost isn't too bad if you are comparatively young, say in your 50s. But can you imagine paying that premium each month until you are in your 80s and never needing nursing care?

Many decide to wait till they are old and going downhill. But that just brings other problems. The older you are, the greater the cost of insurance. And there is the risk that you will be refused coverage because of a "pre-existing" condition, i.e., the insurance company may consider you to be too great a risk for them to insure.

Different insurance companies have come up with insurance plans that may provide a solution for the person who is relatively young and in good health. Some companies offer long-term care insurance that is paid-up within a fixed period of time. Once payments are made for a certain number of years, the person is insured for long-term care without further payment. Other companies combine long-term care insurance with a life insurance policy. They offer long-term care insurance that converts to a life insurance policy, if it happens that the insured person dies before needing long-term care.

When shopping for a long-term care policy, consider including different insurance alternatives in your investigation.

WHEN INSURANCE IS NOT AN OPTION

For some people long term care insurance is not an option. An elderly person living on a low fixed income may not have enough money to pay the monthly premium for a long term care insurance policy. And long term care insurance is not an option for the person who has been diagnosed with a chronic, debilitating disease.

People in such a position worry that they may need to deplete their life savings, just to pay for a year or two of nursing care.

Both of these problems can be solved by using current law to become qualified for Medicaid. Medicaid is a public assistance program that is funded jointly by the federal and state government. There are state and federal laws governing who may become eligible for the program.

A *Medicaid Qualifying Plan* is a plan that takes both state and federal laws into consideration. Operating within the boundaries of these laws, those who are concerned about becoming impoverished in order to pay for long-term care, seek to preserve and protect their Estate by implementing a Medicaid Qualifying Plan.

There has been controversy about plans designed to qualify a person for Medicaid. Some think that to intentionally arrange finances to qualify for Medicaid is immoral — a legal method of working the system.

Those people may argue: "Why are such things allowed? After all, wasn't Medicaid designed to help poor people? Why should people be allowed to make themselves poor to get on the public dole??

Those who feel they need to qualify for Medicaid have a different point of view. They may argue:

"I worked all my life and hoped to leave a few pennies for the kids. Why did I work so hard? To give it all to a nursing home? I paid my taxes just like everyone else. The government pays hundreds of thousands of dollars for people on Medicare to have open heart surgery, and they pay for lengthy and expensive cancer treatments. Why should those who have Alzheimer's or Parkinson's or those who suffer a debilitating stroke, not be entitled to receive equal benefits?"

Although we can understand and appreciate both points of view, our job, as we see it, is to just explain the law as it is at the time of publication. We think it is important to do so because many people take a position (pro or con) based on what they perceive the law to be, and not based upon the law as it actually is.

Once the reader understands what it takes to qualify for Medicaid in the state of California, he can decide for himself whether the law is basically fair to the people who need to qualify, or whether it is flawed (either too restrictive or too liberal) and needs to be changed.

Hopefully, those with a strong opinion will share those views with their legislators.

A Medi-Cal Qualifying Plan 10

A better name for this chapter might be "A Health Care Contingency Plan." A lengthy stay in a nursing home is something most of us do not want to even think about, much less prepare for. Why prepare for something that may never happen? Yet as we age, there is that nagging "What if?" "What if I need long term nursing care? How will I pay for it?"

An effective way to put this anxiety at rest is to have a contingency plan. To form a contingency plan, you need to know your options. In this case, your options are directly related to your ability to pay for that care. But it is hard to predict future fortunes. People win the lottery. Those with a large portfolio may have their fortunes disappear in a market melt-down. There is no need for concern if it turns out that you can afford to pay for your own nursing care; and there is no concern should you become impoverished because there are government programs that provide for your health care. The worst case scenario is that you will be able to afford long-term care, but at the cost of your life savings.

In this chapter, we will discuss options available to you under that worst case scenario. We will explain current state and federal law as it relates to qualifying for medical assistance programs.

MEDICAID — A STATE OF LIMBO

On February 8, 2006, President Bush signed the Deficit Reduction Act of 2005. The Act reduces spending on Medicare, Medicaid and other domestic programs. The Act gives states certain options, such as disqualifying an Applicant for Medicaid if the equity in his home exceeds $500,000 or $750,000. Each state must pass new regulations to conform to the new law, including choosing an option for the $500,000 limit, or for the $750,000 limit. Beginning in 2011, the law requires that the above dollar amounts be increased by the cost of living rounded to the nearest $1,000 (42 U.S.C. 1396p(f)).

As of mid 2006, California regulators are working on but have not adopted new Medicaid regulations. That is not the only impediment to putting the new law into effect in this state. The Deficit Reduction Act is being challenged in federal Court on Constitutional grounds. Before the President can sign a bill into law, both the Senate and House of Representatives must adopt <u>identical</u> measures. However, the House version and the Senate version of the Deficit Reduction Act differ on Medicare payments for administering oxygen. Regardless of which way the judge rules, changes to the Medicaid law will no doubt be the same as passed by the Congress, and the discussion that follows in this chapter is based on that assumption.

The new law relates to transfers to qualify for Medicaid made after the "date of enactment," so theoretically, whenever the state and federal government settle on the details, the new law can be applied retroactively back to February 8, 2006. We anticipate that by 2007, the new law will be implemented in California, however, Medi-Cal officials have indicated that they do not intend to apply the law retroactively, sothe new law will likely be implemented as of the day it is enacted in California.

WHO IS ENTITLED TO MEDI-CAL?

Medicaid is a program that provides medical and long term nursing care for people with low income and limited resources. The program is funded and regulated by both federal and state government. The governing agency for the federal government is the Centers for Medicare and Medicaid Services. In California, the program is referred to as *Medi-Cal*. We will use the terms *Medicaid* and *Medical Assistance* and *Medi-Cal* interchangeably. The DEPARTMENT OF HEALTH SERVICES is the state governing agency for the Medi-Cal program. Its name will soon be changed to the DEPARTMENT OF HEALTH CARE SERVICES. Applications are taken and the program administered at the local level by local County Welfare/Social Services Agency office.

Whoever meets the financial standards set for the program is entitled to receive benefits under that program. Those who do not qualify are not entitled to Medi-Cal benefits.

There are many benefits offered under Medi-Cal, from health care for mothers and children; to community based services for those who need some assistance with their medical needs; to full nursing care for those who need assistance with dressing, bathing, feeding, walking and toileting. We will limit our discussion of Medi-Cal to those who need institutional long term care.

You can get information about other Medi-Cal programs by calling your local County Welfare/Social Services Agency office. You can also get information about Medi-Cal from the Telephone Service Center by calling them at (800) 541-5555. The hearing impaired can call TDD (800) 952-8349.

You can also find information about the Medi-Cal on the Department of Health Services Web site.

 DEPARTMENT OF HEALTH SERVICES — MEDI-CAL
http://www.medi-cal.ca.gov

Persons who are receiving SSI/SSP (Supplemental Security Income/State Supplement Program) may be automatically eligible for Medi-Cal because the requirements for these programs are much the same. A person who is not receiving SSI/SSP, may be eligible for Medi-Cal if he is 65 or older, or blind, or disabled.

When a person applies for Medi-Cal (the *Applicant***) the Department of Health Services ("DHS") will investigate his income and assets. If the Applicant is too ill to apply for himself, a family member, friend, or court appointed Guardian may apply for him (42 US Code of Federal Regulations ("CFR") 435.908, California Code of Regulations ("CCR") 22:50143).

MEDICAL ELIGIBILITY

Generally ,an Applicant who is currently receiving skilled nursing level of institutional care is medically eligible for Medi-Cal. However, if there is any question regarding his condition, a Disability Review Team will review the Applicant's medical report to determine whether he requires skilled nursing care. The Disability Review Team is composed of a psychological or medical consultant and another person qualified to interpret and evaluate medical reports and other evidence relating to the Applicant's medical eligibility (42 CFR 435.541)

** For simplicity, we will use the male gender for the Applicant and the female gender for his spouse.

CITIZENSHIP ELIGIBILITY

To be eligible for Medi-Cal, the Applicant must be a resident of the United States, and either a U.S. citizen or an alien who is lawfully admitted for permanent residence (42 U.S. 1396a(10), 1382c(a)(1)(B)).

INCOME ELIGIBILITY

In California, there is no limit on the amount of income earned by the Applicant each month, because once he is approved, his income will be used to contribute to the cost of his care. The amount he contributes, called the "share of cost," is supplemented by the Medi-Cal program at a rate established by DHS. Of course should the Applicant have a high income, there would be no reason to apply for Medi-Cal because he could afford to pay for his own nursing home care.

THE PERSONAL NEEDS ALLOWANCE

Once the Applicant is approved and becomes a recipient of Medi-Cal benefits, he is referred to as a *Medi-Cal Beneficiary* (CCR 22:50024). The Medi-Cal Beneficiary is allowed to keep a certain amount of his income each month (currently $35**) for his personal needs, such as clothing or hair cuts (CCR 22:50024).

** The figures used in this Chapter are for the year 2006. The federal and state government adjust these values on an annual basis. Check the UPDATE section of the EAGLE PUBLISHING COMPANY Web site for later values.
http://www.eaglepublishing.com

RESOURCE ELIGIBILITY

Although there is no limit on the Applicant's income, there is a limit on his **Resources**. Resources are assets owned by the Applicant, either by himself or together with another, that are countable for purposes of qualifying for Medi-Cal. An Applicant may have no more than $2,000 in Resources. If he is over the Resource limit on the day he applies for Medi-Cal, he will need to "spend down" his assets to $2,000. If he is eligible at any time during the month that he applies, his Medi-Cal benefits will begin on the first date of that month (CCR 22:50193, Welf. & Inst. 14006).

If the Applicant is married, he can transfer anything over $2,000 to his spouse, but there are limits to his spouse's assets as well.

THE COMMUNITY SPOUSE

The spouse of an Applicant who lives in their home or elsewhere in the community (i.e., not in a nursing home) is called the **Community Spouse**.

NOTE ⇨ DOMESTIC PARTNER IS NOT A COMMUNITY SPOUSE Medicaid is a federal and state program. The federal government does not recognize the Domestic Partner relationship, so the laws relating to the Community Spouse apply only if the Applicant is legally married to a person of the opposite sex.

Prior to 1988, the Community Spouse was required to use whatever assets she had to pay for the nursing care of her spouse. The Applicant could not qualify for Medi-Cal until they both were virtually impoverished. In addition to being unfair to the Community Spouse, this was not good government policy because it often resulted in the impoverished spouse turning to local government social service programs for support.

The Medicaid provisions of the Medicare Catastrophic Coverage Act of 1988 remedied the situation by considering the assets of the couple as being part of a common pot and allowing the Community Spouse to keep her own share of that pot. The amount allowed has been increased over the years. The federal government currently allows the Community Spouse to keep up to $99,540 of their combined assets.

The federal government also considers that the Community Spouse needs money each month for her maintenance. If her income is not sufficient to support her, the income of the Medi-Cal Beneficiary will be used to supplement the income of the Community Spouse up to a maximum of $2,489.00 per month. Each year, the federal government adjusts the spouse's Resource allowance and monthly maintenance allowance for cost of living increases. The values quoted are those used in California in the year 2006 (42 U.S.C. 1382b).

Notice that $99,540 and $2,489.00 are the maximum values set by the federal government. States have the right to administer the Medical Assistance program according to their state law, provided their state law is within federal guidelines and does not exceed the maximum values set by the federal government. This being the case, the actual amount allowed to the Community spouse can vary significantly state to state.

THE SPOUSE'S INCOME

The Community Spouse is not required to contribute her income to the cost of the nursing care of her spouse. Income attributed to the Community Spouse is determines by the "name on the check" rule, without considering the California marital property rules. If name of the Community Spouse is on the check, it's her money. If an income check is paid jointly to the husband and wife, then each is entitled to half of the value of the check (42 U.S.C. 1396r-5(b)).

The current value set by the state of California as the Community Spouse's *Monthly Maintenance Needs Allowance* is the federal maximum value of $2,489.00 None of the Medi-Cal Beneficiary's income is available to his spouse, if the Community Spouse has an income that is greater than the amount determined by DHS as her Monthly Maintenance Needs Allowance. But if her income is less than the monthly Needs Allowance, the Medi-Cal Beneficiary's income can be used to supplement her income

For example, suppose the Community Spouse has a monthly income of $2,000 and DHS finds that she needs the current maximum value of $2,489.00 a month for her maintenance. In such case, she is allowed to keep $489.00 of the Beneficiary's income each month. If for some reason (high medical bills, the need for special care, etc.) she needs more than $2,488.50 a month, she can appeal to have that value increased. See the next chapter for a discussion of the appeal process.

THE PROPERTY RESERVE

In California, property that is countable for the purpose of qualifying for Medi-Cal is called the **Property Reserve**. The Property Reserve consists of all real or personal property, owned by the Applicant, or his Community Spouse, that can be converted to cash to be used for their support. This includes their bank accounts, certificates of deposit, stocks and bonds, etc. These assets count as part of the couple's Property Reserves regardless of whether it is Separate or Community Property.

THE SPOUSE'S RESOURCE ALLOWANCE

The Community Spouse is entitled to a guaranteed share of the couple's Property Reserve. The state of California allows the Community Spouse to keep as much of their Property Reserve to get to the maximum value allowed under federal law, currently $99,540. This value is called the **Community Spouse Resource Allowance** (CCR 22:50403, 22:50453, 22:50456, 22:50457, 42 U.S.C. 1396r-5(c)(2), 1396r-5f).

Under state and federal law, there are items that can be converted to cash, that do not count as part of the Property Reserve for purposes of Medi-Cal eligibility. These items are considered to be "excluded resources" or in some cases "unavailable property." We will refer such non-countable items as EXEMPT PROPERTY..

EXEMPT PROPERTY

The following assets are considered to be *Exempt Property* and do not count as part of the Applicant's Property Reserve.

AUTOMOBILE

➪ A car that is in use by the Community Spouse or the Applicant is Exempt Property. If the Applicant can no longer drive, the car remains exempt, provided it is being used by another person to meet the needs of the Applicant or Medi-Cal Beneficiary. The full market value of a second automobile, as well as recreational vehicles (boats, campers, trailers, snow mobiles, etc.) are included as part of the Property Reserve (CCR 22:50461, 22:50463, 22:50469).

HOUSEHOLD ITEMS

All items used to furnish and equip a home are exempt (CCR 22:50465).

PERSONAL EFFECTS

Personal effects owned by the Applicant or his Community Spouse are exempt items. They include:

➪ wedding and engagement rings, regardless of their value;

➪ all items of clothing;

➪ all musical instruments.

Items of jewelry that are handed down generation to generation (i.e. heirlooms), are exempt; but any other piece of jewelry worth more than $100 is counted as a part of the Property Reserve (CCR 22:50465, 22:50467, 22:50471).

LIFE INSURANCE

➡️ An insurance policy owned by the Applicant is Exempt Property, provided the face value (the amount paid at death) is $1,500 or less. The Applicant can own more than one policy on the same person, provided that the sum of the face values of those policies is not greater than $1,500 (CCR 22:50475). If the face value of one or more policies is more than $1,500, the Cash Surrender Value of the policy is counted as a part of the Property Reserve. You can write to the insurance company and they will give you the current Cash Surrender Value of the policy.

Term life insurance policies have no cash surrender value, so they are not included in the Property Reserve.

BURIAL ARRANGEMENTS

➡️ Burial spaces for the Applicant or his family (Community Spouse, adult or minor child — including adopted and stepchildren, parent, sibling and the spouse of a family member) are exempt. This includes burial plots, vaults, crypts, etc. (CCR 22:50477).

➡️ An Irrevocable Preneed Funeral Arrangement as described in Chapter 8 is Exempt Property. Money or securities placed in an irrevocable trust to pay for the Applicant's funeral, cremation or interment expenses, is exempt. If the Applicant has a revocable Preneed Funeral Arrangement, the DHS will allow him to make that plan irrevocable so that it may qualify as Exempt Property.

➡️ A burial fund for the Applicant and/or his Community Spouse of up to $1,500 is Exempt Property provided the fund is in a separate account and clearly identified as a burial account. This is account is not exempt if there is an insurance policy of $1,500 or if there is an Irrevocable Preneed Funeral Arrangement of $1,500 or more (CCR 22:50479).

THE HOMESTEAD — EXEMPT MAYBE

It used to be that the primary residence (home, condominium, cooperative apartment, or mobile home) occupied by the Applicant was an Exempt Resource for purposes of qualifying for Medi-Cal. The Applicant could not be denied Medical Assistance because he owned a home — regardless of his *equity* in the home, i.e., the current market value less mortgages and liens on the property.

The recent spiral of residential property values has not gone unnoticed by the government. A home purchased years ago is now worth a substantial amount of money. Congress decided that a person whose equity in his home is $500,000 or more should not be able to qualify for Medi-Cal. As explained, California legislators may decide to opt for the higher value of $750,000.

The equity limit does not apply if the Applicant's Community Spouse or his minor or disabled child is living in the home. Specifically, the home does not count as a Resource regardless of its value if the spouse, or the Applicant's minor or disabled child lives in his home (42 U.S.C. 1396p(f)(2)). If the Applicant is in a nursing home, and no family member lives in the home, it remains Exempt, provided the Applicant has indicated that he intends to return home and his equity in the home does not exceed $500,000 (or $750,000) (42 U.S.C. 1382b, CCR 22:50426).

ASSETS THAT ARE NOT SALEABLE

⇨   Property owned by the Applicant or his spouse must be able to be converted to cash in order to be counted as part of their Property Reserve. Shares held in a close (small) corporation, Life Estate interests, certain irrevocable annuities, and other non-saleable items can be considered to be unavailable, subject to the approval of the DHS (CCR 22:50402).

PENSION PLAN

⇨   IRA's, Keogh accounts, 401(k) accounts and other pension plans of the Applicant and/or his spouse are not considered to be part of the Property Reserve, provided they are receiving periodic payments of the principal and interest. The payments they receive count as income (CCR 22:50507).

BUSINESS PROPERTY

⇨   Equipment, inventory, licenses and materials owned by the Applicant is not included in the Property Reserve provided it is necessary for self-support and it provides a reasonable rate of return. Currently 6% is considered to be reasonable (CCR 22:50485).

JOINTLY OWNED ASSETS

The DHS considers the full value of a jointly owned account to be available to the Applicant or his Community Spouse, unless it can be proven that the other owner of the account is not a family member who lives at home with them; and that joint owner contributed his own money to the account. For example, if the Applicant owns a joint account with his brother, the entire balance counts as part of the Applicant's Property Reserve unless the brother can prove that he contributed his own money to that account. The brother's net contribution (how much he contributed less how much he withdrew) does not count as part of the Property Reserve (CCR 22:50041, 22:50453).

OTHER EXEMPT ASSETS

We have listed many of the more common items that the DHS considers to be Exempt Property. But this is not a complete list. There are other items that do not count as part of the Property Reserve. You can find the complete list of items that are exempt by reading Sections 50425 through 50489 of Title 22 of the California Code of Regulations. Your local law librarian can help you obtain a copy of these sections.

THE SPEND-DOWN OPTION

Now that we know what is (and is not) included in the Property Reserve, the next question is what options are available to an Applicant who has too many assets. We will consider the problem of a married Applicant whose Property Reserve exceeds $99,540.

Those with no knowledge of the law, might think the only option available to the couple is to pay for his nursing care until the amount over the limit is spent. Those who carefully read the previous pages, might suggest that the couple check to see whether they can use the money to purchase items that do not count as part of their Property Reserve.

Both state and federal law allow the Applicant and his spouse to use their assets to purchase Exempt Property, without losing the right to receive Medi-Cal benefits, provided they pay a fair market value for the item. This being the case, the couple can make funeral or burial arrangements, if they have not already done so. They can purchase household items such as furniture, a television set, a new refrigerator or stove, etc.

REPAIRING OR REPLACING EXEMPT PROPERTY

Paying money to repair Exempt Property is a good spend-down strategy. Perhaps the exempt family car needs new brakes or tires. The Community Spouse may even decide to replace the car with a new model. If the house is in need of repair or improvement, then this is the time to fix it up. A new heating, plumbing or electrical system can use up funds quickly.

If the couple do not own their own home, the Community Spouse might consider using the excess cash as a down-payment on a home.

SPEND-DOWN BY PAYING DEBTS

A couple may use there excess assets to pay off any outstanding debts. If they have a credit card balance, they can reduce the balance to $0. If they have a car loan, they can pay it off. If they have a mortgage on their home, they can use the money to pay down that debt. Paying off loans is a valid spend-down strategy because it is just a return of monies given to the Applicant by the lender for the purchase of an Exempt Property (car, house, clothing, household items). The Applicant can use his excess Property Reserve to pay off all his debts one day and apply for Medi-Cal the next (CCR 22:50408).

When he applies, the DHS, will want proof that the monies he spent were used to pay a valid debt. If he paid off a credit card debt, DHS will want to see the original contract with the company and the monthly bill showing what items were purchased. If the Applicant used the money to pay down the mortgage on his home, DHS will want to see the original loan documents as well as documents showing the new balance, or a satisfaction of mortgage, if paid in full.

Suppose the couple with too much in Property Reserves has too little income. For example, suppose the couple's combined income is only $1,500. In such case, she can ask DHS to allow her to keep as much of the couple's excess Property Reserves as is necessary to generate enough income to get her to the minimum income of $2,489. In effect, she needs to ask "May I keep more than $99,540 so that the income from this property will help to get me to the minimum monthly income as allowed by state and federal law?"

Although it is the legal right of the Community Spouse to receive the minimum Monthly Maintenance Needs Allowance, because she is asking DHS to keep more than is allowed as a Property Reserve, they will probably deny the request.

In such case the Community Spouse can employ an attorney to appeal their decision. But the appeals process can drag on for months; meanwhile, the status of the Applicant remains in limbo. Because of the legal cost of the Appeal and the uncertainty of whether the Court will agree that additional resources are necessary for the support of the Community Spouse, it may be better to use a spend-down strategy that enables the spouse to obtain additional income.

One such strategy is the **MEDI-CAL ANNUITY.** The Community Spouse uses the excess resources to buy an Annuity that will give her additional income. This spend-down strategy is permissible provided it conforms to state and federal law.

A spend-down strategy that is currently allowed by both federal and state law is the purchase of an *Immediate Pay Annuity*; i.e., an Annuity whose payments begin the month after the purchase and continues for a fixed period of time. For purposes of Medi-Cal eligibility, that fixed period of time must be less than, or equal to, the life expectancy of the Annuitant (in this case, the Community Spouse).

The life expectancy of the Annuitant is determined by referring to the actuarial table as published by the Centers for Medicare and Medi-Cal Services; State Medicaid Manual, Part 3 (SM3 3259.1) "Life Expectancy Tables— Males and Life Expectancy Tables—Females." You can find excerpts from that table at Public Service Information section of the Eagle Publishing Company Web site.

http://www.eaglepublishing.com

By purchasing an Immediate Pay Annuity, the excess Resources are converted to a monthly income that continues for the term of the policy.

In order to qualify as a permissible spend-down strategy, the annuity must meet both state and federal criteria; specifically:

NO CASH VALUE

The annuity contract must have no value other than the monthly payments to the annuitant.

UNASSIGNABLE AND IRREVOCABLE

The Annuity contract cannot be transferred, sold or assigned. It must be irrevocable. In other words, nothing can be changed; not the monthly payment, nor the number of payments, nor the identity of the Annuitant.

ACTUARIALLY SOUND

The Annuity contract must be *actuarially sound,* meaning that the money invested in the Annuity (plus a reasonable rate of interest) must be returned to the Annuitant during his life expectancy as printed in the State Medicaid Manual (SM3 3258.9(B), 3259.1). There is no rounding "up." For example, according to the State Medi-Cal Manual a 65 year old man has a life expectancy of 14.96 years. An Annuity that makes regular payments to the Annuitant for 14 years is actuarially sound, but an Annuity that makes payments for 15 years is not.

NO CASH VALUE/EQUAL PAYMENTS

The Annuity contract must have no value other than the monthly payments to the Annuitant. The monthly payments must be of equal value, with no deferred payment and no balloon payment (42 U.S.C. 1396p(c)(1)(G)).

THE STATE IS THE RESIDUARY BENEFICIARY

The Deficit Reduction Act requires that the state be the Residuary Beneficiary of the Annuity up to the amount paid by the state for his care. If the Applicant is married, his Community Spouse or minor/disabled child may be in first position as beneficiary, provided the state is in second place (42 U.S.C. 1396p(c)(1)(G)). It may be that this requirement does apply to an Annuity purchased by the Community Spouse for her own benefit. However, as explained, no regulation has been adopted on the matter, when we went to print in late 2006.

We will refer to an Annuity that meets all of these criteria (no cash value, unassignable, irrevocable, actuarially sound) as a *Medi-Cal Annuity*.

CAUTION VERIFY THAT THE ANNUITY MEETS
DHS CRITERIA PRIOR TO PURCHASE

Once the Annuity is purchased it is irrevocable, so before you buy it, have your Elder Law attorney, or the agent who is selling the annuity, check with DHS to be sure the Annuity meets state and federal requirements. If you purchase the Annuity and for some reason the Department determines that the Annuity does not meet current state and federal criteria, whatever you paid for the Annuity might count as an impermissible transfer of assets and a PENALTY PERIOD of ineligibility will be imposed, i.e., a period of time that the Applicant is disqualified from receiving Medi-Cal benefits. The Penalty Period is discussed later in this Chapter.

USING THE ANNUITY TO GENERATE INCOME

Purchasing a Medi-Cal Annuity could solve the problem for the Community Spouse who has too little income and too much in Resources. She can use her excess Resources to buy the Annuity. She will keep the income from that investment, just as she would if she had invested in a stock, bond or Certificate of Deposit. Unlike these investments, part of the money she paid for the Annuity is returned to her each month along with interest. Most importantly, the Annuity does not count as a Resource.

This spend-down strategy can be used by the Community Spouse even when her income is not a problem. But it may not make economic sense if the sum of her monthly income, including the income from the Annuity, exceeds the value set by the DHS as her Minimum Monthly Maintenance Needs Allowance

For example, suppose the DHS determines that the Community Spouse needs $2,489.00 per month and her income is $2,000 from her pension and Social Security. The DHS will allow her to keep $489 of her husband's income. If the Annuity pays $489 per month, she may keep none of her husband's income. All of his income will be used for his nursing care. In other words, purchasing the Medi-Cal Annuity may enable the Applicant to qualify for Medi-Cal, but it may not result in extra income for the Community Spouse. And there are other things to consider.

⇨ THE COMMUNITY SPOUSE MAY DIE
OR NEED NURSING CARE

Buying a Medi-Cal Annuity for a Community Spouse who is herself aged or in frail health may not be the best option. If she dies before all of the payments are made, whatever remains will go first to the state of California as reimbursement for her spouse's nursing care.

It could happen that she lives her full life expectancy, but needs long-term nursing care and will need to apply for Medi-Cal. If she purchases an Annuity and later becomes a Medi-Cal Beneficiary, that extra income will be used as her contribution to her nursing care.

⇨ RISK OF LOSS

By purchasing an Annuity, the Community Spouse is giving her money to a company in exchange for the company's promise to return part of the principal each month, together with interest. The company promises to make these payments every month for a certain number of years. Should the company become bankrupt during that period of time, the monies invested might be lost.

⇨ LOSS OF LIQUIDITY

Should the Applicant die shortly after his Community Spouse buys the Annuity, she cannot cash it in. She must keep the investment for the full term.

⇨ FIXED RETURN ON INVESTMENT

Annuities offer a fixed rate of return on the money invested. There is no way to adjust that rate for periods of inflation. The rate of return on the Annuity is set at the time of purchase. If you purchase an Annuity in a period of low single digit interest rates, it will remain at that same low rate even if the interest rate goes into the double digit range. You may find that you are able to earn more on your savings account than the rate of return that you are receiving from your Annuity.

All these concerns need to be addressed before investing in a Medi-Cal Annuity. Consultation with an Elder Law attorney prior to the purchase is a must.

NOT THE BEST OPTION FOR THE SINGLE APPLICANT

Although purchasing a Medi-Cal Annuity may work for a healthy Community Spouse with a low fixed income, it may not be the best strategy for the single Applicant, because any income he receives from the Annuity will be used for his nursing care. He could live in the nursing home longer than his life expectancy and all the money invested in the Annuity would be used for his care.

One exception may be the single Applicant who intends to return home after a few months. For example, suppose an unmarried person with $100,000 needs extensive nursing care because of a car accident. If doctors expect he will be able to return home after several months of therapy and nursing care, he might consider purchasing a Medi-Cal Annuity for $98,000.

Once he makes the purchase, he can immediately apply for Medi-Cal. He will of course report the purchase to the DHS. The DHS will examine the terms of the Annuity to be sure they satisfy current regulations. If they do and he meets all other requirements, he should qualify for Medi-Cal.

He's happy because he did not need to spend down his $98,000 in nursing home bills. He's hoping that his condition improves enough so that he can return home. In such case, his nursing care will be paid by Medi-Cal, and he will continue to receive the income from the Annuity when he returns home.

The DHS is happy because any income he receives while in the facility will go toward payment of his nursing home bill, leaving that much less for the DHS to contribute to his care.

By purchasing a Medi-Cal Annuity, the Applicant is betting that he will not need nursing care for the rest of his life expectancy. If he loses his bet, none of his assets are protected. All his money will be used to pay for his nursing care. In such case it may be better for him to use a strategy better designed for the single Applicant.

If the Applicant has a medical condition, but he does not expect to need nursing care for several years, he may decide to simply transfer all of his money to his child with the hope that he will not need long term nursing care for at least five years. The five years is the **Look-back Period** that DHS uses to investigate the finances of a person who applies for Medi-Cal. The Look-back Period starts on the date the Applicant enters the nursing home and applies for Medi-Cal and goes back five years from that date (42 U.S.C. 1396p(c)).

During that time the Applicant or his spouse can make a *compensated transfer* without penalty, such as purchasing an item for its fair market value, or paying off a legal debt. The California Code of Regulations (CCR 22:50408) gives a complete list of compensated transfers.

A gift to a child is an ***uncompensated transfer*** because the Applicant gets nothing in return for the transfer (love and affection don't count) (CCR 22:50409). If the Applicant, or his Community Spouse, makes an uncompensated transfer during the Look-back Period, the DHS will impose a **Penalty Period**.

COMPUTING THE PENALTY PERIOD

The rules for determining the Penalty Period are fairly complex (see CCR 22:50411), and may change when the new Deficit Reduction Act regulations become effective. Presently, the Penalty Period is computed by dividing the amount transferred by the average monthly cost of nursing home care as determined by DHS. The current average cost is $5,031.

If a single Applicant with $100,000, decided to give away his excess Property Reserve of $98,000 (he's allowed to keep $2,000) he would be disqualified for over 19 months:
$98,000/$5,031 = 19.48$ months or 19 months 14 days

beginning on the day he applies for Medi-Cal and is otherwise eligible for Medical Assistance.

THERE IS NO LIMIT ON THE PENALTY PERIOD
Although, under the new law, the DHS will Look-back five years, there is no limit on the Penalty Period imposed for that transfer. For example, suppose the Applicant gives his child $400,000. If he applies for Medi-Cal within five years from the date of transfer, he can be denied Medi-Cal benefits for more than six and a half years beginning on the day he applies.
$400,000/$5,031 = 79.50$ months or 6.63 years

The Penalty Period can be reduced, provided the money is returned to the Applicant. But, this is not a complete solution because the father will have too much to qualify for Medi-Cal. He will need to spend-down (probably on nursing home care) before he can qualify for a Medical Assistance Program.

Under the Deficit Reduction Act, profound changes were made to the Medi-Cal law:
** FIVE YEAR LOOK BACK INSTEAD OF THREE
**PENALTY PERIOD STARTS WHEN YOU APPLY
** DENIAL OF MEDICAID IF HOME HAS EQUITY OF $500,000
(OR $750,000) AND NO DEPENDENT LIVES THERE.

People may have transferred property under the old law, believing that they could apply for Medi-Cal once three years passed. Now the DHS can look back five years and apply the Penalty Period starting on the day of application.

The federal government recognized that the transition from the old law to the new could cause **undue hardship,** so they included the following provision to 42 U.S.C. 1396p:

Each State shall provide for a hardship waiver process ...
(1) under which an undue hardship exists when application of the transfer of asset provision would deprive the individual —
    (A) of medical care such that the individual's health or life would be endangered; or
    (B) of food, clothing, shelter, or other necessities of life; and
(2) which provides for —
    (A) notice to the Beneficiary that an undue hardship exemption exists;
    (B) a timely process for determining whether an undue hardship waiver will be granted; and
    (C) a process under which an adverse determination can be appealed.

In other words, the state may not deny the Applicant Medical Assistance if to do so will be dangerous to his health, or deprive him of food, clothing, shelter and other necessities. Although the definition of undue hardship seems clear enough, applying it is complicated. It may take the efforts of an experience Elder Law attorney to convince DHS that a particular case meets the definition.

For example, suppose a father set up a Medi-Cal Qualifying Plan under the old law. He kept enough money to pay for his nursing care for three years, and transferred $100,000 to his son. When the father applies for Medi-Cal, the DHS looks back five years and sees the transfer. They will deny him Medical Assistance for 16 months, 17 days beginning on the day he applied for Medi-Cal. If the son refuses to return the money, and the father has no other way to pay for the care he needs, will the DHS consider this a case of undue hardship?

A father, in another state, with a similar set of circumstances was denied Medicaid. The state determined that this was not a case of undue hardship because the father gave away the money of his own free will.

It could happen that a person is diagnosed in the early stages of a progressive disease that is expected to ultimately result in a lengthy stay in a nursing facility. A person in such a situation may decide to give his property away, with the hope that he will not need long term nursing care for at least five years. If he becomes incapacitated and someone applies for Medi-Cal for him during that period, they are required to report the transfer to DHS.

And this is not a game of "Catch me if you can."
Under both state and federal law, the Applicant or whoever applies for him, is required to make a full disclosure of transfers made during these periods. Anyone who knowingly and wilfully makes a false statement in an application for Medical Assistance Programs can be prosecuted for perjury and fraud.

The reader may be thinking "Yes, but if I come down with an illness that I know will cause me to deteriorate over a period of time, all I need to do is give all my money to my child and be sure to wait five years. My child will keep my money safe. Should I need that money, my child will return as much as I need to me. Money that I don't use will be protected for my child."

The Medi-Cal Qualifying Plan of giving away all assets and waiting five years is allowed under current law, but this is a "brute force" approach to the problem. It is a drastic step to take and fraught with peril. Once the money is transferred, a completed gift is made. The child becomes the legal owner of the money and with all of the obvious "what ifs."

— What if the child becomes bankrupt?

— What if he dies?

— What if the child is sued? Will a Court order the child to use the money you gave to pay the judgment?

— What if the child is divorced? Will a judge decide that your child's spouse is entitled to half of that money?

Most importantly, what if you give the money away and never need long term nursing care?

The medical field is advancing with amazing speed. Although few cures have been found for mankind's ills, there have been many breakthroughs in treatment. With modern drugs, many patients are able to function on their own. Even those who have been diagnosed with a progressive disease may not need nursing care for several years — maybe not at all. Meanwhile, your money is gone, and your independence along with it.

Being impoverished at a time in your life when you are unable to supplement your income, and when your health is declining, can lead to much sadness. Imagine going to your child and asking for money.

Imagine the child thinking, or worse yet, asking: "What's the money for?"

Many of these concerns can be remedied by a transfer into an Irrevocable Trust with the understanding that you will not be able to apply for Medi-Cal for at least five years. But even that has its risks. A lot can happen in five years. The federal law could change the Look-back Period to six years — or more. You could require full nursing care the day after you transfer your assets into the Trust. The Trust assets could be depleted in less than five years, yet you will not be able to apply for Medi-Cal because of the transfer.

For those in good health, an alternative may be to do nothing until you actually need nursing home care and then implement a Medi-Cal qualifying strategy at that time. Of course, there is the chance that you take suddenly ill, say with a stroke, and are unable to implement a Medi-Cal Qualifying plan. A Durable Power Of Attorney that is properly drafted to include Medi-Cal planning language, signed while you have capacity, should solve the problem. You can appoint someone to be your Agent to implement a Medi-Cal Qualifying plan for you.

It is important that the Durable Power of Attorney be properly drafted. In December 2002, A New Jersey Court refused to allow a son to transfer property on behalf of his incapacitated mother for the purpose of qualifying for Medicaid. Although his mother gave him a Power of Attorney authorizing him to apply for Medicaid on her behalf, the Court refused to allow the transfer because the Power of Attorney "... did not provide for him to make gifts on her behalf to himself or anyone else, either to qualify her for Medicaid or for any other reason" (*In the Matter of Mildred Keri*, Superior Court of New Jersey, Appellate Division, A-5949-01T5).

This case was reversed by the New Jersey Supreme Court and eventually the son was able to transfer the assets on behalf of his mother. But a transfer of property under an improperly drafted Power of Attorney can still be challenged. DHS may challenge transfers made under a Power of Attorney that does not give the Attorney In Fact specific authority to implement a Medi-Cal Qualifying plan. It is important that your Power of Attorney be drafted by an Elder Law attorney who knows what provisions to include in the document so that it will stand up to DHS scrutiny.

 THE ONLY THING CERTAIN IS CHANGE

Profound changes were made in 2006 to the Medicaid law. This is not the end of changes to the law. There is a proposal in the federal government to give states new powers to reduce, eliminate or increase Medical Assistance benefits within the state. Under this proposal, benefits for welfare recipients, poor children and other groups who are automatically eligible for Medicaid would remain regulated by federal law. The state would be given autonomy to administer the Medicaid program for other groups; and in particular for the elderly in need of nursing care. Proponents of state autonomy explain that with autonomy, the state could increase benefits, but in these days of budget deficits, more likely the states will opt to decrease Medical Assistance benefits to the elderly.

If states are given autonomy in administering the long-term nursing care program, uniformity would no longer be imposed by the federal government. Medicaid benefits for the elderly could vary significantly state to state. Not only would there be variation state to state, there could be variation within the state.

State programs could be administered with different eligibility criteria county to county. There could even be a difference in benefits county to county!

The point is that there is no certainty when it comes to future Medi-Cal qualifying options. But we did not write this chapter to give the reader a definitive Medi-Cal Qualifying strategy. Rather, it was to give the reader an understanding of the law as it relates to qualifying for Medi-Cal; and to let the reader know that under current law, options are available should the need for long-term nursing care arise.

We also wrote this chapter to let the general public understand how this federal program is administered here in the state of California. And, incidentally, we touched only on the basics. There are other, more sophisticated, Medi-Cal Qualifying options available that an experienced Elder Law attorney can explain to you. The prudent thing to do is to visit an Elder Law attorney if and when you become concerned about a long term care problem. He can explain current law to you as it relates to qualifying for Medi-Cal. He can suggest the best path for you to follow, given your set of circumstances.

It is also important to keep up with changes in policy both in the state and federal government. Whenever California legislators indicate that they are working on changes to the Medi-Cal law, it is important to let them know how you feel about such changes.

Protecting the Homestead 11

As explained in Chapter 10, whether a home in the name of the Applicant counts as a Resource for purposes of qualifying for Medi-Cal depends on his equity in the home, and if over $500,000 (or $750,000) whether his spouse or a dependent family member is living there. Even if no family member is living in the home, the Applicant cannot be denied Medical Assistance provided his equity in the home is less than the state limit, and he says he intends to return home. Once on Medi-Cal, the state has the right to have a physician determine whether he can reasonably be expected to return home within a year. If not, the state has a right to place a TEFRA Lien on the property for monies spent on his behalf. TEFRA stands for TAX EQUITY AND FISCAL RESPONSIBILITY ACT, a federal law. A home encumbered by a TEFRA lien cannot be sold or transferred until the monies spent by the state for the care of Medi-Cal Beneficiary are paid.

Even if the state does not place a lien on his home during his lifetime, if the Beneficiary received Medical Assistance after age 55, the state can place a TEFRA Lien on the property to seek recovery from the sale of his home once the home is sold or he dies. The state will not seek recovery from a home owned by a deceased Beneficiary while his spouse, or minor or disabled child are living there. However, once the child reaches 22, or the spouse and disabled child are deceased, whoever inherits the home will need to pay off the lien or the state can force the sale of the property and take the money from the proceeds of the sale (42 U.S.C. 1396p). In this chapter we discuss ways to protect the home from a *TEFRA Lien.*

Protecting the homestead is easy to do if the Medi-Cal member is married. Under state and federal law, the Applicant can transfer his home to the Community Spouse without penalty. He can make the transfer either before or after he applies for Medi-Cal (CCR 22:50408, 42 U.S.C. 1396p(c)2A).

If the home is in the name of the Medi-Cal Beneficiary only, he can sign a deed transferring the property to his spouse. If he and the Community Spouse own the property jointly, they can sign a deed transferring his interest to his Spouse. It is important to make the transfer of the Beneficiary's interest — otherwise the state can place a TEFRA lien on the property, and seek recovery for medical assistance given to the Beneficiary, once both husband and wife are deceased.

Protecting the home is more of a problem for the aged, single parent; and it is a problem for aging parents, both of whom are not in the best of health. Who knows which of them will require long term nursing care? Maybe both will need such care. Maybe neither of them will require nursing care.

Many parents want to have their children inherit the one thing the parent has of value, namely the family home. Parents fear that if they ever need Medi-Cal benefits, their home will be sold to reimburse the state. This idea is so distressing to some people that even though they are in relatively good health, they may decide to transfer their home to a child with the understanding that the parent will continue to live there for the rest of his life.

Those planning such a move need to understand that they are trading one risk (need to apply for Medical Assistance) for several other risks.

⊠ RISK OF LOSS

Once you transfer the property to your child it becomes his property and that property can be lost or used to pay for his debts just like anything else he owns. Your child could run into serious financial difficulties. Your child could be sued. This is especially a risk if your child is a professional (doctor, nurse, accountant, financial planner, attorney, etc.). If your child is found to be personally liable for damages, your home could become part of the settlement of that law suit.

If your child is (or gets) married, this complicates matters even more so. If the child divorces, the value of your home might be included as part of the property settlement agreement. This may be to your child's detriment because the child may need to share the value of the property with his/her former spouse. If you do not transfer the property, it cannot become part of his marital equation.

Even if your child is single there is a risk of loss. Your child may want to take out a business loan. If the loan is significant, the lender will want to include everything your child owns as collateral (security for the debt). If the lender learns that you are occupying the house, he will especially want to include your house as collateral because that will motivate your son to repay the loan.

The point is, transferring the house to your child could be bad for both of you. And that is not the only downside.

⊠ LOSS OF HOMESTEAD TAX EXEMPTION

People who own a residence in California are entitled to a *Homestead Property Tax Exemption* (currently $7,000 of its value), provided they occupy the homestead as their primary residence (Rev. & Tax 218).

There are additional Homestead Property Tax Exemptions for disabled Veterans. Should a Veteran die, his surviving Spouse/RDP is eligible for the same tax exemption for so long as the Spouse/RDP does not remarry or enter into another DP relationship. These exemptions apply to property the couple own together or separate property held in the name of the surviving Spouse/RDP (Rev. & Tax 205.5). If you give your home away, you lose your right to receive these tax breaks.

⊠ LOSS OF HOMESTEAD CREDITOR PROTECTION

Up to $150,000 of the value of your homestead is protected from creditors during your lifetime (Civ. Proc. 704.730, 704.995). This may not seem like much, but, as explained in Chapter 5 it could keep a roof over your head if the equity in your home is less than the protected value of your homestead. If you simply transfer your homestead to a child, you lose your homestead protection against creditors. If you are married, or a Domestic Partner, it is a double loss of creditor protection. Not only do you lose creditor protection for yourself, you lose it for your Spouse/RDP as well.

If the child does not occupy that property as his homestead, there is no homestead creditor protection whatsoever. The child's creditors can force the sale of the property (that's your home) for a relatively small unpaid debt.

⊠ POSSIBLE GIFT TAX

A federal Gift Tax needs to be paid if the value of the equity in your home (plus the value of all the gifts you gave over your lifetime in excess of the Annual Gift Tax Exclusion) exceeds the lifetime Gift Tax Exclusion. The current lifetime federal Gift Tax Exclusion is $1,000,000, so for most of us, this is not a problem. Yet there still is the hassle of filing a Gift Tax return.

⊠ POSSIBLE CAPITAL GAINS TAX

Although Congress has expressed its intent to phase out the Estate Tax, there is no discussion to do away with the Capital Gains Tax. If you gift the property to the child during your lifetime, when he sells the property he will pay a Capital Gains Tax on the increase in value from the price you paid for your home to the selling price at the time your child sells the property.

If you do not make the gift during your lifetime, the child will inherit the property with a step-up in basis, i.e., he will inherit the property at its market value as of the date of your death. Under today's tax structure and continuing through 2009, that step-up in basis is unlimited. If your child sells the property when he inherits it, he will pay no Capital Gains Tax, regardless of how large the step-up in basis.

In 2010, there will be a limit on the amount that can be inherited free of the Capital Gains Tax but that limit is quite high so for most of us this is not a concern.

⊠ POSSIBLE LOSS OF GOVERNMENT BENEFITS

Under the new Deficit Reduction Act, if you are married and you make an uncompensated transfer of property to someone other than your spouse, both you and your spouse could be denied Medical Assistance if you apply within five years from the date of transfer of the property.

It could happen that during that period of time, one of you takes suddenly ill and requires long-term nursing care. Why jeopardize your right to receive Medicaid for both of you? Owning a homestead will not disqualify you from receiving Medicaid, but transferring it may make you and your spouse ineligible for a long time.

The elderly parent, who is single, may not be convinced that gifting the house is a bad idea. He may be thinking "By giving my home to my child, I risk not being able to qualify for Medi-Cal for five years. If I don't make the gift and need Medi-Cal at any time during the rest of my lifetime, the state will get the house for sure."

But there are better Estate Plans than the outright gift. The Life Estate strategy may be one of them.

THE LIFE ESTATE STRATEGY

You can give the property to your child, and keep a Life Estate for yourself. Your child will have no right to your homestead while you are alive so you have no fear that the property can be lost or taken from you during your lifetime. Upon your death, your child will own the property 100%, and without the need for Probate.

Depending on the value of your home, this Life Estate approach might allow you to shorten the Medi-Cal transfer Penalty Period, because you are not giving your child the full value of your home, you are just giving away the value of the Remainder Interest, i.e., what is left of the property after your death.

More importantly, a gift of the Remainder Interest results in a reduction of your equity in the property. This reduction in equity may bring the value of the portion of the residence "owned" by the you as a life tenant to less than $500,000. Should you transfer the Remainder Interest, and need nursing care once five years from the date of transfer, the value of your home should not bar you from being eligible for Medi-Cal.

DETERMINING THE VALUE OF THE REMAINDER INTEREST

The value of the Remainder Interest depends on your life expectancy. A gift of a Remainder Interest when you are 90 is worth more to your child than when you are 50. The Centers for Medicare and Medicaid Services publishes a table of values for the Life Estate Interest and the Remainder Interest based on the age of the Grantor at the time of the transfer (State Medicaid Manual, Part 3 (SM3 3258.9) LIFE ESTATE AND REMAINDER INTEREST TABLE).

You can find excerpts from this table, at the <u>Public Information</u> section of the Eagle Publishing Company Web site. http://www.eaglepublishing.com

Fortunately, this table goes up to age 109, so the value they assign to the remainder interest is relatively low. For example, according to this table, if a 70 year old makes a transfer to his son and keeps a Life Estate for himself, his Life Estate is equal to 61% of the value of the property. The remainder interest is worth only 39%.

The actual percentage given in the table for the Remainder Interest is .39478. If the home is worth $600,000 it means the value of the gift of the Remainder Interest is $236,868.
$$\$600,000 \times .39478 = \$236,868$$

The value of your Life Estate Interest as of the date of transfer is $363,132: $600,000 - $363,132 — well under the $500,000 limit.

Remember that the Penalty Period for the transfer of the Remainder Interest ($236,868/$5,031 = 47.08 months) will be enforced if you apply for Medi-Cal at any time during the five years after the date of transfer (CCR 22:50410).

And that is not the only problem.

CONTROL
You will not be able to sell your home, or get a mortgage on the property, without permission from your child.

TAX ISSUES
And, as explained at the end of Chapter 2, if you sell the home, you or your child might need to pay a Capital Gains Tax.

RECOVERY BY THE STATE

The state has the right to recover monies spent on your behalf if you receive nursing care under Medi-Cal after the age of 55. Monies can be recovered from property you own at the time of your death. Under federal law, this includes property you own jointly with another, and property in which you own a Life Estate interest (42 U.S.C. 1396p(b)(4)(B)). The state has the right to place a TEFRA lien on your Life Estate interest. Once you die, the state may demand that your child reimburse them for monies spent on your behalf, or they can force the sale of the house and collect the money from the proceeds of the sale.

Up until 2006, the state of California has not sought recovery from Life Estates or joint tenancy interests, but the federal law is on the books, and in these days of tight state budgets, California may decide to do so.

THE REVERSE MORTGAGE

Another possible solution to the problem of owning a home whose equity exceeds the state limit is the REVERSE MORTGAGE. A *Reverse Mortgage* is a mortgage such that the lender gives the borrower a certain amount of money, with the agreement that the loan does not need to be repaid until the house is sold or the borrower dies. The money may be given as a lump sum or the borrower may opt to receive a certain amount of money each month based on his life expectancy.

For example, suppose a couple with low monthly income own a home with equity that exceeds the state limit. If they have a child who earns a substantial income, the couple may take out a Reverse Mortgage with their son as lender. The son will pay his parents a certain amount of money each month.

Because the parents are getting value from the transaction, no Penalty Period will be imposed should either parent need to apply for Medi-Cal at any time. Meanwhile, the parents are receiving a regular income that will enable them to increase their standard of living, and pay for home health care, if it is needed. The mortgage on the property reduces the equity in the home, so should one parent die, and the other parent need to apply for Medi-Cal the $500,000 (or $750,000, depending on state law) limit may not be a problem. Of course, should either parent become a Medi-Cal Beneficiary, the state can place a TEFRA lien on the property, but that lien cannot be paid until both parents are deceased, and their lender son is fully paid. This is one way to protect the equity in the home for their child.

If the child does not have sufficient income to become the lender of a Reverse Mortgage, the parent can take out a Reverse Mortgage with a lending institution. A single Applicant whose equity in his home is greater than $500,000 (or $750,000) may be able to reduce his equity in the home by taking a Reverse Mortgage, but there are downsides for the single Applicant:

ABSENCE FROM HOME MAY RESULT IN FORECLOSURE
The lender may require the homestead to be occupied by the borrower. The mortgage agreement may allow the lender to foreclose in the event the borrower/Medi-Cal Beneficiary does not occupy the home for 365 days or more.

STATE REIMBURSED FROM SALE PROCEEDS
The state has the right to place a TEFRA lien on the property. Once the property is sold, the Reverse Mortgage will be paid from the proceeds of the sale. The state will be reimbursed from whatever remains of the net proceeds of the sale. It could happen that there will be nothing left for the child to inherit.

TRANSFERS THAT PROTECT

As explained, you can own a home and still qualify for Medi-Cal, but there still is the concern that once you become a Medi-Cal Beneficiary, the state may place a TEFRA Lien on your homestead for monies spent on your behalf. Under current law, there are several ways to protect your home from such lien. For a married person, the home can be protected by transferring it to the Community Spouse.

TRANSFERRING THE HOME TO THE SPOUSE

The Applicant is free to transfer his home to his spouse without penalty, either before or after he qualifies for Medicaid (42 U.S.C. 1396p(C)(2)(A)(i)). Once the house is in the name of the Community Spouse, she can arrange to have it inherited by a family member and not the Medi-Cal Beneficiary.

Should the Applicant be too ill to make the transfer himself, the deed can be signed by his Attorney-In-Fact under a properly drafted Durable Power of Attorney. If he did not give an Agent authority to make the transfer, and he is too ill to sign his name, it may be necessary to have a Conservator appointed who can ask the Court for permission to make the transfer.

Establishing a conservatorship may be expensive and time consuming, but as explained earlier in this Chapter, it is important that the homestead be transferred to the Community Spouse. The downside is that there is no guarantee that the judge will allow the transfer of the homestead to the Community Spouse. Before you apply for a conservatorship it is important to ask your attorney whether such transfers have been allowed in the past.

Under state and federal law, if an Applicant owns his home together with a sibling and the sibling lived with the Applicant for at least one year before entering the nursing facility, the Applicant can transfer the home to the sibling without a Medi-Cal transfer penalty (42 U.S.C. 1396p). This law presents an opportunity for an unmarried Applicant who has a brother or sister to protect the homestead. The only question is how the sibling becomes co-owner. If the Applicant and his sibling purchased the property together, and the sibling lived in the home for a year prior to the Applicant entering the nursing home, then the sibling's interest in the property is protected. The Applicant can transfer his share of the homestead to his sibling without penalty, and that will protect all of the homestead.

If the house is in the Applicant's name only, it is important to consult with an Elder Law attorney to determine the best way for the sibling to become part owner of the home. Federal law only requires that the sibling have an equity interest in the property. An equity interest could be joint ownership or a Tenancy In Common or a Remainder Interest in the homestead. An Elder Law attorney will be able to suggest a method of transferring an equity interest to the sibling that will result in a short Penalty Period. Remember, the Penalty Period does not begin until the homeowner applies for Medi-Cal.

The attorney will also assist with preparing documentation to present to the Department of Health Services ("DHS") to verify that:

⇨ the sibling owns an equity interest in the home
⇨ the sibling occupied the home for a year prior to the Applicant entering the nursing home.

A law similar to a transfer to a sibling applies to the Medi-Cal Beneficiary who owns his home and wants to transfer it to his child. The federal law allows a transfer of the homestead to the child without penalty, provided the child lived with and took care of his parent for at least two years before the parent entered the nursing home.

There is no requirement that the child own an equity interest in the property; but the federal statute does require that the state verify that the child lived in the home and provided care to the parent for the two years; and that this care enabled the parent to remain at home rather than be placed in a nursing home (42 U.S.C. 1396p(c)(2)(A)(iv)).

It is important to consult with an Elder Law attorney, preferably prior to the two year period. The attorney will explain how to document that care over the two year period so that the information can be presented to the DHS when the parent applies for Medical Assistance. The attorney may suggest that parent and child sign a Caretaker's Agreement that sets out the terms and conditions of the transfer; i.e., what care the child promises to give to the parent over the next two years in exchange for the transfer of the homestead to the child.

The attorney will explain how to document that care over the two year period so that the information can be presented to DHS when the parent applies for Medi-Cal. Some of the things DHS will want to know are:

⇨ the Applicant's medical condition during the 2 years

⇨ whether the child lived in the home during that time.

And especially, that the child provided most of the following services without receiving compensation from the DHS to do so:

⇨ prepare meals; run errands

⇨ shop for food and clothing

⇨ help maintain the home

⇨ assist with financial affairs

⇨ provide personal services and transportation

⇨ arrange for medical appointments.

The DHS may want someone (friend, family member, physician) to verify that the child did provide the necessary care during the two years. Once it is established by the DHS that federal requirements are satisfied, the property can be transferred to the child without affecting the right of the Applicant to receive Medi-Cal benefits.

TRANSFER TO A DISABLED CHILD

In California, the Applicant or his spouse may transfer their home or any other of their Resources to a child (minor or adult) who is blind, or disabled without penalty (42 U.S.C. 1396p(c)(2A). In the event the child does not have a determination of blindness or disability from the Social Security Administration, the DHS will review the child's medical records to determine whether the child is blind or disabled.

If the child is receiving Social Security disability benefits, the parent can transfer their home or other assets to a Supplemental Needs Trust for the child (see Chapter 7). This transfer will not disqualify the child (or the parent) from receiving government benefits, provided the Trust is drafted according to state and federal law.

IMPACT OF DEFICIT REDUCTION ACT

Laws relating to the transfer of the home to the spouse, sibling and child were enacted prior to the Deficit Reduction Act. Whether these laws will still apply if the home is worth more than $500,000 (or $750,00 depending on state law) is unknown as of the time we went to print in 2006.

CAUTION   DON'T TRY THIS ON YOUR OWN

A Medi-Cal Qualifying Plan is not something to attempt on your own. The Medi-Cal program is complex and volatile. There are many levels of law that govern Medicaid. There are the federal statutes (Social Security Act Title XIX/P.L. 89-97); the U.S. Code of Federal Regulations (42 CFR 430-435) and the Centers for Medicare and Medicaid Services State Medicaid Manual, Part 3 that say how the federal statutes are to be administered in the United States.

There are the California Medi-Cal statutes (Welfare and Institution Code); and the California Code of Regulations (Title 22, Division 3, Health Care Services) that say how the Medi-Cal program is to be administered in this state. These five different sets of laws and regulations are constantly changing — often with little or no notice to the general public.

And the laws are not well written. Judges in the federal District Court observed: "The Social Security Act is among the most intricate ever drafted by Congress. Its Byzantine construction ... makes the Act 'almost unintelligible to the uninitiated.' ... The District Court ... described the Medicaid statute as 'an aggravated assault on the English language, resistant to attempts to understand it'." (*Schweiker v. Gray Panthers*, 453 U.S. 34(1981)).

In *Rehabilitation Association of Virginia v. Kozlowski*, 42 F.3d 1444, 1450 (4th Cir 1994), the Court had nothing but sympathy for officials who must interpret or administer these laws. "There can be no doubting that the statutes and provisions in question, involving the financing of Medicare and Medicaid are among the most completely impenetrable texts within human experience. Indeed, one approaches them . . . with dread, for not only are they dense reading of the most tortuous kind, but Congress also revisits the area frequently, generously cutting and pruning in the process and making any solid grasp of the matters addressed merely a passing phase."

To make matters worse, the program is not uniformly administered within the state. The California Code of Regulations gives the local DHS office discretion in applying the Code. What may be an acceptable Medi-Cal qualifying option in one county, may be challenged by the Department of Health Services in another county. And the same county can decide to change their policy, so what is acceptable today, may be challenged tomorrow.

An attorney who regularly practices Elder Law within the county will be aware of the changes, and will be able to advise you accordingly.

THE MEDI-CAL APPEAL

An Applicant who is denied Medi-Cal benefits will receive notice from the DHS that he has the right to appeal. The first step in the appeal process is for the Applicant, or someone acting on his behalf, to request a "Fair Hearing." The DEPARTMENT OF SOCIAL SERVICES conducts the hearing on behalf of the Department of Health Services (CCR 22: 50951, 22:50953). This administrative procedure is called a "Fair Hearing." A County Appeals Representative will represent the position of the DHS. An Administrative Law Judge presides over the hearing. The Applicant, or his spouse or adult child is expected to appear at the hearing.

The Department of Social Services has a pamphlet that explains the Appeal process. It is entitled YOUR RIGHTS. You can get a copy by writing to:

THE DEPARTMENT OF SOCIAL SERVICES
744 P Street
Sacramento, CA95814.

If you read the handbook you will see that even though a Fair Hearing is an informal proceeding, it is none-the-less a complex legal proceeding. To win you will need to have a complete understanding of all applicable law. You will need to know how to discover and present evidence to prove your case. It is important to have an experienced attorney present at the hearing to represent the Applicant. If the Applicant cannot afford to employ an attorney, then ask Legal Aid for assistance.

After the hearing, the Administrative Law Judge will within 45 days, submit his proposed decision to the Department of Social Services. The Department will review his decision and accept, alter or reject the decision — or order a new hearing.

If you lose at the Fair Hearing level and the Department of Social Services accepts the decision of the Administrative Law Judge, you can bring your appeal to a judge in the Superior Court. The judge of the Superior Court will take a broader look at the picture and consider state and federal law, as well as your Constitutional rights under the law. If you are turned down in state Court, you can appeal to a federal court — all the way up to the United States Supreme Court.

As you can see, appealing the decision of DHS is stressful, complicated, and time consuming. It is important to employ an attorney to help with the appeal and that can be expensive.

In Chapter 10 we presented many different options that are legally available to the Applicant at this time. The goal is to get the Applicant qualified for Medi-Cal as quickly as possible, and with the least amount of hassle. It is better to choose a strategy that has been allowed in the past, rather than chance a denial of the application and be forced to appeal the decision.

An experienced Elder Law attorney can explain what strategies have been allowed in the past in your county and which strategies are likely to be challenged. The key word is "experienced." Before employing an attorney, determine what percentage of his practice is devoted to Medicaid eligibility; how long he has practiced Elder Law in that county; and whether he is familiar with the appeal process, should the need arise.

Guiding Those You Love 12

Once you are satisfied with your Estate Plan, then the final thing to consider is whether your heirs will be able to locate your assets after you're gone.

Most people have their business records in one place, their Will in another place, car titles and deeds in still another place. When someone dies, their beneficiaries may feel as if they are playing a game of "hide and seek" with the decedent. The game might be fun were it not for the fact that unlocated items may be forever lost. For example, suppose you die in an accident and no one knows you are insured by your credit card company for accidental death in the amount of $25,000. The only one to profit is the insurance company, which is just that much richer because no one told them that you died as a result of an accident.

And how about a key to a safe deposit box? Will anyone find it? Even if they find the key, how will they locate the box?

It is not difficult to arrange things so that your affairs are always in order. It amounts to being aware of what you own (and owe) and keeping a record of your possessions. A side benefit is that by doing so, you will always know where all your business records are. If you ever spent time trying to collect information to file your taxes or trying to find a lost stock or bond certificate, you will appreciate the value of organizing your records.

Heirs need all the help they can get. It is difficult enough dealing with the loss, without the frustration of trying to locate important documents. Your heirs will have no problem locating your assets if you keep all of your records in a single place. It can be a desk drawer or a file cabinet or even a file storage box that you purchase from the stationary store.

If you do not feel like doing a complete job of organizing your records at this time, consider an abridged version. You can set up a single folder and place all of your important papers in that folder. You need to make the folder easily accessible to whomever you wish to manage your affairs in the event of your incapacity or death. You can do this by letting that person know of the existence of the folder and how to get it in an emergency.

You can keep the folder in an easily accessed place in your home with the folder identified as containing important papers. We labeled it "THE QUICK-FIND FOLDER" because the folder gives you and your family easy access to important information and/or documents. But you can create your own heading such as: "MY IMPORTANT PAPERS" or if you want a particular person to access the folder, you might label it: "RECORDS FOR MY SON, ROBERT"

It is helpful if you include a list of all you own and the location of each item in that folder.

We discussed people's natural disinclination to make an Estate Plan until they are faced with their own mortality. Many believe that they will make just one Will and then die (maybe that's why they put off making a Will). The reality is, most people who make a Will, change it at least once before they die. If you have an Estate Plan, it is important to update it when any of the following events take place:

✍ CHANGE IN MARITAL STATUS
GETTING MARRIED

Unless you enter a marriage with no property and no children, it is fool-hardy to marry without signing a Premarital Agreement. The example given in the stepchild section of Chapter 7 shows how the lack of planning on the part of a parent who remarries can be to the detriment of his children. A Premarital Agreement could have provided for a fair distribution of his property.

The same applies to a couple entering a Registered Domestic Partner relationship. In California, all of the laws relating to Community Property apply to Registered Domestic Partners. It is important to have a Prepartnership Agreement to define your rights and responsibilities to your partner during the union, as well as your rights in the event of dissolution or death of one your partner.

Hopefully, your union will prosper and you along with it. You should review your Agreement on a regular basis as your finances change or as you have children. With the consent of your Spouse/RDP, you can amend your Premarital Agreement.

Changes to the Premarital or Prepartnership Agreement need to be prepared and signed in the same manner as your original agreement.If your Agreement needs a complete revision, you can revoke and replace it with a Marital or Domestic Partnership Agreement. To be legally enforceable the Agreement should be fair. There should be full disclosure by both parties as to the extent of their wealth. Each party should be represented by his own attorney (Fam. 1615).

ENDING A RELATIONSHIP

In California, a judgment for the dissolution of a marriage or even for a legal separation will contain a statement notifying the parties that a dissolution or an annulment of the marriage may automatically cancel rights each has the other's Will, Trust, retirement benefit plan, Power of Attorney, Transfer on Death vehicle registration, and survivorship rights to property owned in joint tenancy. The notice cautions the parties that the dissolution will not remove a former spouse as beneficiary of a life insurance policy so if they want to change the beneficiary, they need to do that themselves (Fam. 2024).

A Registered Domestic Partner relationship is terminated by order of Court or by filing a Notice of Termination of Domestic Partnership with the Secretary of State. As with a married couple any provision in the Will or Trust relating to the former Domestic Partner is revoked. Should a former Domestic Partner die before changing his Will, any provision for the former partner will be read as if the former partner died first (Prob. 6122, 6122.1).

The changes described in the notice contained in the final judgment apply to the termination of a Registered Domestic Partner relation as well as to a married person.

Although a legal separation contains the same notice as a divorce decree, the legal changes described, do not apply unless the parties later divorce or terminate their partnership. Regardless of whether you divorce, or separate, you need to change all of your legal documents. This includes credit accounts, and credit reports giving your marital status.

In addition to changing your legal documents, you need notify anyone who might rely on these documents of the change. The law does not protect you if a transfer is made by someone who has not been notified of the change in of relationship. For example, suppose you gave your Spouse/RDP a Power of Attorney and (s)he used the document after the divorce to sell your securities. You could sue your former Spouse/RDP for doing so, but not your broker, unless you gave written notice to the broker that you revoked the Power of Attorney.

NOTIFY EMPLOYER OF CHANGE
If you change your marital/partnership status, you need to tell your employer of the change so that the employer can change your status for purposes of paycheck tax deductions. If you have a health insurance plan or a pension plan, that provides benefits to your Spouse/RDP, these need to be changed as well.

California law allows up to $5,000 in wages to be transferred to your surviving Spouse/RDP without the need for Probate (Prob. 13600). If you change your partnership status, you need to inform your employer, in writing, of the change, and ask him to make that information part of your personnel file.

✍ A CHANGE IN RELATIONSHIP

Getting married, separated or divorced; having a child; having a beneficiary of your Estate die, are all profound changes in one's life. When the dust settles, it is important to examine your Estate Plan to see if it needs revision. If you have a Trust, you can change it by having your attorney prepare an amendment to the Trust. If you have a Will, your attorney can prepare a *codicil* (a supplement) to the Will.

It is important to have changes made by a properly drafted and signed document. If you make changes by crossing things out or writing over your Will, or Trust, the validity of the document can be challenged once you die. If you simply rip up the old Will, that will effectively revoke the Will (Prob. 6121). But it could happen that someone (perhaps your attorney) has a copy of the Will. If no one knows that you revoked the Will, they may think the Will is lost and then offer the copy of the Will for Probate. If you draft a new Will, the first paragraph should say, "I revoke all prior Wills ..." This makes it clear that you want the new Will to replace all other Wills.

 NEW CHILD CAN
CHALLENGE OLD WILL

A child born or adopted after you prepared your Will is entitled to receive as much as any of your other children provided for in your Will. If you have no other child, the *after-born* child is entitled to as much as he would have received had you died without a Will.

The Court will determine how much the after-born child is to receive, but in general, each beneficiary of your Will, will contribute a proportionate share to the after-born child, unless:

⇨ your Will indicates that the omission was intentional; i.e., that you wanted to omit any after-born child - or -

⇨ you had one or more other children when the child was born, and you left all of your Estate to the other parent of the after-born child - or -

⇨ you made other provisions for your after-born child outside the Will (i.e., insurance POD accounts, joint property, etc.) (Prob. 21620, 21621).

The laws relating to an after-born child are complex; and could lead to disagreement and hard feelings for those forced to contribute to the child's share. It is better to change your Will when a child is born so that your child receives no more and no less than you intended.

✍ BENEFICIARY MOVES OR DIES

Most people remember to name an alternate beneficiary should one of their beneficiaries die. But how many of us remember to notify the pension plan or insurance company when a beneficiary moves?

It is important that your beneficiary's address be available to those in charge of distributing funds upon your death. Many life insurance proceeds are never paid because the company cannot locate the beneficiary. The Actuarial Office of the Federal Employees' Group Life Insurance Program reported that as of September, 2003, they had over 55.8 million dollars in unpaid benefits, mostly because they could not locate the beneficiary at the last given address.

✍ RELOCATION TO A NEW STATE OR COUNTRY

There is no need to change your Estate Plan for a move within the state of California. There is much to check out if you are moving to another state. If you are moving out of state, you need to take the Will with you. If your attorney has your original Will or any other original of your Estate Planning documents, then unless you plan to continue to employ him, you need to retrieve these items to take with you to the new state.

HOLOGRAPHIC WILL MAY NOT BE ACCEPTED

You need to determine whether your Will conforms to the laws of the state of your new residence. A Will that is signed and witnessed according the laws of the state, is generally accepted into Probate regardless of where it is drafted. However, many states will not accept an unwitnessed Holographic Will into Probate. If you have a Holographic Will, it is best to draft a new Will that conforms to the laws of the state of your new residence.

If you are married, you need to determine whether your Will conforms to the laws of the state of your new residence. Most states will honor a Will drafted according to California law, however, the rights of a spouse vary considerably state to state. If you are married and have not provided the minimum amount as required by the laws of the new state, should you die before your spouse, your Will may be challenged on that basis. The same applies to a Trust. Many states allow a surviving spouse to demand funds from the Trust of the decedent spouse, if the deceased spouse did not provide the minimum amount to his spouse as required by the laws of that state.

If you do not have a Will, it is important to check out the Laws of Intestate Succession for that state. In some states they are referred to as the *Laws of Descent and Distribution*. Each state has its own laws of inheritance of property and those laws are very different from each other. Who has the right to inherit your property in the state of California may be different from who can inherit your property in another state. If you do not have a Will, this is the time to think about who will inherit your property should you die in the state of your new residence.

This is especially important for those who are married. The right of a spouse to inherit property varies significantly from state to state. Even if you move to another Community Property state (Arizona, Idaho, Louisiana, Nevada, New Mexico, Texas, Washington or Wisconsin) the rights of a spouse may differ significantly from those of a spouse in California.

MAKE PROVISION FOR DOMESTIC PARTNER

You need to keep in mind that a Domestic Partnership that is registered in California is not recognized in most other states. Even those states that allow legal rights for Domestic Partners may have rules different from the laws of California. For example, Arizona statute 36-843 allows a Domestic Partner to make an anatomical gift on behalf of the deceased partner, provided no one else has assumed financial responsibility for the decedent. In New Jersey, a Domestic Partner relationship is established by a couple who obtain a *Certificate of Domestic Partnership* from the New Jersey State Registrar. New Jersey will recognize a Domestic Partnership that is valid in another state, however, Domestic Partners have only those rights and responsibilities as allowed under New Jersey law. See *Guiding Those Left Behind In New Jersey* by AMELIA E. POHL.

In all states, you can make provision for your Domestic Partner in a Will or Trust. You also give your Domestic Partner authority to make your medical decisions and handle your finances in the event of your incapacity.

TAX CONSIDERATIONS

You need to check out the taxes of the new state. Each state has its own tax structure. Some states have an inheritance tax, or a transfer tax on all inherited property. If Estate or Inheritance Taxes are high, you may need to set up an Estate Plan that will minimize the impact of those taxes.

CREDITOR PROTECTION

Creditor protection is another item that is significantly different state to state. If you have much debt, determine what items can be inherited by your family free of your debts.

OTHER ESTATE PLANNING DOCUMENTS

Many states have laws directing physicians to honor a Health Care Directive that is properly drafted in another state. Other states will not recognize a Medical Directive unless it is drafted according to the laws of that state. But even if the laws of the state honor your California Advance Health Care Directive, consider drafting another in the new state. Medical Directives vary significantly state to state. Other states may have laws that enable you to appoint someone with powers similar to a Health Care Agent, but the laws of the state may refer to such person as a *Patient Advocate* or a *Health Care Surrogate* or a *Health Care Representative*.

It is best to sign a new Health Care Directive using the form and terminology recognized in the new state, rather than chance any confusion should you become ill and find yourself in an emergency situation.

Similarly, if you have appointed someone to handle your finances under a Power of Attorney, you may want to have another prepared in conformity with the laws of the new state, so there will be no question of the right of your Attorney-In-Fact to conduct business on your behalf.

RELOCATING THE MEDI-CAL BENEFICIARY

If your family member is a Medi-Cal Beneficiary, and you want to move him to another state, you need to check out whether he will continue to be eligible for Medicaid in that state. As explained in Chapter 10, Medicaid is both a state and federal program. Once a person qualifies for Medicaid in one state, he can be transferred to another state; provided he qualifies under that state's Medical Assistance Program.

For example, California does not have an upper limit for income, provided the Applicant's medical expenses are greater than the level of his non-exempt income. Other states have an *income cap*. Applicants whose income exceed that limit can be refused Medicaid benefits. If you plan to move a Medicaid Recipient to another state, it is important to first check with an Elder Law attorney in that state. He can explain the laws relating to Medicaid eligibility. As in California, there are Medicaid qualifying techniques available under the laws of the state. For example, if the state has an income cap and your family member's income exceeds that value, an Elder Law attorney will be able to tell you what can be done in order to have the Recipient qualify for Medicaid in that state.

As you can see, state law has an important impact on your Estate Plan. When moving to another state, you need to educate yourself about the laws of that state, or consult with an attorney who can assist you in reviewing your Estate Plan to see if that plan will accomplish your goals in that state.

✍ A SIGNIFICANT CHANGE IN THE LAW

We pay our legislators (state and federal) to make laws and, if necessary, change those in effect. We pay judges to interpret the law and that interpretation may change the way the law operates. The legislature and the judiciary do their job and so laws change frequently. Tax laws are particularly volatile. The 2001 change in the federal Estate Tax law gradually increases the Exclusion amount so that by 2010 no federal Estate Tax will be due regardless of the value of your Estate. You may be thinking that there is no need for an Estate Tax plan because you don't intend to die prior to 2010. But any certainty relating to death and taxes is false security (especially taxes, in this case). As explained in Chapter 3, the law as passed in 2001, is effective only until December 31, 2010. If lawmakers do nothing, then on January 1, 2011, the federal Estate Tax goes back into effect; and Estates that exceed one million dollars will once again be subject to federal Estate Taxes.

And that is not the only uncertainty. Each state has its own Estate Tax structure. It remains to be seen how each state will react to the position taken by the federal government in 2010. If federal Estate Taxes are phased out altogether, some states may follow the lead of the federal government and dispense with Estate Taxes. However, with states struggling to balance the budget, more likely they will see this as an opportunity to increase their Estate Taxes, so Estate Taxes that would have been paid to the federal government will be paid to the state.

You need to keep up with the news to learn about changes in the law that affect your Estate Plan. It is a good idea to check with your attorney on a regular basis to see if any change in the state or federal law affects your current Estate plan. And also check out the Eagle Publishing Company Web site for changes we will post to keep this book fresh.   http://www.eaglepublishing.com

SPRING CLEAN YOUR RECORDS

Used to be, that housewives did a once a year, floor to ceiling, "spring housecleaning." We know of no survey telling whether today's houseperson conducts an annual purge of dirt and clutter. We suspect it went by the wayside when housewives entered the work force as full time employees. But it was a good practice. In many cases, it was the only time of the year when the house was truly clean and tidy. It is a good idea to apply that old-fashioned housecleaning practice to your financial records and clean them up on a regular basis. There is no need to keep the deed to real property that you have long since sold; a lease agreement to an apartment you no longer rent; a credit card to a closed account, etc.

Many hesitate to toss out some scrap of paper for fear it will not be available for future reference. There are documents you may need to keep for a lengthy period of time to establish a basis for tax purposes. You can avoid the problem of keeping too much, or not enough, by taking your box (or folder) of records with you the next time you visit with your accountant or attorney. You can ask your advisor to help you organize your records and assist with your "housecleaning."

Keys are another item to keep up to date. You may have a sentimental reason to keep old keys, but there is no business reason to keep a key to a car you no longer own, a safe deposit box you no longer lease, etc. Keeping such keys can only cause confusion should you become disabled or die. Whoever takes possession of your property will be left with mysterious keys. He will probably think the keys are protecting something of value.

Unless you enjoy picturing an heir's frustration as he seeks an imaginary treasure, pitch the key.

Glossary

ABSTRACT OF TITLE An *Abstract of Title* is a condensed history of the title to the land. It consists of a summary of recorded documents that affect the land, including mortgages.

ACTUARIAL TABLE An *actuarial table* is a table organized according to statistical data that indicates the life expectancy of a person.

ADDENDUM An *addendum* to a contract is an addition to the contract.

ADMINISTRATION The *administration* of a Probate Estate is the management and settlement of the decedent's affairs. There are different types of administration. See ANCILLARY ADMINISTRATION.

ADMINISTRATIVE LAW JUDGE An *Administrative Law Judge* is someone who is appointed to conduct an administrative hearing. He has the power to administer oaths, take testimony, and then decide the facts of the case. Although he can decide the facts of the case, the final outcome of the hearing is decided by the government agency that appointed the Administrative Law Judge.

ADMINISTRATIVE CODE OF REGULATIONS The *Administrative Code of Regulations* are the set of rules used by governmental agencies to apply laws enacted by the legislature. The Administrative Code of Regulations interprets the law and describes the agency's requirements to implement that law. See *CFR*.

ADVANCE HEALTH CARE DIRECTIVE An *Advance Health Care Directive* is a document that gives directions about the type of health care the person signing the document (the Principal) wants in the event he is too ill to speak for himself. The California statutory form of an Advance Health Care Directive (Prob. 4701) contains a Medical Power of Attorney that can be used to appoint an Agent to make health care decisions for the Principal should he be unable to do so himself.

AFFIANT   An *Affiant* is someone who signs an affidavit and swears or acknowledges that it is true in the presence of a notary public or other person with authority to administer an oath or take acknowledgments.

AFFIDAVIT An *Affidavit* is a written statement of fact made by someone voluntarily, under oath, or acknowledged as being true, in the presence of a notary public or someone else who has authority to administer an oath or take acknowledgments.

AGENT   An *Agent* is someone who is authorized by another (the principal) to act for or in place of the principal.

AGENCY ACCOUNT An *Agency account* is a bank account in which the owner of the funds in the account authorizes another to make bank transactions as his Agent under a Power of Attorney.

AMENDMENT   An *amendment* to a Trust is an addition to the Trust that changes the provisions of the Trust.

ANATOMICAL GIFT An *anatomical gift* is the donation of all or part of the body of the decedent for a specified purpose, such as transplantation or research.

ANCILLARY ADMINISTRATION An *Ancillary Administration* is a Probate procedure that aids or assists the original (primary) Probate proceeding. Ancillary administration is conducted to determine the beneficiary of the decedent's property located within that state, and to determine whether the property is taxable in that state.

ANNOTATED STATUTE A statute that is *annotated* is a statement of the law followed by cases which illustrate or explain the statute.

ANNUAL GIFT TAX EXCLUSION The *Annual Gift Tax Exclusion* is the amount a person can gift to another each year without being required to file a federal Gift Tax Return. The Annual Gift Tax Exclusion is $12,000 for the year 2006.

ANNUITANT An *Annuitant* is someone who is entitled to receive payments under an annuity contract.

ANNUITY CONTRACT An *annuity contract* is a contract that gives someone (the annuitant) the right to receive periodic payments (monthly, quarterly) for the life of the annuitant or for a given number of years.

ASSET An *asset* is anything owned by someone that has a value, including personal property (jewelry, paintings, securities, cash, motor vehicles, etc.) and real property (condominiums, vacant lots, acreage, residences, etc.).

ASSIGN To *assign* is to transfer one's rights in or to something to another. For example, a person who has the right to receive income from a partnership may assign that right to another person.

ATTORNEY or ATTORNEY AT LAW An *attorney*, also known as an *Attorney at law*, or a *lawyer*, is someone who is licensed by the state to practice law in that state.

ATTORNEY-IN-FACT An *Attorney-In-Fact* is someone appointed to act as an Agent for another (the Principal) under a Power of Attorney.

BASIS The *basis* is a value that is assigned to an asset for the purpose of determining the gain (or loss) on the sale of the item or in determining the value of the item in the hands of someone who has received it as a gift.

BENEFICIARY A *beneficiary* is one who benefits from the act of another or from the transfer of property. In this book we refer to a beneficiary as someone named in a Will, Trust, or deed to receive property, or someone who inherits property under the Laws of Intestate Succession.

BENEFICIARY ACCOUNT A *beneficiary account* is a bank account with a named beneficiary. The owner of the funds in the account directs the bank to give the funds remaining in the account to the named beneficiary upon the death of all of the owners of the bank account. *Pay On Death* and *In Trust For* accounts are beneficiary accounts.

BONA FIDE A *bona fide* act is something that is done in good faith; honestly, openly and without deceit or fraud.

BUS. & PROF. *Bus. & Prof.* is the abbreviation for the California *Business and Professional Code.*

CAPITAL GAINS TAX A *Capital Gains Tax* is a tax on the amount the net sales proceeds exceeds the basis of a capital asset sold by a taxpayer.

CASH SURRENDER VALUE The ***Cash Surrender Value*** of a life insurance policy is the amount of money the insurance company will pay to the owner of an insurance policy in the event the owner cancels the policy before the death of the person who is insured under the policy.

CCR   The ***California Code of Regulations ("CCR")*** is the set of regulations used to implement California law.

CFR   The ***Code of Federal Regulations ("CFR")*** is the annual cumulation of regulations set by federal executive agencies combined with previous regulations that are still in effect. The CFR contains the general body of laws that govern the practices and procedures of federal administrative agencies.

CHARITABLE REMAINDER ANNUITY TRUST A ***Charitable Remainder Annuity Trust*** is a Trust that pays an annuity to a beneficiary (the *Annuitant*) for a certain period of time or until his death. Once the annuity is paid, whatever remains in the Trust is donated to a tax exempt charity.

CIV. ***Civ.*** is the abbreviation for the California *Civil Code*.

CIV. PROC. ***Civ. Proc.*** is the abbreviation for the California *Code of Civil Procedure*.

CLAIM A ***claim*** against the decedent's Estate is a demand for payment. To be effective, the claim must be filed with the Probate court within the time limits set by law.

CLOSE CORPORATION A ***Close Corporation*** is a corporation whose voting shares are held by a single shareholder or a small, closely-knit, group of shareholders.

CODE A *Code* is a body of laws arranged systematically for easy reference, e.g., the Internal Revenue Code.

CODICIL A *codicil* to a Will is an addition to the Will that changes or replaces certain parts of the Will.

COLUMBARIUM A *columbarium* is a vault with niches (spaces) for urns that contain the ashes of cremated bodies.

COMMON LAW MARRIAGE A *Common Law marriage* is one that is entered into without a state marriage license or any kind of official marriage ceremony. A Common Law marriage is created by an agreement to marry, followed by the two living together, and telling everyone they know that they are husband and wife. California does not recognize a Common Law marriage unless it was entered into in another state that considers the union to be a valid marriage.

COMMUNITY PROPERTY Certain states (Arizona, California, Idaho, Louisiana, Nevada, New Mexico, Texas, Washington, and Wisconsin) have laws stating that property acquired by husband or wife, or both, during their marriage is *Community Property* and is owned equally by both of them.

COMMUNITY PROPERTY ACCOUNT A *Community Property Account* is an account owned by a married couple or Registered Domestic Partners. Should one die, half of the account becomes the property of the surviving Spouse/RDP. The other half is distributed according the decedent's Will or Trust — or if neither of these, according to the Laws of Intestate Succession.

COMMUNITY PROPERTY WITH RIGHT OF SURVIVORSHIP

Community Property With Right of Survivorship is a method of ownership created by the California legislature that enables a married couple or Registered Domestic Partners to own property with the right of the Spouse/RDP to inherit the property without going through a Probate procedure, and yet preserving the Community status of the property. For married couples, federal law enables the surviving spouse to take a step-up in basis of the entire value of the property.

CONFLICT OF INTEREST A *conflict of interest* is a conflict between the official duties of a fiduciary (guardian, Trustee, attorney, etc.) and his own private interest. For example, it is a conflict of interest for a Successor Trustee to use Trust property for his own personal profit.

CONSERVATOR A *Conservator* is someone appointed by the Probate Court to care for the person or property of a disabled adult. A Conservator can also be appointed to care for the property of a missing person.

CORPORATION A *Corporation* is a company created by one or more persons according to the laws of the state. The company is owned by the *shareholders* or *stockholders*. Each owner has limited liability (see Limited Liability).

COURT The *Court* as used in this book is the Court that handles Probate matters. In California, the Probate Court is a department of the Superior Court (Prob. 7050). When referring to an order made by the Court, the term is synonymous with "judge," i.e., an "order of the Court" is an order made by the judge of the Court.

CREDITOR A *creditor* is someone to whom a debt is owed by another person (the *debtor*).

CUSTODIAN   A *Custodian* under the ***California Uniform Tranfers to Minors Act*** is a financial institution or person who accepts responsibility for the care and management of property given to a minor child pursuant to the Act.

DAMAGES   *Damages* is money that is awarded by a Court as compensation to someone who has been injured by the action of another.

DEBTOR A *debtor* is someone who owes payment of money or services to another person (the *creditor*).

DECEDENT The *decedent* is the person who died.

DECLARANT   The *Declarant* is the person who signs an ***Advance Directive For Health Care*** in accordance with California law.

DESCENDANT A *descendant* is someone who descends from a common ancestor. There are two kinds of descendants: a *lineal descendant* and a *collateral descendant*. The lineal descendant is one who descends in a straight line such as father to son. The collateral descendant is one who descends in a parallel line, such as a cousin. In this book, unless otherwise stated, the term *descendant* refers to a *lineal descendant*.

DISTRIBUTION The *distribution* of a Trust or Probate Estate is the giving to the beneficiary that part of the Estate to which the beneficiary is entitled.

DHR   The ***Department of Health Services ("DHR")*** is the state agency that administers the Medi-Cal program.

DISSENT A *dissent* is a refusal to agree with something stated or ruled upon. A dissent by a judge sitting on the Supreme Court is often in the form of a written opinion that opposes a ruling made by the Court. The dissent does not change the ruling of the Court.

DOMESTIC PARTNER See REGISTERED DOMESTIC PARTNER

DOWER *Dower* is the right of a wife, upon the death of her husband, to a Life Estate in one-third of all real property that he owned during their marriage. This English Common Law has been abolished in most states, including California.

DURABLE As used in the Power of Attorney, the word *durable* means that the Power of Attorney will remain in effect in the event that the principal (the person giving the Power of Attorney) becomes incapacitated.

DURESS *Duress* is the use of force or threats to get someone to do something.

ELECTIVE SHARE The *Elective Share* is the minimum amount of the decedent's Estate that a surviving spouse is entitled to receive under law. In California that amount is one third of the decedent's *Augmented Estate*.

ENTITLEMENT An *entitlement* is a legal right to receive a benefit of income, property or services.

EQUITY The *equity* in a home is the market value of the home less monies owed on the property (mortgages, tax liens, etc.).

EQUITABLE ADOPTION An *Equitable adoption* occurs when a Court determines that a parent-child relationship existed even though there was no legal adoption. The ruling is for the benefit of the child in determining the right of the child to inherit under the Laws of Intestate Succession.

EQUITY INTEREST An *equity interest* is an ownership interest. It is the value of the ownership interest over and above monies owed on the property.

ESTATE A person's *Estate* is all of the property (both real and personal property) owned by that person. The decedent's Estate may also be referred to as his *Taxable Estate* because all of the decedent's assets must be included when determining whether Estate Taxes are due. Compare to PROBATE ESTATE.

EXECUTOR An *Executor* (feminine *Executrix*) is a legal term found in many Wills. The term refers to the person named by the Will maker to carry out directions given in the Will. In modern Wills, that person is referred to as the *Personal Representative*.

FACE VALUE The *face value* of a life insurance policy is the value stated on the insurance certificate or policy. It is the amount to be paid upon the death of the insured person.

FAIR HEARING A *Fair Hearing* is an administrative procedure. In California, it is conducted by the Department of Social Services. It is the first step in the appeals process for someone who has been denied Medi-Cal benefits.

FAM *Fam.* is the abbreviation for the California *Family Code*.

FIDUCIARY A *Fiduciary* is one who takes on the duty of holding property in Trust for another or acting for the benefit of another, such as a Personal Representative, Trustee, Guardian etc.. A fiduciary relationship is also one that is developed out of trust and confidence. For example, an attorney has a fiduciary relationship with his client.

FORECLOSURE *Foreclosure* is a court proceeding in which a creditor either takes title to, or forces the sale of, property owned by the borrower, in order to satisfy the debt.

GOV'T *Gov't* is the abbreviation for the California *Government Code*.

GRANT DEED A *Grant deed* is a deed in which someone (the *Grantor*) transfers the property to another (the *Grantee*) and guarantees good title, i.e., the Grantor guarantees that he has the right to transfer the property, and that no one else has any right to the property.

GRANTEE The *Grantee* of a deed is the person who receives title to real property from the *Grantor*.

GRANTOR A *Grantor* is someone who transfers property. The Grantor of a deed, is the person who transfers real property to a new owner (the *Grantee*). The Grantor of a Trust is someone who creates the Trust and then transfers property into the Trust. Also see SETTLOR.

GUARANTOR A *Guarantor* is someone who promises to pay a debt or perform a contract for another in the event that person does not fulfill his obligation.

GUARDIAN A *Guardian* is someone who has legal authority to care for the person or property of a minor or for someone who has been found by the court to be incapacitated.

HEALTH CARE AGENT A *Health Care Agent* is someone who is appointed by another (the *Principal*) to authorize medical treatment for the Principal, in the event the Principal is to too ill to do so himself.

HEALTH CARE POWER OF ATTORNEY A *Health Care Power of Attorney* is a document in which someone (the *Principal*) gives another (his *Health Care Agent*) authority to make medical decisions on behalf of the Principal.

HEALTH & SAFETY *Health & Safety* is the abbreviation for the California *Health and Safety Code.*

HEIR An *Heir* is anyone entitled to inherit the decedent's property under the Laws of Intestate Succession in the event that the decedent dies without a valid Will.

HOLOGRAPHIC WILL A *Holographic Will* is a Will written, dated and signed by the hand of the Will maker himself. Many states refuse to admit a Holographic Will into Probate unless it is witnessed according to the laws of the state.

HOMESTEAD The *homestead* is the dwelling that is owned, and occupied, in the state of California, as the owner's principal residence.

INCAPACITATED The term *incapacitated* is used in two ways. A person is *physically incapacitated* if he lacks the ability to perform certain tasks. A person is *legally incapacitated* if a Court finds that he is unable to care for his person or property.

INTER VIVOS TRUST An *Inter Vivos Trust* (also known as a *Living Trust*) is a Trust that is created and becomes effective during the lifetime of the Grantor (or Settlor) as opposed to a Trust that he includes as part of his Will to take effect upon his death.

INTESTATE *Intestate* means not having a Will or dying without a Will. *Testate* is to have a Will or dying with a Will.

IRA ACCOUNT An **Individual Retirement Account ("IRA")** is a retirement savings account created in conformity with the federal Internal Revenue Code. Income taxes on certain deposits and interest to the account are deferred until the monies are withdrawn.

IRREVOCABLE CONTRACT An **irrevocable contract** is a contract that cannot be revoked, withdrawn, or cancelled by any of the parties to that contract.

IRREVOCABLE TRUST An **Irrevocable Trust** is a Trust that cannot be changed, cancelled or terminated until its purpose is accomplished.

IRREVOCABLE INSURANCE TRUST   An **Irrevocable Insurance Trust** is a Trust that is set up to purchase life insurance. The proceeds of the life insurance policy can be used to pay taxes that may be due upon the death of the insured person.

ISSUE The decedent's **issue** are his descendants, children, grandchildren, great-grandchildren, etc.
See DESCENDANT.

IRA ACCOUNT An **Individual Retirement Account ("IRA")** is a retirement savings account in which income taxes on certain deposits and interest to the account are deferred until the monies are withdrawn from the account.

JOINT AND SEVERAL LIABILITY   If two or more people agree to be **jointly and severally liable** to pay a debt, then each individually agrees to be responsible to pay the debt, and together they all agree to pay for the debt.

JOINT TENANCY   In California, a *Joint Tenancy* means that each tenant owns an equal share of the property with right of survivorship; i.e., should one Joint Tenant die the surviving tenants own the property.

KEOGH PLAN   A *Keogh Plan* is a retirement plan available to self-employed taxpayers. Certain tax benefits are available such as tax deductions for annual contributions to the plan. The plan is named for its author, Eugene James Keogh.

KEY MAN INSURANCE *Key man insurance* is a disability and life insurance policy designed to protect a company from economic loss in the event that an important employee of the company becomes disabled or dies.

LAWS OF INTESTATE SUCCESSION The *Laws of Intestate Succession* are the laws of the state that determine who is to inherit the decedent's Probate Estate if the decedent died without a valid Will.

LEGALESE *Legalese* refers to the use of legal terms and confusing text used by some attorneys when drafting legal documents.

LETTERS *Letters* is a document, issued by the Probate court, giving the Personal Representative authority to take possession of and to administer the Estate of the decedent.

LIEN   A *lien* is a charge against a person's property as security for a debt. The lien is evidence of the creditor's right to take the property as full or partial payment, in the event that the debtor defaults in paying the monies owed.

LIFE ESTATE A *Life Estate* interest in real property is the right to possess and receive the income from that property for so long as the holder of the Life Estate lives. A one-third Life Estate interest means the person can occupy one-third of the property or receive one-third of the income generated by that property.

LIMITED LIABILITY *Limited Liability,* as related to a corporation or other company created according to state law, means that a shareholder of the company generally is not responsible to pay the debts of the company beyond the amount that he/she invested in the company.

LIMITED LIABILITY COMPANY A *Limited Liability Company* is a company created according to the laws of the state. In California, it can be formed to engage in any lawful business activity, except banking and insurance business (Corp. 17002, 17050). All of the members of the company have limited liability.

LIMITED PARTNERSHIP A *Limited Partnership* is a partnership created according to the laws of the state. Each *Limited Partner* has limited liability. Each *General Partner* has control of the business and is personally liable for all of the debts of the company. (See Limited Liability).

LINEAL DESCENDANT See *descendant.*

LITIGATION *Litigation* is the process of carrying on a lawsuit, i.e., to sue for some right or remedy in a court of law. A Litigation Attorney is one who is experienced in conducting the law suit and in particular, going to trial.

LIVING WILL A *Living Will* is a Health Care Directive, that gives instructions to the physician about whether life support systems should be withheld or withdrawn in the event that the person who signs the Living Will is terminally ill or in a persistent vegetative state and unable to speak for himself. In California, this type of directive is called END-OF-LIFE DECISIONS as included in Part 2 of the statutory Advance Health Care Directive.

LOOK-BACK PERIOD The *Look-back Period* is a period of consecutive months that can be reviewed for transfers of Resources to determine whether a period of ineligibility should be imposed for the Medicaid Applicant.

MARITAL AGREEMENT A *Marital Agreement* is an Agreement made by a couple after marriage to decide their respective rights and responsibilities in case of a divorce or the death of a spouse.

MEDICAID *Medicaid* is a medical assistance program sponsored jointly by the federal and state government to provide health care for people with low income and limited resources. In California, the program is called *Medi-Cal.*

NET PROCEEDS The *net proceeds* of a sale is the sale price less costs and expenses paid to make the sale.

NET WORTH A person's *net worth* is the fair market value of all of the property that he owns less the sum of his liabilities, i.e. what he owes.

NEXT OF KIN *Next of kin* has two meanings in law: *next of kin* refers to a person's nearest blood relation or it can refer to those people (not necessarily blood relations) who are entitled to inherit the property of a person under the Laws of Intestate Succession.

NON-PROBATE TRANSFER A *non-Probate Transfer* is a transfer made to a beneficiary of the decedent without going through a Probate procedure. This includes transfers from a joint account, a Trust, a Pay On Death account, a Transfer On Death security, etc.

PARTNERSHIP A business *partnership* is an agreement between two or more persons to use their assets, expertise and/or labor to carry on a business for profit as co-owners.

PERJURY *Perjury* is lying under oath. The false statement can be made as a witness in court or by signing an Affidavit. Perjury is a criminal offense.

PERSONAL EFFECTS *Personal effects* is personal property that is kept for one's personal use such as clothing, jewelry, books, and other items generally found in the home.

PERSONAL PROPERTY *Personal property* is all property owned by a person that is not real property (real estate). It includes personal effects, cars, securities, bank accounts, insurance policies, etc.

PERSONAL REPRESENTATIVE The *Personal Representative* is someone appointed by the Probate Court to settle the decedent's Estate and to distribute whatever is left to the proper beneficiary.

PER STIRPES *Per Stirpes* is a method of distributing property to a group of beneficiaries in the event that one of them dies before the gift is made. The deceased person's share goes to his descendants. If he has no descendants, the surviving beneficiaries share equally in the gift.

PETITION A *Petition* is a formal written, request to a Court asking the Court to take action or issue an order on a given matter; e.g. a request to appoint a Guardian.

POWER OF ATTORNEY A *Power of Attorney* is a document in which someone (the *Principal*) gives another person (his *Agent* or *Attorney-In-Fact*) authority to do certain things on behalf of the Principal.

PRECEDENT A *Precedent* is a previously decided case which is recognized as an authority for future cases that have the same or similar set of facts.

PREMARITAL AGREEMENT A *Premarital Agreement* (also known as a *Prenuptial Agreement*) is an Agreement made prior marriage to take effect once a couple marry. The Agreement states how the couple's property is to be managed during the marriage and how their property is to be divided should either die, or they later divorce.

PRINCIPAL OF A POWER OF ATTORNEY The *Principal* of a Power of Attorney is someone who gives another (his *Agent*) authority to act on his (the Principal's) behalf.

PRINCIPAL OF A TRUST The *Principal of a Trust* is the Trust property. The Trust income is the money that is earned on the Trust Principal.

PROB. *Prob.* is the abbreviation for the California *Probate Code*.

PROBABLE CAUSE *Probable cause* exists if it is reasonable to believe certain facts. Mere suspicion is not enough. For probable cause to exist, there must be more evidence for the facts than against.

PROBATE ***Probate*** is a procedure in which a Court determines whether the decedent left a valid Will. The Court will appoint someone, a *Personal Representative* to settle the decedent's Estate by paying valid claims and expenses, and distributing whatever remains to the proper beneficiary.

PROBATE ESTATE The ***Probate Estate*** is that part of the decedent's Estate that is subject to a Probate procedure. It includes property that the decedent owned in his name only, or as a Tenant In Common. It does not include property owned jointly. It does not include property held in trust for someone.

PRO BONO The term ***Pro Bono*** means "for the public good." When an attorney works Pro Bono, he does so voluntarily and without pay.

REAL PROPERTY ***Real property***, also known as ***real estate,*** is land and anything permanently attached to the land such as buildings and fences.

REGISTERED DOMESTIC PARTNER A ***Registered Domestic Partner*** is a relationship established by the California legislature. California statute gives a same gender couples, each 18 or older, the right to become Registered Domestic Partners by filling out a *Declaration of Domestic Partner* with the California Secretary of State. The law allows a heterosexual couple, each over the age of 62 to become Domestic Partners. Registered Domestic Partners have all of the rights and responsibilities under California Law as does a married couple.

REMAINDER INTEREST A ***Remainder Interest*** in real property is the property that passes to a beneficiary at the end of the life interest i.e. the property that passes to the beneficiary once the owner of the Life Estate dies.

RESIDUARY BENEFICIARY A ***Residuary Beneficiary*** of a Will is a beneficiary who is entitled to whatever is left of the Probate Estate once specific gifts have been distributed and the decedent's bills, taxes and costs of Probate have been paid. Unless the Will makes some other provision, Residuary Beneficiaries share equally in the Residuary Estate.

RESIDUARY ESTATE The ***Residuary Estate*** is whatever is left of the Probate Estate once specific gifts made in the Will have been distributed and the decedent's bills, taxes and costs of Probate have been paid.

RESOURCE A ***Resource*** for purposes of determining Medicaid eligibility, is an asset owned by the decedent, or his spouse, that can be converted into cash to meet their needs. Federal statute 42 U.S.C. 1382b identifies what counts (and does not count) as a Resource.

REV & TAX ***Rev. & Tax*** is the abbreviation for the California *Revenue & Taxation Code*.

REVERSE MORTGAGE A ***Reverse Mortgage*** (also known as a ***Reverse Annuity Mortgage***) is a mortgage whose loan proceeds are paid to the borrower incrementally over a period of time. The loan is not repaid until the borrower dies or the property is sold.

REVOCABLE TRUST A ***Revocable Trust*** is a Trust which can be amended or revoked by the Grantor or Settlor during his lifetime.

REVOCABLE LIVING TRUST A ***Revocable Living Trust*** (also known as an ***Inter Vivos Trust***) is a Revocable Trust that is created and becomes effective during the lifetime of the Grantor or Settlor.

SETTLOR A *Settlor* or a *Trustor* is someone who creates a Trust.

SIBLING   A *sibling* is one of two or more people born of the same parents; i.e., a brother or a sister. Unless, otherwise noted, we used the term to include those who have only one parent in common; i.e. a half brother or a half sister.

SOLE PROPRIETORSHIP   A *Sole Proprietorship* is a form of business ownership in which one person owns all of the assets of the business and that person is personally liable for all of the debts of the business.

SOLEMNIZE To *solemnize* a marriage is to enter into the marriage publicly, before witnesses, in contrast to a secretive or Common Law marriage.

SPECIFIC GIFT   A *Specific Gift* is a gift of a specific item of the Will maker's Estate that is made to a named beneficiary of the Will.

SPENDTHRIFT   A *Spendthrift* is someone who wastes money and/or spends lavishly.

SPENDTHRIFT TRUST   A *Spendthrift Trust* is a Trust created to provide monies for the living expenses of a beneficiary, and at the same time protect the monies from being taken by the creditors of the beneficiary.

SPRINGING POWER OF ATTORNEY A *Springing Power of Attorney* is a Power of Attorney that is not operational until, and unless, the Principal is incapacitated.

STATUTE OF LIMITATION A *Statute of Limitation* is a federal or state law that sets maximum time periods for taking legal action. Once the time set out in the statute passes, no legal action can be taken.

STEPPED-UP BASIS A *stepped-up basis* is the fair market value placed on property that is purchased or inherited from another. The "step-up" refers to the increase in value from the basis of the former owner (usually what he paid for it), to the basis of the new owner (usually the market value when the transfer is made).

SUCCESSOR TRUSTEE   A *Successor Trustee* is someone who takes the place of the Trustee.

SURROGATE A *surrogate* is a substitute; someone who acts in place of another.

TEFRA LIEN *TEFRA* is the abbreviation for the TAX EQUITY AND FISCAL RESPONSIBILITY ACT. It is a federal law that allows states to place a lien on real property owned by those who receive Medicaid benefits after age 55.

TENANCY IN COMMON   *Tenancy In Common* is a form of ownership such that each tenant owns his share without any claim to that share by the other tenants. There is no right of survivorship. Should a Tenant In Common die, his share belongs to the tenant's Estate and not to the remaining owners of the property.

TERM LIFE INSURANCE POLICY A *Term Life Insurance policy* insures the life of a person for a certain period of time. No insurance proceeds are paid unless the insured person dies within the given period of time. The monies paid for the policy are not refundable, so a Term Life Insurance policy has no cash surrender value.

TITLE INSURANCE *Title Insurance* is a policy issued by a title insurance company after searching title to the property. The insurance covers losses that result from a defect of title, such as unpaid taxes, or a claim of ownership of the property.

TRADE MARK A *Trade Mark* is any word, name, symbol or device, or combination thereof adopted and used by a person to identify goods made or sold by him and to distinguish them from goods sold by others.

TRUST AGREEMENT A *Trust Agreement* is a document in which someone (the Settlor) creates a Trust and appoints a Trustee to manage property placed into the Trust. The usual purpose of the Trust is to benefit persons or organizations named by the Settlor as beneficiaries of the Trust.

TRUSTEE   A *Trustee* is a person, or institution, who accepts the duty of managing Trust property for the benefit of another.

UNASSIGNABLE ANNUITY An *unassignable annuity* is an annuity that cannot be assigned; i.e., the annuitant's benefits cannot be transferred to another.

UNDUE INFLUENCE   *Undue influence* is pressure, influence or persuasion that overpowers a person's free will or judgment, so that a person acts according to the will or purpose of the dominating party.

VEH. *Veh.* is the abbreviation for the California *Vehicle Code*.

VOID GIFT A *void gift* is one that is not legally enforceable. For example, if a Will makes a gift and the Court finds that provision to be void, the beneficiary has no legal right to receive that gift.

WAIVER   A *waiver* is the intentional and voluntary giving up of a known right.

WELF. & INST. *Welf. & Inst.* is the abbreviation for the California *Welfare & Institutions Code*.

INDEX

B

C

STATUTES, CALIFORNIA
CIVIL PROCEDURE CODE ("Civ. Proc.")

703.010	98
703.070	97
703.140	98, 100
704.100	96, 102
704.115	97, 102
704.150	100
704.730	99, 236
704.840	99
704.995	99, 100, 102, 236
706.052	97

CORPORATIONS ("Corp.")

200	111
1502	111
15612	117
15621	117
15632	117
15643	117
15672	119
15673	119
15674	119
17002	121, 284
17050	121, 184
17052	121
17101	121
17158	121

FAMILY CODE ("Fam.")

125	17
297	10
297.5	10, 86
298	10
298.5	10
300	8
302	8

FAMILY CODE ("Fam.")

308	9
308.5	9
331	53
721	85
750	18
760	17
770	17
771	17, 86
772	17
852	18
914	86
1000	87
1100	59
1101	59
1615	260
2024	260
2200	8
2201	8
7611	16
7613	12, 14

HEALTH AND SAFETY CODE ("Health & Safety")

7100	160, 170
7100.1	169
7103	170
7113	175
7117	162
7151	137
7203	170
18080.2	37

PROBATE CODE ("Prob.")

80	35
100	17, 31
331	53, 54, 81
1470	184

PROBATE CODE ("Prob.")		PROBATE CODE ("Prob.")	
6450	16, 98	13600	261
6451	15	13651	25
6452	16		
6453	16	15212	147
6454	15	15300	55
6455	15	15305	55
6500	100	15680	58
6510	100	15687	56
6540	98		
6543	98	16061.7	51, 52
		17200	58
7050	6, 276	18100.5	53
7051	54	20110	75
8121	26	20111	75
8200	80	20116	75
8461	26, 69	21131	74
8800	26	21620	263
9050	25, 26	21621	213
9052	26		
9760	110		

REVENUE & TAXATION
("Rev & Tax")

205.5	236
218	236

PROBATE (left column continued)	
10800	27, 69
10804	70
10810	27
10811	27

VEHICLE CODE ("Veh.")

4150.7	37
9852.7	37
12811	172

13050	23
13105	24
13100	23
13101	23
13110	24
13200	22
13202	22
13500	25, 39, 43
13550	87
13551	87

WELFARE & INSTITUTIONS
("Welf. & Inst.")

2203	198
5352	184
14006	207

A Will is Not Enough in California

WEB SITES

236 California Statutes and Regulations are referenced in
A Will Is Not Enough In California

Each state has its own set of laws relating to the control, and protection of a person's Estate. The laws of California relating to Guardianship, Probate and especially Medicaid are very different from the laws of other states.

The author is in the process of "translating" *A Will Is Not Enough* for the rest of the states; that is, writing state specific books that explain how to set up an Estate Plan for the given state and how to qualify for Medicaid in that state.

A Will Is Not Enough is now available for:
ARIZONA, CALIFORNIA, CONNECTICUT
COLORADO, FLORIDA, GEORGIA, HAWAII
INDIANA, ILLINOIS, MARYLAND, MICHIGAN
MASSACHUSETTS, NEBRASKA
NEW JERSEY, NEW MEXICO, NEW YORK
OREGON, PENNSYLVANIA, TEXAS
VIRGINIA, WASHINGTON, WISCONSIN.

To check whether this book is currently available for other states call Eagle Publishing Company of Boca at
(800) 824-0823

To order books call Eagle Publishing Company or visit its Web site for a 20% discount.
http://www.eaglepublishing.com

OTHER BOOKS BY AMELIA E. POHL
How To Defend Yourself Against Your Lawyer

is a book about the unhappy experiences people have with their lawyers, beginning with that of the author AMELIA E. POHL. She became involved in a law suit and found herself in the role of client, rather than lawyer. She become concerned about lawyers who do not provide their clients with loyalty and respect. This book is a result of those concerns.

The book is divided into chapters that cover the most common problems that take people to a lawyer: divorce, probate, criminal, personal injury, starting a business, making a Will, buying a house, etc. Each chapter tells of the misadventures of the unwary as they sought the services of a lawyer without a clue as to what they were "buying." This book is funny, sad, interesting, but most of all informative. It tells the reader how to become a savvy consumer, i.e., how to find the right lawyer for the right job. If you ever find the need to employ a lawyer, you will be glad you read this book.

Copyright 2004   272 pages 6" X 9" soft cover
$20 includes Shipping and Handling

BOOK REVIEW

TED KREITER of the SATURDAY EVENING POST said "Horror fans, forget about those tawdry tales of ghosts and vampires. Pick up Amelia E. Pohl's *How To Defend Yourself Against Your Lawyer* to read some really scary stuff. Like the story . . . of the grieving widow, Ethel, whose husband died shortly after a lawyer drafted a sweetheart will for the two of them. . . . Six months in attorney's fees later, Ethel learned that she already had her husband's money because it never needed to go through probate! . . Ethel then went out and found a good lawyer for $1,000 who was able to get her $5,000 back. You do the math. . . Following Pohl's useful advice could save a person much more than money."

Guiding Those Left Behind In . . .

Amelia E. Pohl has written a series of books explaining how to settle an Estate. Each book is state specific, telling how things are done in that state. Each book explains:

- ✧ who to notify
- ✧ how to locate the decedent's property
- ✧ how to get possession of the inheritance
- ✧ when you do, and do not, need an attorney
- ✧ the rights of a beneficiary, and much more.

Each book is written with the assistance of an experienced attorney who is licensed and is practicing in that state.

The *Guiding* series is currently available for the following states: ALABAMA, ARIZONA, ARKANSAS, CALIFORNIA
CONNECTICUT, FLORIDA, GEORGIA, HAWAII, ILLINOIS
INDIANA, IOWA, KANSAS, KENTUCKY,
LOUISIANA, MAINE, MASSACHUSETTS
MARYLAND, MICHIGAN, MINNESOTA, MISSOURI
MISSISSIPPI, NEW JERSEY, NEW YORK
NORTH CAROLINA, OHIO, OKLAHOMA
PENNSYLVANIA, SOUTH CAROLINA, TENNESSEE
TEXAS, VIRGINIA, WASHINGTON, WISCONSIN

Visit the EAGLE PUBLISHING COMPANY Web site at
http://www.eaglepublishing.com
to check whether books for other states are available at this time.

A 20% publisher's discount is a available at the Web site.

It is the goal of EAGLE PUBLISHING COMPANY to keep our publications fresh.

As we receive information about changes to the federal or California law we will post an update to this edition at our Web site.

http://www.eaglepublishing.com